T0301671

Poverty and Subsidiarity in Europe

GLOBALIZATION AND WELFARE

Series Editors: Denis Bouget, *MSH Ange Guépin, France,* Jane Lewis, *Barnett Professor of Social Policy, University of Oxford, UK and* Peter Taylor-Gooby, *Darwin College, University of Kent, Canterbury, UK*

This important series is designed to make a significant contribution to the principles and practice of comparative social policy. It includes both theoretical and empirical work. International in scope, it addresses issues of current and future concern in both East and West, and in developed and developing countries.

The main purpose of this series is to create a forum for the publication of high quality work to help understand the impact of globalization on the provision of social welfare. It offers state-of-the-art thinking and research on important areas such as privatization, employment, work, finance, gender and poverty. It includes some of the best theoretical and empirical work from both well established researchers and the new generation of scholars.

Titles in the series include:

Poverty and Subsidiarity in Europe

Minimum Protection from an Economic Perspective

Didier Fouarge

Researcher at the Tilburg Institute for Social and Socio-Economic Research (TISSER) and the Institute for Labour Studies (OSA), Tilburg University, the Netherlands

GLOBALIZATION AND WELFARE

Edward Elgar
Cheltenham, UK • Northampton, MA, USA

Published by
Edward Elgar Publishing Limited
Glensanda House
Montpellier Parade
Cheltenham
Glos GL50 1UA
UK

Edward Elgar Publishing, Inc.
136 West Street
Suite 202
Northampton
Massachusetts 01060
USA

A catalogue record for this book
is available from the British Library

Library of Congress Cataloguing in Publication Data

Fouarge, Didier.
  Poverty and subsidiarity in Europe : minimum protection from an economic perspective / Didier Fouarge.
    p. cm. — (Globalization and welfare)
  A revision of the author's thesis (doctoral)—Tilburg University, 2002.
  Includes bibliographical references and index.
  1. Poverty—Europe. 2. Income distribution—Europe. 3. Subsidiarity. I. Title. II. Series.

  HC240.9.P6F68 2004
  339.4'6'094—dc22

                                                                2004043435
  ISBN 1 84376 605 1

Printed and bound in Great Britain by MPG Books Ltd, Bodmin, Cornwall

Contents

Figures

Tables

Acknowledgements

This book is an updated version of the dissertation I defended in June 2002 at Tilburg University, the Netherlands. It focuses on the performance of welfare states in the redistribution of income and the combat of income poverty. In particular, we deal with the dynamic nature of poverty. Through an investigation of the theoretical basis of the principle of subsidiarity, the book also asks whether or not there is a role for the EU to play in the area of social policy. Many people have – in their own way – supported and helped me while I was writing this monograph. It is now time to express my gratitude to all of them.

Most importantly I am thankful to Jos Berghman (K.U. Leuven University) and Ruud Muffels (Tilburg University) who supervised my research activities. It was a great privilege to have them at my side when I needed them. Their continuous support and interest was a great source of motivation. I am indebted to both of them for commenting on my work and sharing their knowledge with me. I am grateful to Wil Arts (Tilburg University), Iain Begg (South Bank University), Denis Bouget (MSH Ange Guépin) and Stephen Jenkins (University of Essex). I have met with all of them on several occasions and have benefited from their knowledge and experience to improve my own research. My colleagues at the Tilburg Institute for Social and Socio-Economic Research (TISSER), Tilburg University, and at the Institute for Labour Studies (OSA) have also been very supportive.

Over the years, I have been involved in a number of European research projects. I have been taking part in European research programmes within the framework of the European Panel Analysis Group (EPAG) and the Social Exclusion and Social Protection (EXSPRO) network. I have learned a lot from all the people I have met there and some of the chapters are based on my work within these research projects.

Finally, Monique, my wife, and Céleste and Blaise, my children, have been important elements in the completion of this study. Their love and affection, patience and understanding have contributed to an optimal climate for me to concentrate on my work. This book is dedicated to them.

1. Introduction: Poverty, Subsidiarity and the European Union

1.1 INTRODUCTION

The end of the last decade was marked by rapid economic growth in the European Union (EU), which resulted in job creation and decreased unemployment. Real gross domestic product (GDP) growth rate averaged 2.5 percent per year during the second half of the 1990s. Total employment rose by 4.6 percent between 1994 and 1999 while, at the same time, unemployment fell from 11.1 to 9.2 percent. This sustained economic activity has, however, had little effect on poverty and the short-term prospects are not very optimistic. Estimations by Eurostat show that, in 1996, about 17 percent of all EU individuals lived in poor households (Eurostat, 2001). In the EU, a total of more than sixty million individuals were poor, half of whom had been living in poverty for longer than three years.

Issues of income distribution and poverty have been receiving a great deal of attention in politics and social science literature. These issues are serious in developing countries where millions are dying of hunger and ill health. Although hunger and extremely poor living conditions are not large-scale phenomena in richer Western countries such as Europe and the USA, a great deal of the research on poverty and inequality is being carried out in these nations. It is quite remarkable that, in the so-called rich countries, there is still a fringe that lives in poverty. Careful analysis – as well as an array of policy measures – is required in order to combat this.

Although the welfare state in most Western countries was given its present form and content during the post-war period, its origins are more remote. What originally started as Christian charity for poverty relief has, through the years, largely been taken over by public authorities. Now, minimum protection policy is a task that has most often become the responsibility of public authorities. These authorities are successful – to a greater or lesser degree – in reducing poverty and inequality by their income maintenance policy, by promoting education and by favouring access to the labour market, but also by ensuring that all citizens have access to decent housing and proper health care.

The recent developments in Europe, with the creation of the single market implying free movement of labour, capital, goods and services – as well as the single currency – raise questions about the possibilities for the Member States to lead independent economic policies. In order to take part in the European Monetary Union (EMU), Member States have agreed to give up the use of a number of key economic policy instruments they formerly used as economic stabilisers. This is particularly the case for budgetary and monetary policy. In particular, these developments have consequences for the social context of the Member States.

Lately, questions of social protection have been heavily debated at the national and European level. However, in spite of the ongoing discussion about a Social Europe – and in spite of the European Council's recommendations on common criteria concerning sufficient resources and social assistance in social protection systems (92/441/EEC) and on the convergence of social protection objectives and policies (92/442/EEC) – the degree of minimum protection offered in the various Member States of the EU varies greatly as a consequence of divergent welfare state design. The 1998 level of social protection expenditure in percentage of GDP, for example, varied from 33 percent in Sweden to only 16 percent in Ireland (Eurostat, 2001: 111). Moreover, various studies have also shown that there is a great variation in the extent of poverty in European countries. Using half of the average equivalent expenditure poverty threshold, in the late 1980s, 4.2 percent of the Danish households were poor compared to 26.5 percent in Portugal (Hagenaars et al., 1994). Qualitatively similar results for the 1990s have been found by Eurostat using more recent data and a slightly different poverty line (Eurostat, 1997, 1998, 2000a, 2000b, 2001). In this respect, one can wonder whether the fact that the Member States have different redistributive policies is at all a concern within the framework of the economic and monetary integration. From the point of view of equity, this is important as well. If social exclusion is of any concern, what are then the instruments which the EU has at its disposal to prevent such situations? This amounts, on the one hand, to the question of the legal prerogatives of the EU in matters of minimum protection and, on the other hand, to the question of whether one can make a case, from an economic perspective, for supranational intervention in this policy field. More fundamentally, the question of whether or not the market can do the job of eliminating poverty on its own must also be addressed. Such are the questions that are developed in this study.

The principle of subsidiarity

In order to tackle these questions, the principle of subsidiarity is used as a leading concept. In economic terms, the subsidiarity principle states that economic activities that can be efficiently carried out by the market should indeed be undertaken by it. That means that there is no case for intervention from public authorities unless this would improve efficiency. The principle can also be applied to questions of centralisation versus decentralisation in federal governments. In this case, it implies that decentral authorities should be given priority over central authorities.

Wondering whether or not there are economic reasons for public authorities to intervene in the redistribution of income boils down to asking whether or not the government should assist or supplement the market in order to bring about a more equal distribution of income or to decrease poverty. This appeals to the concept of *horizontal subsidiarity* between the market and the State. Whether or not there is a role for social partners also relates to the notion of horizontal subsidiarity. The question whether, within the framework of a compound state such as the EU, a role is given to the higher level of authority in fixing minimum protection standards, ponders the need for the EU to assist or supplement the Member States in their combat of poverty. This appeals to the concept of *vertical subsidiarity* between public authorities at different levels. In particular, within the framework of the EU, its – non-exclusive – competencies are subject to the test of subsidiarity. Subsidiarity is, therefore, a key concept in this study and is discussed in greater detail in Chapter 2. There we show that the principle of subsidiarity can be given a broader and more positive interpretation leaving more scope for higher-placed authorities to help and stimulate action at a lower level.

1.2   EUROPE AND MINIMUM PROTECTION

A great deal has changed since 1957, when the Benelux countries, France, Germany and Italy started negotiations concerning the creation of a common market. What started with the gradual opening of labour and commodity markets was extended, in the 1980s, by opening the capital market and the market for services. It was further extended to include more countries. Alongside the six original Member States, Spain, Portugal, Greece, Great Britain, Ireland, Denmark, Sweden, Finland and Austria joined, and 10 more countries – Cyprus, the Czech Republic, Estonia, Hungary, Latvia, Lithuania, Malta, Poland, the Slovak Republic and Slovenia – have joined the EU as of May 1, 2004.[1] Since the approval of the Treaty of Maastricht, EU Member States have agreed to the completion of an EMU. This implies that there is far-reaching economic and monetary integration among the Member States requiring strict monetary, budgetary and inflatory constraints. Today, capital, labour, goods and services are allowed to move freely throughout the EU. However, from the outset, integration in the field of social protection has been considered as problematic.

When the negotiations for the Treaty of Rome started among the six original founding Member States, the existing differences among the social protection systems as a potential source of competition distortion were heavily discussed. In a common market, the countries with high levels of social protection – and, therefore, high social security premiums – would be penalised compared to those with low levels of social protection and correspondingly lower taxes and wage costs. As a consequence, there was a debate on whether social security systems should be harmonised through an equalisation of social security contributions across the countries. The French argued in favour of the inclusion of a social paragraph in the Treaty. They argued that social protection had an impact on labour costs so that it directly distorted the balance of competitiveness of the Member States. The German point of view, however, was that labour costs are only one of the determinants of competitive advantage. When taking into account other determinants of competitiveness – such as technology, infrastructure, productivity and the fiscal climate – the situation in the six original Member States was more or less balanced. Therefore, according to this argument, there was no need to include a social paragraph in the Treaty. It was argued that it is better to let social protection act as one of the variables determining competitive advantage. This debate has to be seen alongside the possible distortive effect of the underpayment of female labour which, at the time, was easier to settle than the harmonisation of social security rates. The question of underpayment of female labour was eventually settled in the Treaty of Rome, which laid down the principle of equal pay for men and women (Chassard, 2001). For political reasons, the German point of view won and harmonisation of social protection was not deemed necessary for the implementation of the common market.

While the first six countries which formed the Common Market at the end of the 1950s had social protection systems that were more or less in the Bismarkian tradition, it is imaginable that the demand for harmonisation would be met eventually. However, after the first extension, when countries with different conceptions of social protection joined, it became clear that harmonisation would not be attainable. Nonetheless, fears of social tourism induced the Member States to implement strict regulations concerning the residence criteria of non-workers, in particular the non-exportability of unemployment benefits. As far as the diversity of the Member States is concerned – and the fact that social contributions are but one of the factors affecting labour costs – it must be concluded that harmonisation by decree was not only politically impossible, it was also undesirable. After the ratification of the Social Charter in 1989 by all Member States except the UK, the Commission initiated the promotion of the convergence of social protection policies in accordance with common objectives. However, this idea of policy convergence was believed to be too ambitious and it was feared that the setting of these objectives would lead to a situation in which the lowest common denominator would be set as the sole objective.

Employment and minimum income protection

At the EU level, the debate on minimum protection is usually conducted in relation to the issue of employment and work incentives. One of the issues dealt with in the White Paper on Growth, Competitiveness and Employment is the negative effect of social security on the labour market. Various EU summits have also drawn attention to the possible effect of social security benefits on employment. The 1992 Green Paper on European Social Policy stresses the need to restore growth and diminish the impediments to job creation. In that paper, the Commission endeavours to encourage debates on social policy. It indicates the negative consequences of social exclusion and the lack of social policy, but also suggests that the development of society would be threatened. A dual society could indeed result from the economic process in which wealth creation would benefit the well qualified, requiring increasing transfers to the less qualified. This is a situation which, in turn, is expected to lead to diminishing social cohesion. The White Paper on European Social Policy urges the combat of social exclusion and poverty by way of labour market insertion measures. The preferred instrument suggested in the White Paper is the reinforcement of wage flexibility. However, the paper hardly mentions the impact of such a proposal on the distribution of income and poverty.

At the Social Affairs Council of December 1996, a resolution was adopted concerning the role of social protection in the fight against unemployment. The council invited the Member States to incorporate objectives of combating unemployment. This was to be done not only by seeking a balance in methods of financing through a decrease in the labour costs of low-skilled workers, but also by modifying social security benefits in order to improve work incentives.

Although the White and Green Papers on Social Policy suggest that greater collaboration among the Member States for labour-related social policy matters would benefit the economic and social integration process, convergence and/or harmonisation of social security systems within the EU is hardly contemplated. Moreover, until recently, official EU publications paid little attention to the role of the welfare state in relation to economic and social efficiency, or equity.

The 1989 Social Charter is concerned with, among other things, social protection, education and training, gender discrimination and the combat of social exclusion. The Charter is a formal declaration that social and economic objectives should be given equal weight. It includes a declaration on pay stating that 'All employed shall be fairly remunerated. To this end, in accordance with arrangements applying in each country, workers shall be assured of an equitable wage, that is a wage that is sufficient to enable them to have a decent standard of living'. Despite that, the issue of minimum wage has, thus far, been omitted from the Treaty. The Charter recognises the freedom of movement as the first fundamental social right. It also declares that each worker, according to the arrangements applying in each country, should be granted the right to adequate social protection and that, once retired, they should be granted resources guaranteeing them a decent standard of living. Aside from that, 'the Charter lacks any coherent, consistent or comprehensive social philosophy or policy' (Kleinman and Piachaud, 1993: 3). This is due to the fact that the Social Charter expresses no concern for the social rights of citizens (it deals only with the social rights of workers) that these declarations are restricted to what is feasible according to the arrangements applying in each country and that the EU intervention must be in accordance with the principle of subsidiarity.

For years, the topic of social protection was avoided by the European political agenda and integration was primarily concerned with employment policy, a process that culminated in the launching of the European Employment Strategy (EES) in Luxembourg in 1997. The aim here was to encourage an active labour market policy and an employment-friendly social security policy among the EU Member States. Within the framework of the EES, Member States are invited to draw national action plans for employment (NAPs). The framework for these NAPs consists of employment guidelines formulated by the Commission. These guidelines are based upon four main pillars: employability, entrepreneurship, adaptability and equal opportunity. Guidelines are formulated on an annual basis and must be implemented by the Member States in a way that they judge most appropriate for them. A process of benchmarking through peer review and the publication of 'league tables' then takes place. Taken as a whole, this process is referred to as 'open method of co-ordination'. Since the Lisbon summit, the question of social exclusion has also been put on the European agenda. As in the EES, the method chosen is the open method of co-ordination.

1.3   CO-ORDINATION, HARMONISATION AND OPEN METHOD OF CO-ORDINATION

Although the Treaty includes both an employment and a Social Chapter, and it formulates aims in the area of employment policy and social protection, it is silent when it comes to the means of achieving them. Moreover, in accordance with subsidiarity, competencies in this field are left to the Member States. In the field of social protection, the potential role to be played by the EU relates to the co-ordination and harmonisation of social protection systems. Co-ordination is about putting the various social protection systems into relationship with one another without altering the content of the laws of the Member States. Harmonisation, on the contrary, does imply an alteration of these laws in order to introduce common elements into them.

Regulations 1408/71 and 574/72 – on the application of social security schemes to employed persons, self-employed persons and the members of their families moving within the EU – are two examples of co-ordination of social security policies at European level. These regulations are meant for workers who migrate inside the EU. The aim of these regulations is to suppress social security-related barriers to the free movement of workers, free movement being one of the objectives of the Treaty.

The directive 79/7/EEC on the implementation of the principle of equal treatment for men and women in social security matters – by extension of article 119 of the Treaty of Rome concerning wage equality between men and women – is an example of the harmonisation of social security policy. Some of the Member States were indeed forced to adapt their legislation in order to comply with the directive. This directive obliges the Member States to harmonise their social security arrangements concerning sickness and invalidity payments, old age, unemployment and work-injury benefits. Notice that guaranteed minimum income arrangements fall beyond the scope of this directive unless they are designed for the above-mentioned aims.

Along with these examples, the action of the EU in social matters was limited to the formulation of two recommendations in the field of social protection that were adopted unanimously in 1992: the European Council's recommendation on common criteria concerning sufficient resources and social assistance in social protection systems (Recommandation du Conseil 92/441/EEC) and the recommendation on the convergence of social protection objectives and policies (Recommandation du Conseil 92/442/EEC). The latter is an application of the principle of subsidiarity. It suggests that the EU be limited to providing the main orientations of social policy and that organisation and financing – as well as the decisions on the relative importance of legal and complementary protection – be left to the Member States. The recommendation on minimum protection aims to implement a subsistence minimum for all persons in the EU, without disregarding labour incentives. The recommendation endeavours to compensate for damages caused by a particular risk, but also to support an active policy of social integration and to provide for sufficient resources to guarantee human dignity. The recommendation reflects a common concern for developing adequate minimum protection systems. The idea of a minimum income, as it is suggested in the recommendation, is also present in the White and Green Papers. It is a minimum standard, in conformity with the principle of subsidiarity, which is presented as a way of intensifying social cohesion. However, in the text no reference is made to a desirable level for such a minimum standard.

Both recommendations are of direct relevance to our topic. Four reasons justify their existence: the will to remove the social security-related impediments to labour mobility; the fear of social tourism; the feeling that the European Parliament and Commission should initiate measures to fight poverty and social exclusion; and ultimately, the fear that the single market might lead to social dumping. However, these recommendations have no obligatory character for the Member States and thereby constitute a soft approach to policy co-ordination. The recommendations recognise that the Member States alone are responsible for their social policy and thereby exclude any idea of solidaristic transfers between Member States. Nevertheless, the recommendations have triggered the discussion on social protection at the EU level. They are, for example, the basis for the 'Social Protection in Europe' reports, the communication on modernising and improving social protection in the EU (European Commission, 1997) and the subsequent proposition for a concerted strategy towards the modernisation of social protection (European Commission, 1999). The Commission has also made an attempt to implement the minimum protection recommendation (European Commission, 1998).

Another sign of advancement is that the attitude of Member States is changing as the political majority changes. An illustration is provided by the fact that the UK, which had originally not signed the Social Charter, has now reviewed its position and agreed for it to be included in the Treaty of Amsterdam. In response to including the fight against exclusion as one of the EU policy objectives in articles 136 and 137 of the Treaty of Amsterdam, the Lisbon European Council has agreed to take decisive steps to combat poverty. According to the Council the goal for the EU is 'to become the most competitive and dynamic knowledge-based economy in the world, capable of sustained economic growth with more and better jobs and greater social cohesion' (European Council, 2000a). As part of the approach outlined in Lisbon, the Commission has set up a five-year Social Policy Agenda setting a number of strategic goals (European Commission, 2000a, 2003). Besides, the recent European summit, held in Nice in December 2000, resulted in the Council requesting the Member States to draft action plans against poverty and social exclusion, much in the spirit of the national action plans in the area of employment policy (European Council, 2000c).

The method chosen – the open method of co-ordination – was first introduced in the wake of the Luxembourg process concerning employment policy, in which countries formulate common targets and indicators. Countries inform each other about their policy practice and identify best practices through the peer review methodology used in the framework of the EES. The open method of co-ordination is, therefore, primarily a learning process. The introduction of this method can best be understood because although threats to the welfare state are common to most of the Member States, no Member States applaud intervention from the EU. The open method of co-ordination is not imposed from above and thus corresponds to the Member States' understanding of subsidiarity. However, as Vandenbroucke (2001) argues, this method is more than a defensive instrument; it is a constructive instrument that should help shape Europe's social model through the exchange of information.

In this process, national action plans were submitted to the Commission in June 2001. These were reviewed by the Commission later that year in the very first document assessing the Member States' measures to eliminate poverty and promote social inclusion (European Commission, 2002a). The report states that, although the magnitude of the challenges varies among countries, 'significant improvements need to be made in the distribution of resources and opportunities in society so as to ensure the social integration and participation of all people and their ability to access their fundamental rights' (European Commission, 2002a: 16). Key risk factors and core challenges are identified. The key risk factors are: long-term dependence on low/inadequate income; long-term unemployment; low-quality employment or absence of employment record; low level of education and illiteracy; vulnerable family situation; disability; poor health; living in an area of multiple disadvantage; precarious housing conditions and homelessness; immigration; ethnicity; racism and discrimination; and poverty and exclusion. The following eight core challenges have been identified: developing an inclusive labour market and promoting employment as a right and opportunity for all; guaranteeing an adequate income and resources to live in human dignity; tackling educational disadvantage; strengthening families and protecting the rights of children; ensuring good accommodation for all; guaranteeing equal access to and investing in high-quality services; improving delivery of services; and regenerating areas of multiple deprivation.

A great deal of effort is put into the monitoring and benchmarking of social exclusion (Atkinson et al., 2002, 2003). The Commission is now required 'to improve knowledge, develop exchange of information and best practices, promote innovative approaches and evaluate experience' (article 13 of the EU Treaty). The interest of the EU for social protection is also apparent through the European System of Integrated Social Protection Statistics (ESSPROSS), the creation of European Community Household Panel (ECHP) and its follow-up EU-Statistics on Income and Living Conditions (EU-SILC), which is a great asset for the scientific community.

Moreover, there are signs of autonomous convergence of key indicators over the years. These include social protection expenditure, taxation regime and active and passive labour market expenditure (Greve, 1996; Alonso et al., 1998), as well as the taxation of enterprises (Broekman et al., 2001). However, the use of social spending as an indicator of convergence raises some problems. The level of spending may indeed vary under the effect of demographic changes and/or economic shocks. Hence, convergence does not necessarily point towards policy changes. It is, nevertheless, interesting to examine the development of social spending in Europe. Our own calculations show that the variance in social protection spending in percentage of GDP between the original 12 Member States was reduced by nearly 50 percent during the 1980s. This convergence continued during the first half of the 1990s, but at a slower rate. In a recent paper, Cornelisse and Goudswaard (2001) also note a strong relative convergence in the sphere of social security spending. Nonetheless, indicators of poverty and inequality are still largely divergent.

Note finally that the draft constitutional treaty by the EU convention chaired by Valéry Giscard d'Estaing which was presented in June 2003 represents a significant step forward for the area of EU social policy. It has opened the door for co-ordination in the area of employment policy. But it has also paved the way for such co-ordination in social policy.

Competencies of the EU
As it turns out, neither harmonisation nor co-ordination are preferred methods of developing social policy at the European level. Instead, the Member States have chosen the non-binding and flexible open method of co-ordination. This does not mean that the EU is devoid of formal competencies in the field of minimum protection. Various authors have shown that the EU – together with the Member States – does indeed possess competencies in the field of minimum protection. Vansteenkiste (1995) and Jaspers et al. (2002) point out that those competencies are based on articles 42, 94 and 308, as well as on the chapter on Social Provisions included in the Treaty. Article 42 of the Treaty of Amsterdam gives the Commission the power to co-ordinate social security systems when this is necessary with respect to the free movement of workers. On the basis of article 94, initiatives of harmonisation by the Community are possible, in any policy field, as far as these are considered to be essential for the establishment and functioning of the Common Market. Article 308 also provides a basis for harmonisation when

measures are taken which are essential for the attainment of one of the objectives of the Treaty, when no other grounds for action can be found. We can point to two relevant objectives for our purpose: the improvement of the living conditions of EU residents, and collaboration in the field of social security (articles 2 and 136). The Commission also has competence concerning collaboration in the field of social security by ordering studies and consultations, and by delivering opinions. Article 308 can be invoked for the realisation of these objectives (Vansteenkiste, 1995: 402). Articles 136 and 137 of the Treaty must also be mentioned. They include the objectives endorsed by the EU and the Member States that are relevant for our subject: the improvement of employment; the constant improvement of living and employment conditions; an adequate level of social protection, social dialogue; and the development of human capital to ensure a lasting high level of employment and the combat of exclusion.

We can conclude that the EU does have competencies in matters of co-ordination and harmonisation of social security systems. These competencies have relevance for the field of minimum protection. However, their use requires unanimity and is subject to the test of subsidiarity as mentioned in article 5 of the Treaty (see Chapter 2).

1.4   OUTLINE

The objective of this study is threefold: 1) to investigate the theoretical basis of the principle of subsidiarity and its implication for redistribution policy and, in relation to this, to investigate the economic rational for income redistribution by the government; 2) to investigate the economic and social efficiency of redistribution policies; and 3) to simulate possible options for co-operation or fiscal competition in the social field among EU Member States.

The first objective pertains to developing the theoretical basis of the principle of subsidiarity. The dual character of subsidiarity will be closely investigated. On the one hand, the principle of subsidiarity refers to the limitation of the legitimacy of intervention by a higher authority while, on the other hand, it has a more positive aspect relating to the obligation of the higher authority to support and assist lower-plane entities. This duality will be developed in Chapter 2. From an economic perspective, subsidiarity refers to the respective roles to be played by the market and the public authorities, in particular with respect to income redistribution. The objective is also to investigate which level of government is most adequate in order to carry out redistributive policies in compound states – such as the EU – with an economic and monetary union. In other words, is there a role for the EU in the field of redistributive policies? Answering such questions requires elucidating the economic arguments for government intervention in the market. For this, we draw on the welfare and public sector economics literature. It also requires stating the arguments relating to the distribution of responsibilities in compound states. These will be drawn from the literature on fiscal federalism. These arguments are discussed in Chapter 3.

Following these theoretical considerations – and this will be our second concern in this research – we undertake to investigate empirically the economic and social efficiency of the redistributive policy of various types of welfare state arrangements. The concept of social exclusion, as recognised by the European Commission, is multidimensional and encompasses aspects of low income, unemployment, low education, poor health and housing. The social protection systems, as a whole, give broad protection to cases of social exclusion. Even though employment policy is considered to be a core anti-exclusion policy, it remains the 'responsibility of the society to ensure equal opportunities for all' (European Commission, 2000b). Minimum income schemes, as part of the social protection scheme, deal with the most acute lack of resources. Our primary focus will be on minimum income protection, operationalised in the form of protection against (long-term) income poverty.

Welfare state arrangements differ with respect to some crucial characteristics, such as their method of financing, the type of replacement income they provide and the conditions imposed on the (potential) recipients. The role played by the market – that is the way the incentives to work are imbedded into the system – is an important distinguishing feature. Although each such system is unique, it has been argued that some display common traits and can be grouped according to some welfare state typologies or regimes (Titmuss, 1974; Esping-Andersen, 1990, 1999;). It can be expected that these various models or regimes have different implications for the distribution of income and poverty, so this will have to be taken into account. The dynamics of poverty will receive special attention, as it provides insight into the processes of entry into and exit from poverty and into the extent of persistent poverty. Most importantly, however, it reveals the incentive structure of the welfare regimes. According to the literature, a distinction is made among the liberal, corporatist and social-democratic approach to employment and welfare (see Chapter 4). In terms of subsidiarity, the liberal model emphasises market mechanisms, the corporatist model emphasises the role of the household and social group and the social democratic regime relies more heavily on public provision. Panel data for Great Britain, Germany and the Netherlands, respectively, are used as the best available examples of these approaches. As requested at the Lisbon and Feira Council (European Council, 2000a, 2000b), the Commission has now released a Communication on 'Structural Indicators' (European Commission, 2000c) which proposes a set of indicators used for the synthesis report at the Stockholm Council (March 2001). Among these, six are concerned with social cohesion: 1) distribution of income; 2) poverty rate before and after transfers; 3) persistence of poverty; 4) jobless households; 5) regional cohesion; 6) early school-leavers, not in further education or training. We develop indicators and present evidence with respect to the first three aspects for the Netherlands, Germany and Great Britain. The questions we answer are:

- What is the effectivity of public transfers in reducing poverty and inequality? Can public transfers be socially and economically efficient? (Chapter 5)
- What is the medium and long-term performance of welfare states in terms of reducing poverty? How successful are welfare states in triggering exits from poverty? (Chapter 6)
- What is the extent of persistent poverty? How is persistent poverty affected by shocks on the labour market and family structure? How are these shocks absorbed in the various welfare state systems? (Chapter 6)

We believe that the information provided in the empirical analyses is relevant for evaluating the economic and social efficiency of various approaches to the welfare state. Note that some parts in the empirical analyses are rather technical. We have put such technical aspects in separate text boxes so that the reader can more easily recognise them.

Our third concern is to simulate the possible effects of EU involvement in anti-poverty policy. According to the actual EU debate, what can be expected in terms of co-ordination of social policies? What are the possible scenarios for the future and how do they affect poverty and inequality across Europe? If countries do compete in the field of social protection, will this affect poverty and income distribution? Three scenarios for the outcome of the competition process among EU Member States are tested with respect to their effect on poverty and inequality. The first scenario reflects the assumption that fiscal competition leads to a race to the bottom among Member States. What are, then, the implications of a race to the bottom on replacement income and wages for poverty in the EU Member States, and what are the consequences of cutbacks in replacement income and wages for income distribution? The second scenario reflects the assumption that, in the long run, convergence of social security systems is taking place, either spontaneously or triggered by the open method of co-ordination. What are then the effects on poverty and inequality of a mean convergence of replacement income and wages among EU Member States? In the last scenario, it is assumed that either the process of co-ordination or the application of positive subsidiarity induces the

Member States to upgrade their minimum protection system and wages. What are, then, the consequences – in terms of poverty and inequality – of a genuine social Europe, involving relatively high levels of replacement income? These scenarios are tested in Chapter 7.

In the final chapter (Chapter 8), the evidence presented is brought together and implications for the design of the welfare state and Social Europe are stated.

NOTES

1. Bulgaria and Romania are hoping to join the EU by 2007. Whether or not Turkey will negotiated accession to the EU depends on the ongoing reforms in the country.

2. The Concept of Subsidiarity

2.1 INTRODUCTION

When questioning the economic desirability of State intervention in the market economy – or intervention by higher entities in federal-type government systems – the principle of subsidiarity can be used as a guideline. The principle of subsidiarity is rooted in Catholic social doctrine, but it also has a footing in economics. In Section 2.2, we focus on the origin and meaning of this principle. We position it in economics and social doctrine and elaborate on its current usage within the European Union (EU) context. In Section 2.3, we formalise the two dimensions of subsidiarity: the horizontal–vertical and the positive–negative. Finally, the implications of subsidiarity for this research are summarised in Section 2.4.

2.2 THE ORIGIN AND MEANING OF SUBSIDIARITY

2.2.1 Subsidiarity in Economics: on the Role of the Government

Although a thorough discussion of the implications of subsidiarity in economic theory is postponed until the next chapter, in this section we briefly introduce the implications of subsidiarity for centralisation versus decentralisation.

John Locke (1632–1704) was a keen advocate of limited competencies for governments. According to him, the State should only have powers that cannot be dealt with at a lower level, such as justice and security. Locke recognised the need for the liberty of aims and his thinking is characteristic for the transition from the Middle Ages to modern society. He favoured an individualistic society where the necessity of the State arises from the incapacity of the entities at lower levels to resolve particular problems. The main task of the State is to safeguard the interests of its citizens.

In ancient times, the world and humanity were seen as a whole; a cosmos. During the Middle Ages, the large empires fell apart and nation states were created. This process, which could be called decentralisation, induced the states to see each other as opponents. This might be one origin of the idea of sovereignty. From antiquity until the birth of modern society in the 18th century, the individual was seen essentially as being part of a group. Structures such as the family and the guild were the frameworks within which individuals lived. They were considered more important than the individuals themselves. Any decision or action was taken by and for the group and, within these limits, the individual had certain liberties.

The mercantilist movement that followed – circa 1500 to 1750 – saw the development of the production of goods for the market together with the rise of the nation state. Since trade was thought to be a zero-sum activity (the gains from trade were thought to be the losses for other nation), one major aim at the time was to increase the power, as well as the wealth of the nation state by means of international trade. This could only be achieved by increasing production, keeping private consumption low and improving the balance of trade. Within the economic theory of mercantilism, the State was thought to have a major role to play in the economy. Its key activities included stimulating production, fixing salaries and maintaining the level of the balance of trade. Keeping the wages low was an effective instrument for limiting consumption, improving the balance of trade by making national goods more attractive and – since it was thought that labour supply was negatively influenced by wage increases[1] – ameliorate work effort and production. Poverty for the many was the price to pay for the wealth of the nation.

During the 18th century, however, government intervention had a primarily distorting effect on the economy and some economists argued in favour of a reduction of government intervention. That century saw the rise of a new school of economic thought: the physiocrats. For them, wealth originated in agriculture and nature. The physiocrats – and in particular their intellectual leader François Quesnay (1694–1774) – were of the opinion that the State should refrain from any intervention in the economy. Physiocrats believed that such a *laissez-faire* policy would bring about equilibrium in a more spontaneous and natural way than would State regulation. They recognised a solely allocative role for the State consisting of defence, law and public order, the protection of (private) property rights and a few basic public works. The physiocrats placed the individual at the centre of their value system and the effect of this new philosophy was the individualistic society. It was Adam Smith (1723–90) who, in the 18th century, most clearly developed the basic argument concerning the allocation of responsibilities between the market and the State.

Since Adam Smith, the guiding principle in microeconomic theory is that of the pursuit of self-interest. He demonstrated how the pursuit of private interest leads to the public good in an unregulated economy (Smith, 1976). The pursuit of self-interest is a major human characteristic. Just as David

Hume (1711–76) and Locke thought of individual interest as a solution to failing morale, in Smith's opinion it would be useless to try to alter this tendency and would be more fruitful to concentrate on developing supportive institutional structures that account for this propensity such that the pursuit of self-interest would ultimately lead to the common good. According to Smith, the market is the obvious institutional setting to provide for that. An 'invisible hand' ensures that when individuals pursue their own interests, the common good is automatically realised. Agents, by pursuing their own interests, will lead markets to an equilibrium situation *par excellence*. A second argument for small government springs from the belief that capital formation is the engine of economic growth. Hence, according to the argument, government spending for unproductive labour that requires levying taxes inhibits economic growth because of its negative impact on capital formation. It follows that, for economists, the principle of subsidiarity is simply: what the market can achieve should be left to the market. A higher, all-enveloping level – such as the government – should carry out activities that cannot be performed efficiently by the market, or that should not be performed by it because of the nature of these activities. In other words, public authorities are to take action when market failures arise. Markets fail to achieve an efficient outcome when competition is imperfect, when information is incomplete, when there are public goods to be produced, when production induces externalities or when the markets face uncertainty. Equity considerations can also call for government intervention. Starting from the usual assumption in economics that market allocation is efficient, the State is a subsidiary of the market.

The arguments used by economists to justify government intervention in the market can also be extended to the issue of role distribution among levels of government in a federal setting (see, for example, Tiebout, 1956). As Alexis de Tocqueville suggests in *De la démocratie en Amérique* '[c]'est pour unir les avantages divers qui résultent de la grandeur et de la petitesse des nations que le système federal a été créé'. In this context, the principle of subsidiarity means that each level of government should do what it can do best. The principle is supportive of decentralisation for informational and efficiency reasons. Hence, the distribution of responsibilities among different layers – that is the market, decentral authority, national States and supranational entities – is primarily a question of economic and social efficiency. In this sense, subsidiarity can be applied to the role distribution between the EU and its Member States.

2.2.2 The Principle of Subsidiarity in Social Doctrine

It is often argued that the principle of subsidiarity arose from, and was developed by, the Catholic Church and Catholic political parties. The principle, however, has more distant origins. In her account of the foundations of the principle of subsidiarity, the French political philosopher Chantal Millon-Delsol shows that the idea of subsidiarity originated with ancient philosophers was found in medieval Christian philosophy and was also present in the German view concerning the allocation of responsibilities within society (Millon-Delsol, 1992: 13).

Aristotle (384–322 BC) had already discussed the distribution of responsibilities between the State and society. For him, the State was of major importance for the community. While he advocated liberty and democracy, he did not think that the role of the State should be limited. Individuals and small entities – such as the family – could cover basic everyday needs, but were incapable of total self-sufficiency. Only by grouping these smaller entities into villages, the villages into cities and, ultimately, the cities into States could they be ensured of total autarky and could their well-being be guaranteed. Society was perceived as an organism, with the individual as the central element, and the family alleviating the shortcomings of the individual, the corporations the shortcomings of the families, the villages the shortcomings of the corporations, and so on. In his conception, not only did entities of higher rank make up for the incapacities of the individuals and the entities of lower rank, they also contributed to their development. In Section 2.3.1, this will be qualified as 'positive subsidiarity'.

Although the notion of subsidiarity can be traced back to Aristotle, Thomas Aquinas (1225–75) can be considered the founder of the principle of subsidiarity within Catholic social doctrine. He emphasised the importance of individual liberties and liberty of action. He stressed, however, that the objectives of collective action should be set at a higher level because individuals are unable to set these objectives themselves. The State could then contribute to the development and improvement of one's well-being. Aquinas's principle of totality implies that society pursues common good – that is the greater good of society – above specific objectives. Moreover, it implies that one seeks to serve the common interest before his or her own (Millon-Delsol, 1992: 38). The common good should be interpreted, according to Catholic social thought, from the perspective of those who are excluded (Hirsch Ballin and Steenvoorde, 2000). This concern for fairness, equity and justice is characteristic of Aquinas's philosophy, but contrasts sharply with the prevailing axiom in economics concerning the pursuit of the self-interest. While Aquinas saw a role for the State in establishing the just price (wage), economists such as Adam Smith felt that this role was to be played by the market. This just wage must be sufficient to offer subsistence necessary for life and virtue.

The Roman Catholic Church used and developed Aquinas's ideas when formulating its teachings concerning the 'right order' of society and the place of the Church and the State within it. Through the principle of subsidiarity, Catholic social thought recognised the role of intermediate associations, which provides us with an interesting link to the discussion of role distribution between State, market and civil society (Hirsch Ballin and Steenvoorde, 2000).[2] At the end of the 19th century Christian politicians urged the Catholic Church to state its point of view on this question. This led Pope Leo XIII (1810–1903) to publish the encyclical *Rerum Novarum* (Leo XIII, 1891). In *Rerum Novarum*, the Roman Catholic Church established its position on the respective roles of the Church and the State. Two major roles are assigned to the Church (Bekkers et al., 1995: 20–21). The first one consists of the formulation of a doctrine with respect to the ordering of human life, social classes, workers' and employers' obligations and the situation of the labourers in general. Its second role is to take care of those in need. On the one hand, the State must ensure that the legislation is favourable to the common good, paying special attention to the position of workers and taking care not to act in a way that would reduce the freedom of action of individuals. On the other hand, State intervention is justified and necessary when the common good is threatened. Earlier in the same century, Von Ketteler (1811–77) – when discussing the social order in Germany – had also expressed similar ideas concerning a positive role for the State (Millon-Delsol, 1992: 127–31). He felt that help from a higher entity was necessary because individuals are not self-sufficient. However, the higher entity should take care not to thwart individual liberties. Such views, however, stand in sharp contrast with Althusius (1557–1630) developed in Germany. His conception was indeed that the autonomy of lower bodies should be protected from intervention of higher ones. This view leaves 'little room for obligations of central units' as Føllesdal (1998: 202) concludes.

While previous thinkers gave content to the idea of subsidiarity, the principle was actually first defined by Pope Pius XI (1854–1939) in the encyclical *Quadragesimo Anno* (Pius XI, 1931):

[J]ust as it is wrong to withdraw from the individual and to commit to the community at large what private enterprise and endeavour can accomplish, so it is likewise unjust and a gravely harmful disturbance of right order to turn over to a greater society of higher rank functions and services which can be performed by lesser bodies on a lower plane.

Pius XI expressed the idea that society's institutions need to be reformed – with each entity being given a proper place – and that State intervention needs to be reconsidered (Coote, 1989). The definition given to the principle of subsidiarity in this encyclical suggests that small entities are responsible for their mutual relations while entities of higher rank should only intervene in matters that go beyond the reach of the smaller entities. This relates to use of subsidiarity in economics, in the sense that it stresses the importance of self-interest. In the area of social protection, this involves that the State should only supplement the market when private insurance mechanisms do not work.

In the 1930s, the Church promoted capitalism along the corporatist track, aiming at increasing social cohesion and diminishing the risks of social unrest. It is in this tradition that *Quadragesimo Anno* must be placed. At the time, private property was seen as the single most important manner of preventing poverty and insuring security of subsistence. In this era of primacy of the individual and the family, the State was not obliged to provide assistance, but it had to support the assistance stemming from the market as well as from the voluntary sector. Employment policy fitted into that perspective.

The 1960s witnessed the development of the welfare state. Private property was no longer recognised as the only instrument to safeguard against economic and material dependency. A strong and interventionist State was thought necessary in order to correct for injustice and inequality. The present Pope, John Paul II, also favours an interventionist State for the protection of the weakest (working conditions and minimum support) and for job creation when it can enhance common good. He furthermore argues in favour of solidarities across social groups and between countries as a way of improving common good.[3]

2.2.3   Catholic and Protestant View on Subsidiarity

Subsidiarity seems to be justifiable from the point of view of individualism. Individualism stresses the importance of the liberty to do what one wants, leaving little space for intervention from public authorities. However, the principle goes further than that. If one considers society to be an organic system – a network of social and economic interactions and relationships – the principle can be justified by the fact that people bear the responsibility for each other's welfare (Spicker, 1991: 4). In economics, this is understood as altruism and it implies that individual welfare is positively influenced not only by one's own social and economic situation, but also by that of others, either because one derives utility from charity or because one is concerned with the distribution of welfare as such (see Section 3.2). In this respect, it is interesting to elaborate further on the link between the principle of subsidiarity and the principle of solidarity, where solidarity is defined simply as the mutual support between individuals and between communities.

In general terms, it can be said that the degree of proximity (closeness) of the social relationship determines the degree of solidarity. The closer the social relationship, the higher the degree of solidarity. The closest relationship is the family relationship. The further removed one is from that relationship, the lower the degree of solidarity. Since social networks of lower rank are given priority in Catholic thinking, then social networks of higher rank should be subsidiary to those of lower rank. Then, according to this principle, decision-making, including economic decisions, should take place at the lowest level possible. It can take place at a higher level for only two reasons: if the lower level is not able to bring about the desired result, or if action at lower levels induces negative effects that are not desirable and that need to be internalised. Action at a higher level can only be residual so that this reading of subsidiarity is clearly favourable to competition among lower-plane entities.

According to Coote (1989), Catholic social teaching, in its quest to bring about structural changes in society, has stressed the importance of both subsidiarity and solidarity. Both these principles are referred to and defined in the encyclical *Quadragesimo Anno*. Solidarity means that individuals can count on mutual support or support from organisations and institutions on a higher plane, when needs occur. Subsidiarity, then, tells us how the responsibilities among these levels of organisation should be distributed. From this emerges the view that solidarities are hierarchically ordered; that there is a widening circle of responsibility such that the degree of responsibility for the well-being of others decreases as one moves from the inside towards the outside of the circle (Figure 2.1). This presentation, as opposed to the individualistic model, has a strong moral foundation. However, solidarity and its consequence for the distribution of responsibilities does not tell the whole story. Other principles – human rights, freedom, justice and welfare – must qualify the concept of subsidiarity.

In the Netherlands, in the 19th century, religious-based political parties developed social theories that contrasted sharply with the prevailing liberal ideas. The Roman Catholics based their theories on the principle of subsidiarity while the Protestants developed the idea of sovereignty within one's own circle (*souvereiniteit in eigen kring*).

The Roman Catholics see society as a system in which the relationship among people is complementary and essential. They conceive a social theory based on the idea of subsidiarity, according to which responsibilities have to be carried out by the individuals and the family. Only when these fail to guarantee the needs of the individuals can, and indeed must, intermediary structures and, ultimately, the State come into action. The encyclical *Rerum Novarum* heavily influenced these ideas.

The Protestants, on the other hand, see society as being composed of various distinct circles: the family, the morality, science, education, the State and so on. Each of these circles fulfilled an essential role within the whole.

As opposed to what is shown in Figure 2.1, these distinct circles are not supposed to be concentric, but adjacent with some possible overlap. This view of society led Abraham Kuyper to the formulation of the principle of sovereignty within one's own circle. Here, each of the circles is assumed to be sovereign (Kuyper, 1880: 11). This sovereignty of the various circles seemed desirable in order to maintain the equilibrium in the relationships among the various circles. The role of the State in this respect is to ensure liberty of action for those within the sovereign circles (Kuyper, 1880: 13).

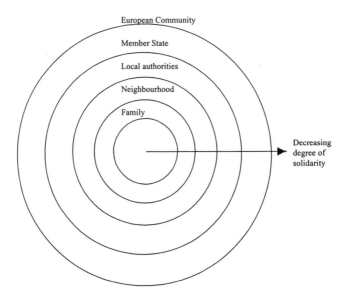

Figure 2.1   Concentric circles of solidarity

2.2.4   The Meaning of Subsidiarity in the EU

At the European level, the principle of subsidiarity assumes a significant place. In his 1974 report on the possibility of a EU, Spinelli referred to the principle of subsidiarity, although it was not explicitly named. He stated that the Community could act when the tasks under consideration can be undertaken more efficiently by it than by the Member States acting separately. The first explicit mention of the principle of subsidiarity was made in the European Act of 1986 (article 130r, ad 4), where it is applied to the environment policy of the Community in order to restrain the EU from intervening.

A broader interpretation was supplied by the former Dutch Prime Minister Ruud Lubbers, who advocated relying on subsidiarity for distribution of competence between Member States and the EU. It must, however, be remembered that the principle not only refers to distribution of competence between national and supranational level, but also – within nations – to the distribution of competence between the private sector and the State (see Chapter 3).

In the report of the Committee of Institutional Affairs on the principle of subsidiarity (Giscard d'Estaing, 1990), it is argued that it operates at two levels: choosing the right level of competence and choosing the right executive level.[4] In the report, two criteria concerning the right level of competencies are set forth: an efficiency criterion that favours centralisation and a criterion limiting the legitimacy of supranational intervention favouring decentralisation.

In legal literature, the fact that the principle of subsidiarity could be used for questions concerning the distribution of competence between the EU and the Member States is disputed (see, for example, Geelhoed, 1991; Lenaerts and van Ypersele, 1994; Vansteenkiste, 1995; Jaspers et al., 2002). In short, the argument can be stated as follows: given that the respective competencies of the EU and the Member States have already been settled in the various EU treaties, the principle of subsidiarity only comes into action for matters in which the EU and the Member States have shared competencies. In such matters, the principle of subsidiarity can be applied to determine the most adequate executive level for carrying out a given policy. As such, subsidiarity does not seem to be an adequate instrument for the vertical distribution of competencies within the EU.

The principle of subsidiarity was officialised in the Treaty of Maastricht (article 3b, now article 5). This article first states that the EU can intervene only in spheres in which it is competent (principle of enumerated powers):

> The Community shall act within the limits of the powers conferred upon it by this Treaty and of the objectives assigned to it therein (Treaty of Amsterdam, article 5, first part).

The content of the principle of subsidiarity is that, in areas where the Community and the Member States have shared competencies,[5] the Community can only intervene when the Member States fail or when action, because of its scope or consequences, can better be undertaken at Community level:

> In areas which do not fall within its exclusive competence, the Community shall take action, in accordance with the principle of subsidiarity, only if and in so far as the objectives of the proposed action cannot be sufficiently achieved by the

Member States and can therefore by reason of the scale or effects of the proposed action, be better achieved by the Community. Any action by the Community, shall not go beyond what is necessary to achieve the objectives of this Treaty (Treaty of Amsterdam, article 5, second and third part).

The formulation of the principle carries the idea that the EU must abstain from action in areas where it does not have any competence. However, it does state that, under some provisions, decision can take place at a level higher than the national one. These provisions are: a) EU action must be more effective than action at the level of the Member State; b) there is some additional value to action at the EU level compared to the national level (Van den Bergh, 1994). In the present situation, however, the Member States use the principle of subsidiarity in order to limit the possibilities of intervention by the Community in social policy matters. Although the principle of subsidiarity is meant as an efficiency test with regard to economies of scale, external effects, information and the working of the internal market in general – and is aimed at determining the most efficient level of responsibility (EU or Member States) – in European practice it is used as a political criterion. The Member States appeal to the principle to restrain transfers of their authority to the EU. On the one hand, the principle of subsidiarity provides room for action at the European level, if this leads to a more efficient outcome than would be the case if the Member States acted independently. On the other hand, however, because of the way it is presently used, it restricts the room for action: action at EU level is subsidiary to action at the level of the Member States.

At the European level, action is only possible in the fields exclusively attributed to the EU or in cases where a policy involves cross-border effects. The reason for this is that the EU, unlike the entities that it is composed of, is not a 'State' with autonomous power. The Community, although it recognises common values and principles, only exists because of the decision of different nations to create and maintain a union and to attribute it with a limited number of competencies. However, as a result of the dynamics of integration, the Community has extended its domain of influence. The Commission has recognised the principle of subsidiarity and thereby it acknowledges that decisions should be taken at the appropriate level. Acceptance of this principle implies that the Community has only a limited number of competencies. It further suggests that the role of the Community in social policy must be restricted. There are, however, economic arguments in favour of social and anti-poverty policy that are based either on normative views on social justice or on genuine efficiency arguments (see Chapter 3).

2.3   THE DIMENSIONS OF SUBSIDIARITY

2.3.1   The Positive Dimension of the Principle of Subsidiarity

Subsidiarity – as it was developed by the Protestants – leaves little space for the intervention of higher authorities, since society is made of various entities who are endowed with quasi-total sovereignty. From the Roman Catholic tradition we can find a positive interpretation of this principle, especially from the works of Thomas Aquinas and Leo XIII, but also Von Ketteler. Here, the principle has a strong moral content and can be taken to mean that authorities of higher rank have the obligation to support and assist entities of lower rank.

In this view, it is not the idea of replacing action at a low level by action at a higher level that is important; it is the idea of giving help and protection. As Jacques Delors points out, in an attempt to apply the Catholic principle to the relations between the Member States and the EU:

> La subsidiarité, ce n'est pas seulement une limite à l'intervention d'une autorité supérieure vis-à-vis d'une personne ou d'une autorité qui est en mesure d'agir elle-même, c'est aussi une obligation, pour cette autorité d'agir vis-à-vis de cette personne ou de cette collectivité pour lui offrir les moyens de s'accomplir (Jacques Delors, quoted in Eijsbouts, 1991: 488).

Authorities of higher rank have the duty to support lower entities when these express the need for assistance and, in particular, when human dignity and human rights are not secured (Millon-Delsol, 1990, 1992; Spicker, 1991; Ranjault, 1992). As the Marquis de Montesquieu wrote, '[t]he State owes all its citizens a secure subsistence, food, suitable clothes and a standard of living which does not damage their health' (*L'Esprit des Lois* XXIII, 1748). This help must be provided until lower plane entities are able to act on their own (van Kersbergen, 1995).

This does not mean that the basic individual liberties are disregarded, but that higher authorities help to protect and uphold these liberties. When the principle of subsidiarity is interpreted negatively – suggesting a limitation of the intervention of an authority of higher rank – it implies a notion of sovereignty and is therefore devoid of its philosophical and sociological content.[6]

It is human dignity which constitutes the foundations of the principle of subsidiarity. Coote (1989) refers to this 'principle of human dignity'. In fact, according to Catholic doctrine, each person is a complete entity and has a direct relationship with God. The idea of human dignity is related to equality and liberty and in Catholic thinking it occupies a central position for God created mankind, whose destiny is to be with Him. It is, therefore, the individual – and not humanity as a whole – who is of highest value. Because society is inferior to the individual, its role can only be to ensure the human dignity of the persons comprising it.

However, individuals are multifaceted. If they are to develop properly they cannot do without any of their natural capacities. They must not be hungry, cold, feel shame, and so on. Moreover, they must have freedom of thought and action. In order to develop their natural talent, political society, in its process of decision-making, must take all these elements into consideration. That is the justification of anti-poverty policies. Society must see to it that the more vulnerable individuals are adequately protected, and must undertake positive action to ensure the full development of its members' capacities. This goes further than merely guaranteeing individual liberties as defended by libertarians such as Friedrich Hayek and Robert Nozick. The interpretation implies that society must refrain from any action in the spheres where individuals can take action, as suggested by the negative meaning of subsidiarity. This illustrates the opportunity of choosing minimum protection when applying the principle of subsidiarity to a particular policy field.

It must be stressed that the terms 'negative' and 'positive' which are used to qualify the principle of subsidiarity in this section – and the rest of this study – are borrowed from Millon-Delsol (1990).[7] One can question whether choosing these terms is opportune, since they have a strong normative connotation. For ease of exposition, however, we will continue using these adjectives, defining them as devoid of any normative undertone.

2.3.2   Vertical and Horizontal Subsidiarity

Economics is concerned with both vertical and horizontal subsidiarity. Vertical subsidiarity is related to role distribution between governments in a hierarchical setting. Vertical subsidiarity can be considered as a principle of efficiency, assigning policy tasks to the lowest level as long as there is no reason to assign them to a higher level. Among economists, Hayek and Friedman were probably the most enthusiast supporters of individual action and the curtailment of government interference in economic activity. According to the Oates' decentralisation theorem (Oates, 1972: 35), public goods or services will be more efficiently provided for by decentral public authorities when consumption is confined to a given geographical area and when the production costs do not differ among jurisdiction levels. Federalism is the expression of this type of subsidiarity. The principle of subsidiarity, as referred to in the Treaties of Maastricht and Amsterdam, can be understood in this (vertical) federalist logic. It is developed as a regulatory tool for the role distribution of executive powers among the Member States (which have priority) and the EU (that carries the burden of the proof).

Horizontal subsidiarity, on the other hand, refers to the role distribution between economic agents at a comparable level (Figure 2.2). It corresponds to the idea of subsidiarity as it was explained within the social doctrine of the Church. According to the doctrine, State intervention is only admissible when private initiative falls short of duly fulfilling its role (Pius XI). This line of reasoning holds within each level of public authority (local public authorities, regions, Member States and Europe). One can apply this reasoning within the field of economics to determine the assignment of policy tasks between the market and the State. In other words, this raises the questions of market and government failures, and the complementarity between the State and the market. The concepts of horizontal and vertical subsidiarity are illustrated in Figure 2.2, and are further developed in Chapter 4. In this study, we will focus on the aspect of horizontal (self-help/market/State nexus) and vertical subsidiarity (Member States/EU nexus).

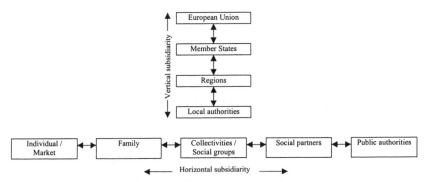

Figure 2.2   Concepts of subsidiarity

2.3.3   Criticism of Subsidiarity as an Ordering Principle

Critics of the principle of subsidiarity – and its application in the field of European policy – claim that it provides no juridical or political foundation. Geelhoed (1991) shows that, in practice, it is not the principle of subsidiarity that plays a decisive role in determining adequate competence at the European level, but rather the political claims of the negotiating partners. He also claims that, in the two most important federal states – the USA and Germany – the principle has not played a significant role. In the USA, federal legislation is valid as long as it is 'necessary and proper', that is when it is essential and when it has a reasonable relationship with a federal competence. The distribution of competencies in the USA shows no trace of subsidiarity.

Germany has a system of co-operative federalism. Here, distinction is made among exclusive competencies of the 'Bund', concurring competencies between Bund and Länder and the competencies of the Länder which are confined within a framework set by the Bund ('Rahmgesetz' competence). The principle of subsidiarity only plays a role in the case of concurring competencies, as is the case in the EU, as stated in article 72 of the German Constitution.

Van Gerven (1992) criticises the fact that the principle of subsidiarity has no significance on its own. Two other European principles are much more significant: the principle of proportionality states that any authority should exercise its competence with reserve, and the co-operation principle states that the EU and Member States should co-operate while exercising their respective competencies. According to him, the principle of subsidiarity is inferior to these two principles.

Despite these criticisms, it remains interesting to scrutinise the implications of subsidiarity in the area of minimum protection.

2.3.4   Implications of the Principle of Subsidiarity

Subsidiarity is not related to any political regime, be it liberal, communist or even democratic. It does, however, sharply contradict despotism and fascism, as these two political regimes imply the existence of a strong, centralised power with little freedom of initiative for the lower levels of society. Subsidiarity is typically a federalist principle. We define federalism as a governmental system consisting of various central and decentralised levels of decision-making. Federalism seems to be the social organisation that most guarantees the autonomy and liberty of the lower levels, without excluding intervention from a higher authority when it is needed.

The application of subsidiarity is far from straightforward. When applied to the market–State nexus, subsidiarity relates to the decentralisation of government activities and the centralisation of market activities. In the European context, one can point to a dilemma in the way the principle of subsidiarity is used by the Member States. On the one hand, most Member States want to keep the organisation of their social protection at the national level and only confer minor executive powers to the lower entities (the municipalities). There are two reasons for this. First, because of the existence of economies of scales and, second, because regional inequalities among municipalities can be avoided. On the other hand, at the European level, the Member States rely on subsidiarity to protect themselves from EU intervention, particularly in the field of social policy which they consider to be sovereign. If the Member States applied the same logic they use within their borders to the European situation, they would actually favour EU intervention, rather than oppose it as they do now.

A second dilemma is that the principle of subsidiarity implies that the higher authority should assist and help the lower authorities. However, this means that the lower entity is made dependent on the help of the higher entity and thereby loses its freedom of action. The problem is actually that the level of authority that is best suited to implement given policies does not always have the necessary financial means to do so. However, the principle does not imply that the higher authority must replace the lower authority when, for instance, it cannot finance its policy, but it suggests that the higher authority give the financial means to the lower one, leaving the choice of the aims to the better suited authority. This, however, raises the problem of control of the use of the financial help and of the determination of criteria for intervention.

As globalisation and international trade increases, we see a rise in regionalism. This implies that the traditional role of the centrally organised state is changing. Thus, the shift of attention is taking place at two levels: internationalisation and regionalisation (Hirsch Ballin and Steenvoorde, 2000). This development has induced the State – and the welfare state – to reconsider its role. The new role of the modern State is an active one: to help create the conditions for an optimal functioning of markets, rather than try to take over market activities. Social doctrine contributes to the understanding of subsidiarity in terms of the positive–negative dimension of the principle. Public authority is to supplement private initiative when it is inadequate and – with respect to the moral content of the principle – help the market fulfil its goals, when needed. Labour market participation, for example, has been shown to be an effective way to pull people out of poverty. Yet, in some cases, the labour market is not able to incorporate everyone or provide an adequate income level (the elderly, disabled workers, those with obsolete skills, and so on). In these cases some other form of public intervention – such as a more active one – is required.

The principle of subsidiarity is often invoked to reflect political realities. It is 'sometimes used as a smokescreen to prevent serious analysis of the relative advantages and disadvantages of federal versus national control of policy functions' (O'Shea, 1996: 283). This is particularly clear in the European context. A major concern for the future is whether economic and monetary integration can be attained without some degree of fiscal integration. In this study, we are interested – from an economic point of view – not only in the distribution of responsibilities between the EU and Member States, but also within Member States, among public authority, decentralised authorities and the market.

Efficiency criteria are decisive when considering the role distribution between market and State or between regions and federation. Competition has various advantages. Yet, in some instances – in the presence of externalities, when information is imperfect, when competition fails (see Chapter 3) – competition does not lead to an efficient outcome. In these cases, intervention by a more highly placed authority is preferable and minimum protection arrangements are demonstrably productive. The positive interpretation of the principle of subsidiarity introduces a social efficiency criterion: should the Member States not successfully guarantee minimum protection – harming human rights and human dignity – then an appeal could be made on positive subsidiarity. This would justify intervention on behalf of the EU using, for instance, directives or harmonisation, or less stringently, soft laws and the stimulation of co-operation among Member States. This answers the question of whether the EU should undertake any action in the field of minimum protection. This would mean that the EU could assist the Member States in their battle against poverty when the States cannot fight it successfully on their own. There is, conceivably, a role for the EU in the area of minimum protection and poverty prevention, based on this positive interpretation of subsidiarity.

2.4　CONCLUSION

One basic precept for communication is that words carry the same meaning, no matter who uses them. It is now clear that this does not hold for the principle of subsidiarity. The dual character of this principle – with its positive and negative meanings – does not mean that one has to choose one over the other. These are two sides of the same coin. Our aim here is to show that the meaning of subsidiarity is broader than has thus far been seen in European debates or in economics.

In summary, one can state that the view of Catholic social thinking on the role of the State is characterised by its ideas on human dignity, common good, solidarity and subsidiarity. The interpretation of the principle of subsidiarity provides material for a long-lasting debate. It means two things: that the State should refrain from doing what individuals and the market can do better and that it should not refrain from doing what it can do better. In debates at the European level, the principle has generally been defined in negative terms, which leads us to the conclusion that there is not a strong basis for a European social policy. However, a positive interpretation is also possible. Then, the EU could assist nations in the development of a successful social and economic policy to combat poverty, through income support, education programmes and active labour market policy. At the very least, the EU could ensure that non-co-operative situations in the field of social protection do not arise during the process of economic integration.

In social science and economic literature, the principle of subsidiarity can be seen – either explicitly or implicitly – in terms of centralisation or decentralisation. The different core values in economics (individual freedom) and social teaching (common good) provide conflicting views on the role of such institutions as the welfare state. In particular, Catholic social teaching emphasises social justice that calls upon proactive institutions to help citizens take an active part in the economic community. This view is not supported in liberal economics. Nevertheless, in Chapter 3 we will show that the welfare state can be seen as a productive (rather than a counter-productive) factor in the economy. In essence, applying the principle of subsidiarity involves an efficiency test. However, this chapter shows that there is another, underexposed 'positive' meaning that rests on the principle of human dignity. As poverty is a breach of human rights which affects human dignity in undesired ways, it is essential to take steps to prevent it. Therefore, public authorities have the duty to do everything they can to combat poverty.

NOTES

1. Mercantilists assumed the labour supply curve was backward-bending.
2. At present, the notion of citizenship is quasi-absent in the EU. Yet, this is not an unimportant notion. As Hirsch Ballin and Steenvoorde (2000) demonstrate, it took quite some time for Catholic social thought to recognise the notion of citizenship. However, once it was recognised the moral dimension of good citizenship – that is solidarity – was formulated. This notion is of great significance to the discussion on social exclusion.
3. Within social doctrine, solidarity (see others as another self) and altruism are seen as virtues. More of it, therefore, leads to higher welfare.
4. See Lenaerts and van Ypersele (1994) on this distinction.
5. In other words, in areas where neither the Community or the Member States have exclusive competence.
6. The notion of sovereignty refers to the situation in which a State is not submitted to any control by any other States or organisations.
7. See also Føllesdal (1998).

3. Subsidiarity in Economics

3.1 INTRODUCTION

The principle of subsidiarity was included in the Treaty of Maastricht as a political instrument for the European economic integration process. However, the principle is vague and needs to be operationalised. In the previous chapter, we shed some light on the origin of subsidiarity and juridical interpretation of the principle within the EU. In this chapter, we show how subsidiarity can be made operational for economic analysis. We also transpose the findings from the previous chapter concerning positive subsidiarity into the economic principle of subsidiarity.

In economics, first of all, when discussing the allocation of responsibilities on the market–State nexus, it is generally concluded that what can be performed efficiently by the market should be left to the market. Subsidiarity, then, means that, for economic activities that cannot be performed efficiently by the market – or that should not be performed by it because of the nature of these activities – some form of State intervention can be considered. Because our application field is minimum protection, we address the question of why it is governments – and not the market – which offer minimum protection and redistribution of income. This questions the existence of a welfare state in a market economy. We show that social protection spending can be a productive factor and not just a financial burden (see Fouarge, 2003). Thus, we see that social, economic and employment policies are highly interrelated. Secondly, applications of the principle of subsidiarity can be found in the economic literature on fiscal federalism, which discusses the distribution of competencies in compound States. In this context, the principle of subsidiarity implies that each level of government should do what it can do best. The lessons of fiscal federalism can be applied to the European Union (EU) context, in particular in the field of social protection and income redistribution.

In welfare economics, justifications for government intervention take the free market situation as the point of departure. According to the first theorem of welfare economics, if markets are competitive, information is perfect and there is a full set of markets, then, if a competitive equilibrium exists it is Pareto-efficient.[1] This means that in such a situation, it is not possible to make someone better off without making someone else worse off. The presumption here is that in the optimal situation, government intervention is not necessary on efficiency grounds. In standard neoclassical economics, the State is subsidiary to the market. In other words, subsidiarity implies that the burden of the proof lies with the defenders of centralisation.

This chapter explains that the underlying assumptions in the above statement are not always met so that corrective mechanisms by the State have to be considered. This is particularly true when it comes to the distribution of resources and the analysis of well-being. Eventually, the optimal role distribution among the various layers – that is the market, decentral authority, national States and supranational entities – is indeed primarily a question of economic efficiency. However, concern for equity or social efficiency also matters. Social efficiency is defined here in terms of reduction of income inequality and poverty (see Chapter 4).[2] The interrelation between efficiency and equity will determine the framework of this chapter. We undertake to show that social protection – as opposed to the impediment of economic efficiency through disincentive effects – can also be viewed as a productive factor. Due to the constraints of time and space, we do not discuss the details of the theoretical arguments here and only present the core of the arguments, supporting them, where possible, with empirical evidence. For a thorough analysis of the arguments supporting the welfare state, we refer the reader to Atkinson and Stiglitz (1980), Barr (1987, 1989, 1992) and Stiglitz (1988).

Social protection as a productive factor can be interpreted as promoting growth or, more broadly, as promoting quality of life. Productivity, in the sense of promoting growth, implies that growth in income per capita is the key policy aim. This option rejects the quality of life approach as being ill defined and impractical (MacGillivray et al., 1996: 16). Viewing productivity as promoting quality of life emphasises the shortcomings of crude economic indicators such as gross domestic product (GDP) growth rate. It also concentrates on evaluating the contribution of social policy on an alternative set of indicators of quality of life (such as human development). The important thing is to realise the double dimension of social policy. It has a consumption (for example, redistribution) and an investment component (education and training, health care, occupational safety and health). On the one hand, the consumption aspect might be conducive to labour disincentives and government failures. On the other hand, the existence of market failures and informational problems call for public mechanisms of insurance and redistribution, and hence more emphasis on social efficiency (see Figure 3.1). The consumption and in particular the investment component of social policy can allow government policy to combine economic and social efficiency. In the following sections, we present evidence that social protection is a productive factor in 'quality of life' terms and show that it can be productive in 'promotion of growth' terms. It must, however, be realised that although the costs of social policy are generally immediately visible, the benefits are more difficult to identify and quantify. The reason is that much of these benefits are long term.

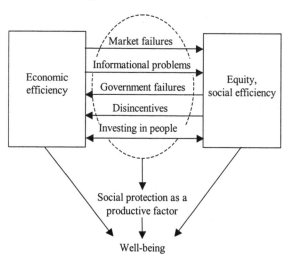

Figure 3.1   Social protection as a productive factor

The theoretical arguments for the co-ordination of activities between the market and the State and for the existence of a benefit system can be articulated according to the three classical economic functions of government intervention: allocation, stabilisation and redistribution (Musgrave, 1959).[3] Although the most important role of the welfare state is to redistribute resources, it also has an allocative and stabilisation function. Considering economic and social efficiency solely in the light of this assumed trade-off is therefore a simplification of reality. Economic and social performance are interrelated in such a way that the potential for win-win situations is high. Higher social efficiency does not necessarily imply loss of economic efficiency. Le Grand (1990) even argued that the trade-off is an elusive one.[4]

We discuss the arguments along two lines. The first is the equity line and the second relates to economic efficiency. Concern for equity is the primary reason for the redistributive function of the social protection system (Section 3.2). However, efficiency considerations can also be relevant. The redistributive, allocative and stabilisation function of social protection is justified for efficiency reasons (Section 3.3). This implies that, irrespective of one's own view on equity, there is an efficiency argument favouring the welfare state.

The fact that it is a productive factor can, to a large extent, be attributed to the existence of market failures and informational problems. This means that social efficiency and the promotion of well-being do not by definition engender loss of economic efficiency. However, the pursuit of economic efficiency will generally harm the distribution of well-being. This synergy between efficiency and equity is the subject of Sections 3.2 and 3.3.

Finally, we turn to the economic implications of subsidiarity in terms of the allocation of responsibilities between central and sub-central entities in a federal setting. We evaluate the economic arguments for centralisation or decentralisation of redistribution and minimum protection policy in Europe. Relying on the insights of theories on fiscal federalism, we show why some degree of EU involvement or co-ordination of minimum protection policies might be required (Sections 3.4 and 3.5). The main conclusions from this chapter are brought together and discussed in Section 3.6.

3.2 EQUITY ARGUMENTS FOR REDISTRIBUTION

3.2.1 Social Justice

Although the market produces wealth well, it distributes it poorly. The distribution of income and wealth resulting from the market process might not correspond to the prevailing concept of equity in society. According to the second theorem of welfare economics, redistribution could be achieved in a non-distortionary way through lump-sum taxes and transfers such that efficiency is not diminished. Lump-sum taxes and transfers are, however, difficult to devise in real world economics, so a trade-off is believed to exist between efficiency and equity (Okun, 1975). In practice, the State might wish to redistribute income, wealth and other human resources so that it is in accordance with society's concern for equity. This is indeed a major role of the welfare state.

One of the problems with standard microeconomic theory is that it leaves no room for the notion of minimum necessary standard. For Adam Smith, one's subsistence would depend on his wages, which he referred to as the natural price of labour. This natural wage should be enough for the labourer to support him or herself and his or her family. For those unable to generate enough income to secure a decent living for themselves, he believed that the innate moral sentiment of others would induce spontaneous private charity (Smith, 1974). This is referred to as altruism.

In the standard economic model (Figure 3.2) with supply curve S and demand curve D, the equilibrium situation on the labour market is depicted by point E. Let us suppose that there is some minimum subsistence level below which a person does not reach a standard of living that is considered acceptable within the community (a poverty line). This minimum subsistence level is depicted by the dotted W_{min}-line. At the new equilibrium situation E', up to $0B$ persons want a job, but only $0C$ will get one, leaving CB unemployed. These people could offer their labour along the supply curve towards the equilibrium point E, but the wage they would get (W) would be lower than the minimum subsistence level. Hence, they are living in poverty.

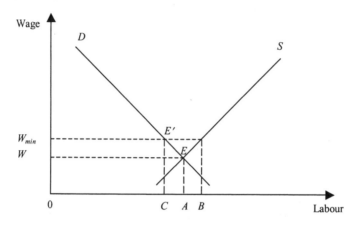

Figure 3.2   Labour market equilibrium and poverty

This simple presentation illustrates one of the shortcomings of the standard model in coping with poverty. Although market outcomes are efficient, Pareto efficiency is not a distributional principle. As such, market mechanisms potentially lead to unequal outcomes and even poverty. Nineteenth-century liberals thought of poverty as a short-term problem. They believed that spontaneous processes, through the labour market, would provide one with the opportunity to improve one's own situation. However, poverty appears to be more persistent than it was thought to be. Minimum wage regulations and the welfare state are instruments that make it possible to correct such inequitable market outcomes. On the basis of extensive analysis of the situation in the USA, Card and Krueger (1995), for example, convincingly document that increases in the minimum wage have led to increases in earnings of low-paid and middle-class workers without inducing job loss. The welfare state, however, is often seen as a financial burden leading, possibly, to inefficiency.

Nonetheless, the question whether the State has any role at all to play in the field of income distribution and poverty relief is a highly normative one on the edge of political and economic theory. While Pareto efficiency is a rather broadly accepted allocative criterion in economics, there is no broadly accepted distributional rule. One's considerations concerning social justice will, to a large extent, determine how one values inequality and redistribution. Within the standard utilitarian framework, the ultimate aim is the maximisation of the sum total utility. Because individuals are generally assumed to have different marginal utility, the distribution of utilities is not an issue.[5] However, there is one exception where equality enters the welfarist framework: concern for equality can be understood from the point of view of cardinalist welfare criteria. If everyone has the same utility function that is increasing in income and concave then, with a given total income, welfare would be maximised if everyone receives the same income. However, this is a special case. Utilitarians do not reject all forms of State redistribution altogether, but they are aware of its limitations due to the distortive effect of taxation which is linked to the problem of incentives. Hence, there is an assumed trade-off between economic efficiency and equity.

Libertarians are much more categorical. They see public welfare provision as paternalistic and eroding personal freedom. Therefore, Robert Nozick advocated a minimal State:

> [A] minimal state, limited to the narrow functions of protection against force, theft, fraud, enforcement of contracts, and so on, is justified; that any more extensive state will violate persons' rights not to be forced to do certain things, and is unjustified (Nozick, 1974: ix).

His view of justice is based on the moral value of rights and entitlements. Any social outcome, including income distribution, is just as long as it is arrived at through a fair exercise of rights and entitlements. It follows that the sole possible role for the State is to see to the proper use of these rights and entitlements. There is, according to his view, no role for the State to play in the redistributive policy field. Any form of welfare state is unacceptable because it is a violation of individual liberties. The relief of destitution through private charities is, to him, the only legitimate way to redistribute income.

Friedrich Hayek and Milton Friedman are more moderate, although they also have a minimalist view of the welfare state. For them, taxation might be legitimate for the limited provision of some public goods and for the relief of poverty up to a (low) level of subsistence. Although Hayek and Friedman see an 'institutional' welfare state as a coercive agency resulting in inefficiencies, they see a 'residual' welfare state as appropriate to relieve destitution and provide certain public goods.

Hayek expected all people to build up money reserves for themselves in order to cover their needs during adverse economic times. He believed private insurance markets would develop in the face of these prospective market opportunities. The State would only have to ensure the development of those insurance companies. Welfare provision by the public authorities is inefficient because it is flawed. It provides for a standard level of welfare to everyone, irrespective of needs and preferences. Moreover, a large social welfare organisation at the national level is an impediment to the creation of other private welfare organisations – also those that, potentially, could offer a higher level of welfare. He also argued that the combination of increasing social security contributions and inflation would eventually lead to more poverty. This, Hayek argued, is because politicians promise adequate levels of social provisions which necessitate, among other things, higher social security contributions.

John Rawls's liberal view on social justice allows us to visualise the welfare state as an ex-ante insurance mechanism. Rawls believes that when individuals are placed behind a veil of ignorance – when they know nothing about their socio-economic background and future capabilities – they will agree on a social contract satisfying a set of principles. The first principle – liberty principle – holds that 'each person is to have an equal right to the most extensive total system of equal basic liberties compatible with a similar system of liberty for all' (Rawls, 1971: 302). The second principle holds that 'social and economic inequalities are to be arranged so that they are both: a) to the greatest benefit of the least advantaged, consistent with the just savings principle; and b) attached to offices and positions open to all under conditions of fair equality of opportunity' (Rawls, 1971: 302).[6] Finally, Rawls rules out possible conflicts between the two principles by giving priority to the first one. Briefly, the principles hold that primary goods (which include economic goods but also opportunities, skills, liberty and self-respect) are to be distributed equally, unless another distribution is to the greatest benefit of the most disadvantaged. Redistributive policies that improve the position of the least well off, therefore, constitute an improvement. In other words, the need for social insurance can be understood from the insurance motive. People are willing to redistribute resources towards the needy since there is a chance that they will find themselves in a similar situation at some time in the future. This well-understood self-interest can, therefore, account for the existence of social insurance schemes. Also, altruistic feelings and the public good feature of the income distribution are some of the other reasons for redistribution.

3.2.2   Altruism and Attitudes Towards Redistribution

Within the utilitarian framework, concern for other people's well-being can result in altruistic behaviour when utility functions are interdependent. When such value judgements enter the utility function, social cohesion and redistribution increase not only the total welfare, but also the individual welfare level. Suppose that both the rich's and the poor's income enter the rich's utility function and that utility increases with income and is concave. In that case, there is an income externality of the poor's income on the utility level of the rich and redistribution from the rich to the poor will be rational as long as the rich's utility increase of additional income transfers to the poor exceeds the disutility of their diminished income (Hochman and Rodgers, 1969).[7]

There is indeed evidence that altruistic behaviour is part of human nature (Hoffman, 1981) and that it can play an important role in explaining economic behaviour (Titmuss, 1971; Arrow, 1972; Becker, 1981; Frank, 1987). The above implies that voluntary redistribution without intervention of the State is a possibility. However, a number of problems arise from private redistribution through, for example, voluntary club formation. First, redistribution by voluntary clubs would, most probably, not be on a sufficiently large scale. Secondly, some risks – such as unemployment – are simply not insurable on the market, because of moral hazard, adverse selection and the interdependence of risks (see below). Thirdly, unless there is club formation with effective control on the club members and enforceability of the social contract, the private solution will be marred by the free-rider problem. Finally, lack of co-ordination among private entities might result in undesirable competition among the clubs (see Section 3.5). Hence, as is the case with other public goods, the market is not expected to produce the Pareto-optimal amount of redistribution. It is the welfare state that is better equipped to cope with these difficulties. Note, however, that the welfare state is more than simply the expression of some altruistic concern. The welfare state is a requirement of social justice.

Human dignity is an accepted value. In as far as the market economy does not secure human dignity, it will have to be preserved by other means (such as the welfare state). The income distribution obtained through the workings of the market might not be the one that maximises the social welfare function. In other words, the social preference for equity might be different than the one produced by the market. Research by the Dutch Social and Cultural Planning Office shows that in 1997, 64 percent of the Dutch population find income differences too large. Sixty-eight percent find that income differences should be (much) smaller (SCP, 1998: 12). In the early 1990s, these percentages were 50 and 56, respectively. In another study, it appears that, in 1995, a small majority of the Dutch population (strongly) agrees that public authorities should promote income equality (52 percent) and increase taxation on higher incomes (52 percent; SCP, 1996: 488). Similarly, using the International Social Survey Program data, Svallfors (1997) shows that 60 percent or more of the population in Norway, Germany and Austria see it as the responsibility of the government to reduce income differences between the rich and the poor (see Table 3.1). The USA (38 percent) and Australia (43 percent) can be found at the other extreme. As far as work opportunities are concerned, the popular support for the State is strongest in European countries. Overseeing the results from attitude survey data for a number of EU countries and some acceding countries, Taylor-Gooby (2002) concludes that there is a strong degree of support for the welfare state, even in countries with low levels of spending on social protection. The majority of people is supportive of redistribution (see Table 3.1; second panel). He, however, concludes that there is no clear pattern of difference between the various welfare regime types.[8]

Table 3.1   Attitudes towards redistribution in a number of nations, percentages agreeing with certain propositions

	It is the responsibility of the government to reduce the differences between people with high and those with low incomes	The government should provide a job for everyone who wants one	People with high income should pay a larger share of income tax than those with lower income	Large income differences are necessary for the country's prosperity
Sweden	53.7	74.1	–	–
Norway	60.0	78.3	–	–
Germany	65.5	66.3	–	–
Austria	69.5	72.1	–	–
Australia	42.6	39.4	–	–
New Zealand	53.1	49.1	–	–
Canada	47.9	40.1	–	–
USA	38.3	47.1	–	–
Sweden	60	–	76	21
Norway	62	–	76	17
Germany	53	–	79	30
Austria	50	–	78	20
UK	69	–	79	18
France	68	–	73	16
Czech Republic	72	–	78	19
Poland	85	–	85	28
Spain	79	–	85	28
Portugal	90	–	88	27

Sources: first panel: Svallfors (1997: 288; data for 1992); second panel: Taylor-Gooby (2002: 17; data for 1999).

One should keep in mind that the above results refer to 'stated preferences': people expressing their preference for some situation or some type of public policy. When actually confronted with the costs of their choice, they might change their preference, attempt to free-ride or migrate. Although the method of stated preferences is gaining in popularity in economics, the revealed preferences methodology remains the most common one for analysing individual behaviour. The numbers might, for example, overestimate the true preference for redistribution, providing results that are less pretentious than suggested above.

3.2.3 Poverty Reduction Through Social Transfers

One of the major effects of social protection is to reallocate resources (income) among individuals. In doing so it affects the level of poverty and inequality. Fully comparative data for all the EU Member States are now becoming available through various waves of the European Community Household Panel (ECHP) of Eurostat (Eurostat, 1997; Eurostat, 2000a, 2001). Here, however, we report somewhat different data for a number of OECD countries included in the Luxembourg Income Study. Table 3.2 indicates that the incidence of poverty is sharply reduced by the existing schemes of social security. Even the Greek system, with its low level of social protection spending, works better than the US system. In this respect, one must be aware that this effect is not the only result of the formal minimum protection schemes but includes the aggregate effect of the entire social protection transfer system. That means that nearly half of social transfers are directed towards households that do not actually need them to reach the minimum level. However, at the same time, the receipt of social protection transfers by all sections of the population upholds public support for the schemes and, in doing so, guarantees that the built-in minimum income safeguards retain their legitimacy.

Computations reveal that there is a negative linear relationship between the poverty rate, on the one hand, and the GDP per capita and level of social security expenditure (as a percentage of GDP), on the other hand. There is a high negative correlation between these two aggregate measurements and the poverty rate. As in Gottschalk and Smeeding (1997), we also found a strong negative correlation between public welfare expenditure and disposable income, implying that only countries spending a substantial part of their budget on social security manage to reduce poverty substantially. However, none of these nations have managed to eliminate poverty completely. It is, however, important to note that such correlations give no indication of the direction of the causality among the variables.

It would be short-sighted to limit social protection to minimum protection. The aim is, in fact, to prevent people from sliding down to – or below –

minimum level. It is not a coincidence that panel analyses have shown that it is above minimum protection that prevents the majority of the elderly, the disabled and the short-term unemployed from sliding into poverty and even further into a situation of multidimensional deprivation and social exclusion. As shown in Chapters 5 and 6, the rather stable rate of poverty generally found in trend studies conceals remarkable processes of mobility.

Table 3.2   Percentage of poor persons after social security transfers and poverty rate reduction due to social security transfers

	Poverty rate after social security (%)[a]	Poverty rate reduction (%)
Australia (1989)	16.1	40.4
Belgium (1992)	5.5	84.1
Canada (1991)	13.2	55.3
Denmark (1992)	5.5	85.0
Finland (1991)	6.4	72.2
France (1984)	11.9	69.0
Germany (1983)	8.0	69.5
Greece (1988)	17.9	47.8[b]
Ireland (1987)	21.2	62.8[b]
Netherlands (1991)	7.7	74.5
Norway (1991)	5.3	79.3
Portugal (1989)	24.5	–
Spain (1988)	15.7	51.0[b]
Sweden (1992)	6.0	86.2
UK (1986)	13.0	65.1
USA (1991)	22.6	28.2

Notes:
a) Poverty line equals 50 percent of mean equivalent income with equivalence scale 1, 0.5, 0.3.
b) Computation at household level based on the equivalence scale 1, 0.7, 0.5 (Deleeck et al., 1992).

Sources: Cantillon et al. (1996); Deleeck et al. (1992).

While comparative information on the effect of social protection on the income distribution may be scarce at the cross-section level, it is even more so at the longitudinal level.[9] Evidence from a few of the better-documented countries, however, points to the plausibility of growing income inequality and a growing dualisation of income distribution and social protection. The evidence also shows that changes in the labour market and in social security status – as well as in human capital and demographic factors, respectively – explain many of the transitions in and out of poverty (Duncan et al., 1993). Also, because equity is such an important factor in accumulating human capital – it is one of the determinants of economic competitiveness – the

equity element of social protection systems cannot simply be disregarded.
Equity is certainly productive in terms of quality of life, but it might also be so when productivity is defined in terms of growth. Advanced empirical research on the equity–productivity relationship would be enlightening. As a matter of fact, according to Okun (1975), economic growth is expected to trickle down to the poor. Okun's hypothesis is that, in the process of economic growth, inequality will initially increase and then decrease as the poor also profit from the fruits of said growth. From this perspective, growth can be seen as a possible solution to the poverty issue. However, there is evidence that long periods of sustained growth have exacerbated income inequalities and failed to reduce poverty (Arjona et al., 2001; de Beer, 2001; Cantillon et al. 2002). Furthermore, economic development and increased individualisation undermine the local structure of traditional solidarities in a community (Chassard and Quintin, 1993). Increased labour market mobility in a modern economy increases the need for employment-related protection. However, economic development also makes it easier to generate the funds necessary to finance such a system. Contrary to expectation, economic growth does not automatically trickle down to the poor. Instead, economic development both strengthens the need for social insurance and facilitates its financing.

3.2.4 The Size of Social Protection Schemes

Social protection systems affect the level of welfare and its distribution. Moreover, although it is not the ultimate aim of social protection to improve economic growth or performance, social protection plays an unmistakably positive role in the economy. Without intending to indicate that there might be an optimal size for the public sector, we can illustrate the effect of public spending (about half of which consists of social security spending) on economic and social performance. Tanzi and Schuknecht (1997) evaluated this performance with respect to a number of welfare indicators for nations grouped according to their level of public spending relative to GDP. Their results are reproduced in Table 3.3. The authors conclude that 'small governments generally show better indicators than big governments' (Tanzi and Schuknecht, 1997: 168). While this might be the case for variables such as the unemployment rate and public debt, let us point out that the differences are negligible for the other variables of economic performance. Moreover, a large public sector tends to perform better in such areas as 'secondary school enrolment' and inequality. Although such data are useful in supplying an overall descriptive picture, their relevance for evaluating the counter-productive effect of public intervention is limited. At any rate, this data do not show that a larger public sector leads to poorer economic performance.

Table 3.3   Size of government and welfare performance, 1990

Indicator	Size of public expenditure in percent of GDP		
	More than 50%[a]	Between 40 and 50%[b]	Between 30 and 40%[c]
Total public expenditure[d]	55.1	44.9	34.6
Economic indicators:			
Real GDP growth (1986–1994)	2.0	2.6	2.5
Standard deviation of GDP growth	1.6	2.1	1.9
Gross fixed capital formation[d]	20.5	21.3	20.7
Inflation rate	3.9	3.7	3.7
Unemployment rate	8.5	11.9	6.6
Public debt[d]	79.0	59.9	53.3
Social indicators:			
Life expectancy (years)	77	77	77
Infant mortality/1,000 births	6.7	7.1	6.4
Secondary school enrolment	92.8	[99.1][e]	89.0
Income share of poorest 40%	24.1	21.6	20.8

Notes:
a) Includes Belgium, Italy, the Netherlands, Norway and Sweden.
b) Includes Austria, Canada, France, Germany, Ireland, New Zealand and Spain.
c) Includes Australia, Japan, Switzerland, the UK and the USA.
d) Percentage of GDP.
e) It seems to us [Tanzi and Schuknecht] that this percentage should be around 90%.

Source: Tanzi and Schuknecht (1997: 167).

Until the early 1900s, public spending remained low. In the period that followed, new ideas concerning the role of the State seemed to justify a higher level of public involvement and spending. In Europe, after the Second World War, the role of the State in the economy was extended from the mere production of public goods to include a redistributive function through the welfare state. This had an inflating effect on public spending. The economic crisis in the 1970s increased the pressure on the government's budget and the State involvement in economic activity. In particular, the sustainability of the welfare state was questioned. Although it has been decreasing since 1993, social protection spending still represents a large percentage of the GDP in Europe. Through their social welfare programmes, governments mobilise, allocate and redistribute resources. In practice, the redistributive function through social security represents a substantial part of the governments' budgets in European countries. In fact, in 2000, in the EU, social expenditure amounted to more than 27 percent of GDP (see Table 3.4).

Table 3.4   *Social protection expenditures of EU countries as a percentage of GDP*

	1991	1996	2000
Belgium	27.1	28.6	26.7
Denmark	29.7	31.4	28.8
Germany	26.1	39.9	29.5
Greece	21.6	22.9	26.4
Spain	21.2	21.9	20.1
France	28.4	31.0	29.7
Ireland	19.6	17.8	14.1
Italy	25.2	24.8	25.2
Luxembourg	22.5	24.0	21.0
Netherlands	32.6	30.1	27.4
Austria	27.0	29.5	28.7
Portugal	17.2	21.2	22.7
Finland	29.8	31.6	25.2
Sweden	34.3	34.7	32.3
UK	25.7	28.0	26.8
EU15	26.4	28.4	27.3

Source: Abramovici (2003).

The welfare state is regularly under attack because of these large levels of expenditure. It is claimed to be counter-productive with disincentive and distortive effects on the market. In particular, it is felt that the EU is at a comparative disadvantage with respect to the USA, which has a lower level of spending. A publication by the Dutch ministry of social affairs – using material on Belgium, Germany, Denmark, the UK, Japan, the Netherlands, Sweden and the USA – has pointed out that total social expenditure as a percentage of GDP does not differ greatly among these nations (Ministry of Social Affairs, 1996: 158). The exceptions are Sweden and the USA, with higher and lower levels of expenditure, respectively. The publication shows that the variations in the level of public expenditure are, to a certain extent, compensated by variations of private expenditure. The figures in Table 3.4 are gross figures based on expenditures by the social protection institutions. Correcting them for taxes and social contributions that are levied on benefits leads to slightly different figures of net public expenditure. Moreover, when expenditure on social risks by private insurance schemes are taken into account, the picture again changes, resulting in a sharp decrease in the difference between the Member States of the EU and the USA (see Table 3.5). The overall actual trend, however, is towards less interventionism from the State and increased attention for decentralisation and market mechanisms.

Table 3.5   *Gross and net public and private expenditure for social*
protection as a percentage of GDP, 1997

	Gross public social expenditure*	Net current public social expenditure	Private social expenditure	Net total social expenditure
Belgium	30.4	26.3	2.2	28.5
Denmark	35.9	26.7	0.8	27.5
Germany	29.2	27.2	1.6	28.8
Ireland	19.6	17.1	1.3	18.4
Italy	29.4	24.1	1.2	25.3
Netherlands	27.1	20.3	3.7	24.0
Austria	28.5	23.4	1.2	24.6
Finland	33.3	24.8	0.8	25.6
Sweden	35.7	28.5	2.1	30.6
UK	23.8	21.6	3.0	24.6
Japan	15.1	14.8	0.9	15.7
USA	15.8	16.4	7.0	23.4

Note: *) Due to differences in definitions, the OECD percentages in this table differ from the Eurostat data presented in Table 3.4.

Source: Adema (2001).

3.3   EFFICIENCY ARGUMENTS FOR SOCIAL PROTECTION

Under conditions of pure and perfect competition market forces are expected to generate a Pareto-efficient outcome. This is because:

- the multiplicity of suppliers on the market makes it possible for the consumers to shop around and choose the price–quality combination that best corresponds to their tastes. This advantage of shopping around disappears as soon as there is only one (central) supplier;
- needs and preferences are better perceived at a level close to the consumers than at a higher level. It would, therefore, be more efficient to let the market take care of the production so that it better fits the preferences of the consumers;
- innovation usually increases when competition increases. This innovation process increases efficiency and benefits the economy;
- it is often argued that efficiency gains of the market might eventually result in lower administration costs than would be the case if the public authority were in charge, so it is often argued. This statement, however, is to be treated with caution. Even if it were true, it does not

mean that the cost for the consumer would be lower because private producers are also profit-makers.

The principle of subsidiarity, when seen in this context, can be interpreted as saying that all activities should be left to the market unless it is inefficient to do so. There are instances where the market is inefficient and the first theorem of welfare economics does not hold. Then, corrective action by the State – in the form of regulation, taxation or subsidisation, or public production – is to be considered. These instances have to do with market failures and imperfect information. Efficiency arguments for the welfare state relate largely to the existence of such market failures and informational problems causing an inefficient allocation of resources. The possible sources of allocative inefficiency are summarised in Table 3.6. The implications in the field of social protection will be developed shortly. However, apart from this, we also show that there is an efficiency argument to be made for the stabilisation and redistributive function of social protection. In other words, it might well be the case that an insufficient level of social protection is inefficient.

Table 3.6   Reasons why market provision is not always efficient

Informational problems	Market failures
Tastes	Public goods
Imperfect consumer information	Merit goods
Adverse selection	Imperfect competition
Moral hazard	Increasing returns to scale
Unpredictable probabilities of social risk	External effects
Interdependent probabilities of social risk	Income externalities
Probabilities of social risk close to unity	Non-clearing markets

Market failures refer to imperfect competition (increasing returns to scale and natural monopoly), externalities, the production of public goods and merit wants (goods and services the government believes are consumed in too little or too large quantities), the non-existence of a full set of markets (for all dates in future and all risks), failure to attain full equilibrium (underutilisation of resources). Informational problems include imperfect consumer information, adverse selection, moral hazard and the fact that the probabilities of social risks might be unpredictable, interdependent or close to unity. Imperfect information will possibly result in the absence of some insurance markets. As Barr (1992) argues, the correction of market failures can justify the existence of a residual welfare state. Informational problems, on the other hand, call for a welfare state that is more than residual. The key here is that the government engages in a selection of activities that the market is unable to provide efficiently. In other areas, conform to the principle of subsidiarity, governments abstain from intervention.

3.3.1   Informational Problems and the Insurance Market

One of the underlying assumptions of pure and perfect competition in economics is that information is priceless and perfect. However, information is not priceless: there might be some inefficiency due to the diversity of suppliers on the market. Moreover, information is not always perfect: the market cannot always deal adequately with problems of moral hazard or adverse selection.[10] The State is then called upon to take care of the production of these goods and services. The problem of moral hazard, however, may even persist in the case of public provision. Alternatively, it can also introduce some minimum quality or safety constraints to be respected by private producers in order to convey the adverse selection effect. It can also oblige the individual to buy a given quantity of a good or service to circumvent the adverse selection problem.

Would the 'invisible hand' lead to the establishment of social insurance markets? Intuitively, it is clear that self-interested individuals would be in favour of the introduction of a social security safety net. Because individuals do not have perfect information about their future – they might become ill, disabled or lose their jobs – and do not perfectly know the probability of occurrence of these hazards, they want to insure an income in case such events occur. This results from the common assumption that individuals are risk-averse. Without having to appeal to any moral consideration, we can explain why self-interested individuals would be supportive of a minimum income protection scheme when put behind the Rawls' veil of ignorance. However, there is no straightforward way to organise such a scheme on the market. Some might not be willing to pay a price for income protection that they think is too high compared to their perceived probability of needing it. Before the veil of ignorance is lifted, all are ready to participate but, once it is raised, people gain insight into their capabilities and earning potential. This could lead to an adverse selection process that would eventually lead to the disappearance of the market for income protection. Also, some people (the free-riders) might not contribute at all to the system – expecting others to pay – and thus profit from services they did not pay for. Eventually, if the probability of calling upon the minimum protection scheme can be influenced by the potential recipient of the benefit – a situation referred to as moral hazard – the market solution would not be sustainable either. In these instances of informational problems, the market is not efficient in producing minimum protection.

Some risks are, therefore, thought to be uninsurable by the market. This may be because the various risks cannot be pooled, because they involve an adverse selection process or because of moral hazard. In the case of unemployment insurance, for example, informational problems on employability, incentives and search intensity prevent the existence of an unemployment insurance market. Moral hazard occurs when the unemployed are able to influence their chances of getting a job without the insurer knowing about it. However, there is also a second problem. Since unemployment can, potentially, affect many people at once – as during an economic recession – private insurers are not willing to assume that risk. This is because the possibilities for risk pooling are rather limited due to the positive correlation of the risk insured between insurance policies. Unemployment risk is, therefore, often presented as uninsurable on the market, because neither a competitive (with a single insurance contract for 'good' and 'bad' risks) nor a separating equilibrium (with different insurance contracts for the 'good' and 'bad' risks) is attainable in unemployment insurance (see Appendix 1 for a detailed presentation). In the area of health care, a similar argument can be made: adverse selection can also occur when insurers cannot discriminate between good and bad risks. These problems reduce the possibility for the development of a viable private insurance market and call for State intervention or regulation. For instance, making insurance compulsory can solve the adverse selection problem.[11]

Therefore, it is rather unlikely that the market outcome will be Pareto-efficient. Indeed, one condition to Pareto efficiency is full information. This condition is hardly ever satisfied in practice. From the above discussion, it appears that the case for a private minimum protection insurance market is not as straightforward as it might seem. If private insurers could develop instruments for screening their clients and distinguish the good from the bad risk groups they would concentrate on the former group, leaving the latter to its own fate. Given this selectivity towards the good risks, Titmuss (1974) rejects the 'residual welfare model' and argues in favour of the 'institutional welfare model' (see also Chapter 4).

It is such information problems that – alongside equity (Section 3.2) and stabilisation (Section 3.3.4) considerations – lead the State to make social insurance compulsory. In the case of old age or unemployment, where the risks are, respectively, certain and positively correlated, the State assumes the provision of insurance itself. However, public provision of social support may not result in an increase in total (public and private) support. Public support may crowd out private support because individuals may then reduce the level of their savings and their support to family and friends.

3.3.2 Market Failures and Social Protection

Increasing returns to scale and externalities

First of all, markets may fail when competition fails. This occurs if production costs decline when the scale of production increases, as is the case with, for example, the distribution of gas, water and electricity (increasing returns to scale). The profit-maximising producer will charge a price that is higher than the Pareto-efficient price level and produce correspondingly less. In this case, it would be more efficient to have one single supplier, a so-called natural monopoly. When competition fails, correction mechanisms or production by the State may be required. The existence of economies of scale in the production of public goods and in administrative activities may justify production on a larger scale. Mitchell (1998) shows that a 1 percent increase in welfare programme participation leads to a less than proportional increase in the costs to the magnitude of 0.6 to 0.9 percent. Moreover, Gouyette and Pestieau (1999) provide evidence suggesting that publicly managed insurance systems are less costly than privately managed ones. They do point to productive inefficiencies in welfare provision programmes (one could do better with less) – although it has been argued that they overestimate the magnitude of these inefficiencies (Ravallion, 2001) – but recognise that privatisation is not a solution.

Market production is also inefficient whenever there are positive or negative externalities. Externalities occur whenever someone's utility or production relationships include factors that are influenced by another party. Production at a higher level or imposition of a transfer scheme – in case of environmental issues from the polluter to the polluted – by a senior authority makes it possible to internalise these externalities.[12] A specific case involving income externalities was discussed in Section 3.2.

Merit goods: education and training

One of the failures of the market is its inability to produce public goods, or to produce them in optimal quantity.[13] There is no incentive here for the private producer to produce these goods since, once these are manufactured, he or she cannot exclude anybody from consuming them. Therefore, the State must be responsible for the production of these goods. Similarly, it might be more efficient to let the State handle the production of goods for which individual preferences are thought to be distorted (merit goods). Two main arguments can be pointed out. First, if allocated an income supplement, individuals are not likely to purchase the most appropriate level of education, health care, and so on. The existence of these merit goods is based on the assumption that individual preferences for these goods are distorted or that income is too low to purchase them. Secondly, since these goods and services directly influence general welfare, the government might wish to have close control of the price, quantity and quality of these goods.

This argument is most applicable in the area of education. Modern economies do, of course, profit from a well-educated, well-trained and healthy workforce. Human capital accumulation is the key to a sustained economic growth, since it stimulates productivity and investments. Specifically, investment in human capital – to improve the quality and the skills of the labour force – can be used to upgrade the productivity of workers whom productivity level is too low compared to the level of the minimum wage. Much research has been devoted to showing the positive effect of human capital on economic performance. Barro and Sala-i-Martin (1995) provide a review of the literature. Education and training contribute to developing talent into human capital that can be used in the production process. Education increases the quality of the labour force, thereby enhancing marginal productivity. This effect can be amplified through on-the-job training. By the same token, education contributes to the development of the infrastructure, which has an undeniable effect on the investment climate, especially investment in the high-technology/high-qualification sector. It must be stressed that investment in education only has positive effects in the medium and long term. This is well illustrated by the UK situation. Here employers have urged the government to support primary schools in order to avoid the extension of illiteracy. In the longer term, this might have important consequences for the maintenance of labour skills. Education and training of the long-term unemployed is also productive in that it maintains human capital stock which can be used in the production process when necessary (economic upturns).

Using an overlapping generations model Chiu (1998) has shown that a more equal distribution of income implies higher human capital accumulation and economic performance. He argues that in a market economy, one's material resources have an impact on the possibility to develop and use one's talent. Assuming that receiving education is a necessary condition for fully developing one's talent and that education is costly – and assuming declining marginal utility – the wealthy will find it cheaper to educate their offspring and purchase more education. This possibility would be denied to children from poorer families. Assuming that talented individuals create more human capital, total human capital increases when wealth is redistributed from rich to poor. Rich families will see the opportunity cost of sending their less talented children to college increase and will stop sending them while the poor, who are made richer, find buying education justifiable for their more talented offspring (more talented than the riches' offspring who drop out). To the extent that human capital is a determinant to growth, greater income equality will then contribute to better economic performance. His conclusion does not sustain the idea that redistributive taxation will improve economic performance because it does not take into account the disincentive effects. The conclusion holds if the disincentive effect of making taxation more progressive is low or if there is a one-off – previously unannounced – increase in progressive taxation.

Lifelong learning and equal opportunities

In the context of skilled-biased technological change (see, for example, Autor et al., 1998), schooling and especially training and lifelong learning take an important place. In a logic of economic specialisation, high levels of education call for high levels of training. The role of the welfare state is to provide for adequate initial schooling, but stimulating 'learning-by-doing' and 'on-the-job training' are also productive strategies. In this respect employers have an active role to play. In the context of the knowledge-based economy strategies to support lifelong learning are crucial to counter the depreciation of skills over time (de la Fuente and Ciccone, 2002).

Investing in human capital gains weight in the context of the ageing workforce in Europe. But not only the older workers need to be trained in order to ensure the continuity of labour supply. Schooling and training is also crucial for migrant workers – who often have lower educational levels – and female workers in order to warrant their participation in the economic process. An approach in terms of equal opportunities is likely to promote economic efficiency and to prevent social exclusion (Rubery et al., 1998). From the point of view of gender equality, it has been shown that male and female workers have more or less equal chances to participate in job-related training but that such training is more likely to be paid or subsidised by the employer in the case of male workers (OECD, 1999). The same publication also presents evidence of the reinforcement of skills differences in the economy. Better-educated workers receive training more often than lower-educated workers, but less so in the case of the Nordic countries, the Netherlands and Ireland. One reason for this could be the better involvement of the social partners in policy-making in these countries. The reinforcement of skills differences appears to be strongest in Southern welfare regimes and Belgium. There are lessons to be drawn here if one wants to limit exclusion from knowledge.

Externalities and return to education and training

One problem with education and schooling programmes resides in the evaluation of their social and private returns (see Temple, 2000). Whether such programmes should be financed with public money or not depends on the existence of social returns. By the same token, whether employers are wishing to engage in training of their workforce depends on whether or not they expect their gain from training to be larger than the costs they incur. Because of externalities to training and schooling, it is difficult to bring about the socially optimal level of schooling or training.

Stevens (1996) showed that the standard distinction between general and specific training does not cover all types of training. She points to the existence of externalities to transferable training: 'a labour market in which skills are transferable but not perfectly general is likely to be imperfectly competitive' (Stevens, 1996: 23). Snower (1996) identified two other sources of externalities: training supply and vacancy supply externalities. The first type of externality implies that the larger the number of skilled workers, the greater the probability that firms find skilled workers to fill their vacancies. Henceforth, the private return to schooling falls short of the social return. The vacancy supply externality implies that the greater the number of skilled vacancies, the greater the probability that skilled workers find a good job. Hence, the return to schooling is expected to increase. This means that when a firm creates a vacancy, its private return falls short of the social return (which also includes the increased return to training of the workers). His conclusion is that there is a case for the government to stimulate the acquisition of skills. This can be done either through education subsidy or skilled employment subsidy. Both types would stimulate workers to acquire more skills (Snower, 1996: 121). However, education subsidy will not change the number of skilled jobs. A skilled employment subsidy would stimulate both the supply of skilled jobs and skilled workers, and, therefore, lead to overall upgrading on the labour market.

Finally, upon studying German and US data, Acemoglu and Pischke (1998: 23) suggest that the fact that both low- and high-skilled workers receive training in Germany while it is concentrated among high-skilled workers in the USA contributes to wage compression in the former country and wage dispersion in the latter.

3.3.3 Social Protection Enhancing Allocative Efficiency

While it is often recognised that the benefit system has a disincentive effect on work effort, it may also induce risk-taking. Sinn's theoretical model indeed shows that the welfare state fulfils a risk-reducing function (Sinn, 1995, 1996). When protected by the benefit system, people engage in risky and profitable economic activities which they would probably not undertake otherwise. Using panel data for the USA and western Europe, Bird (2001) indeed shows that measures of risk are positively correlated to the GDP share of social spending. However, further investigation is needed to determine how much the dominant culture of a nation (for example, USA versus European countries) affects the behaviour of individuals.

One could also argue that income support for the unemployed, ill, those on maternity leave, and so on, has a positive effect on transitions within the labour market and, therefore, on its flexibility. Because of the existence of social security, there can be more flexibility in employment contracts and job search can be more efficient. Because unemployment insurance secures an income when out of work, the unemployed are able to search for another job that is in line with their skills (Atkinson and Mogensen, 1993).

On the basis of the job search theory, one would expect that higher unemployment benefits would increase the duration of unemployment. Yet, a review of the research done in the Netherlands shows no conclusive evidence for this theoretical expectation (Jehoel-Gijsbers et al., 1995). Moreover, a recent study of UK unemployed suggests that those who took longer to find jobs tend to be rewarded with more stable employment (Böheim and Taylor, 2000). Two corollaries are that human capital is used more efficiently and that mismatch is less likely. An active labour market policy obviously has a role to play here. Because the unemployed receive benefits when out of work, they are able to interact in economic and social life and invest in training. In the long run, it helps them maintain their employability and facilitates their reintegration into the labour force. Here again, an active labour market policy might help to attain these goals. For the long-term unemployed, in particular, active labour market measures might increase the chances of re-employment.

As strange as it may seem, unemployment benefits can also be expected to have a beneficial effect on the mobility and flexibility of the labour force. This is in spite of the fact that the welfare state is often under attack because of the suggested distortive effect of labour market regulations and social programmes, which are said to reduce labour market flexibility. In fact, there is little or no evidence that social programmes have a negative effect on labour market flexibility. The contributors in Blank (1994) show that:

- the relaxation of lay-off regulations in Belgium, France and Germany has not led to an adjustment of the number of hours worked in response to macroeconomic shocks;
- despite its stricter labour market regulations, Japan achieved a higher rate of economic growth in the 1980s than the USA;
- while it is expected that the State, through its housing market policy, would impede labour market mobility and flexibility – it tends to tie workers to one location – there is little evidence for such effects;
- in Spain, mandated fringe benefits' taxes have had little impact on the labour market;
- in the USA and the UK, there is little difference between the public and the private sector in labour market response to economic changes.

One comes to the conclusion, when analysing labour market incentives, that labour market elasticities are quite small as are the effects of taxes and transfers on the labour supply (Atkinson and Mogensen, 1993). Although there is evidence that specific welfare transfer payments (retirement, sickness and parental leave) affect the number of hours worked, taxes and transfers generally have a smaller effect on male than on female participation (Atkinson and Mogensen, 1993).[14]

In Europe, provisions such as maternity leave, parental leave and palliative care represent opportunities offered by the social protection system on to which more flexibility on the labour market can be grafted. Such facilities respond to family needs while, at the same time, guaranteeing a high level of job security. This European approach is quite different from that in the USA.

3.3.4 Efficiency Argument with Regard to Stabilisation

Perhaps the most recognised effect of the benefit system is that it smoothes business cycles by diminishing the volatility of demand. This anti-cyclical effect comes into play because expenditure tends to rise when there is a downturn in the business cycle and a fall when there is an upturn. Social protection then helps limit the dead-weight loss resulting from volatility in the economy. Evidence for the USA and Canada shows that federal tax and transfer flows cushion 31 and 17 percent, respectively, of regional income shocks (Bayoumi and Masson, 1995). The long-term redistribution effects are estimated at 22 and 39 percent, respectively. The estimates for the EU Member States are similar to the USA. Sala-i-Martin and Sachs (1991) estimate that tax and transfer adjustments eliminate up to 40 percent of income declines. These estimates show that it is possible to cushion adverse economic shocks by borrowing and budget deficit. However, the fiscal constraints of the European Monetary Union (EMU) greatly limit the possibilities to do so.

If social spending has a positive effect in terms of automatic stabiliser, then this should be most obvious in open economies. Rodrik (1998) explored the positive association between the degree of openness of economies and the size of government spending, using a sample of over a hundred countries. He concludes that government spending indeed provides a social insurance in economies subject to external shocks. When the share of total trade (exports plus imports) in GDP increases by 10 percentage points, government consumption would increase by 0.8 percentage points for a country at the mean of the cross-country distribution of the terms-of-trade instability. He also provides evidence for the fact that the risk-reducing role of government spending is strong for social security and welfare spending. This is particularly true in advanced countries, which have the requisite administrative capacity to manage social welfare transfers. In those countries, it is not government consumption but social spending that correlates with external risk. In the same vein, Andersen (2002, 2003) elaborated a theoretical model in which he shows that tighter integration of product markets is conducive to higher volatility of private consumption. Henceforth, there is a case for expanding the social insurance provided through State contingent public activities. This finding is relevant within the context of the EU.

The argument presented above must be seen in the context of Keynsian economic policy: by guaranteeing income during unemployment, illness, and so on, the benefit system stimulates demand and restores economic growth. The significance of social assistance also has to be valued in this context. It is the protection of last resort. Residents who have no rights to replacement income – or have lost these rights – can still benefit from social assistance if they satisfy the conditions of a means test. Social assistance then clearly plays an economic role in terms of sustaining aggregate demand. An active policy of reinsertion – along with social assistance – can play a major role in training long-term recipients and putting them into the labour market.

Nonetheless, the social protection system has often been under attack because it is believed to impede growth. However, a review of a number of studies by Atkinson (1996, 1999) shows that there is no conclusive evidence for this. More recently, Arjona et al. (2001) have provided evidence with respect to increased market inequality in almost all countries in the Organisation for Economic Co-operation and Development (OECD). They note that total household income inequality has also increased, but this trend was less general. A close examination of the data does not lead to the conclusion that a wider income inequality is good for growth. The authors show that, on balance, social expenditure seems to be bad for growth. However, it does depend on the type of expenditure considered. In the margin, spending on active policies seems to have a positive effect on growth.

The social protection system can also be viewed as a form of institutional saving. Through compulsory old-age and unemployment insurance, for example, workers operate an intergenerational or intertemporal income transfer. They trade off consumption today for consumption when retired or unemployed, and therefore also limit the volatility of aggregate demand.

3.3.5   Social Capital and Social Peace

Although problems of definition and measurement are undeniable, the notion of social capital – which can be defined in terms of trust or participation to social networks – is gaining much attention, also in the field of economics.

There is increasing evidence that social capital formation has a positive contribution to economic performance (for a review, see Temple, 2000).[15] Social capital, so it can be argued, can contribute to improved allocative efficiency, but also to macroeconomic stability. Intuitively, the idea is that in societies with low levels of social capital – or trust – resources are diverted towards verification of other party's action and protection of one's position and rights. This means that resources are diverted from their productive aim. In other words, trust provides a way out of the prisoner's dilemma by increasing the odds of a co-operative solution with a higher pay-off. From the point of view of social networks, intuition tells us that in societies where such networks are better developed, the transfer or spillover of knowledge between actors is greater.

As Woolcock (2001: 13) defines it, 'social capital refers to the norms and networks that facilitate collective action'. Solidaristic or 'dense' social relationships, according to Coleman (1986), are attractive not only from a pure sociological point of view, but also from an economic one. One is more likely to engage in economic exchange with people one trusts. Dense social relationships enhance social trust and reciprocity and, therefore, increase the chance that people will engage in economic exchange. Putnam (1993) also shows that social integration – through social networks – is a key element of economic development. He presents evidence that social integration can go hand in hand with economic success: membership of choral societies as well as co-operatives and football clubs are good predictors of a strong and effective local democracy and economy. Moreover, to the extent that the welfare state contributes to social inclusion, it contributes to the supply of labour and, in the longer term, to an improvement of its quality (Pedroso, 1997).

Since Putnam's work, numerous studies on the relationship between social capital and economic indicators have been carried out. In particular, the effect of social capital on economic growth has received much attention. Using growth data for the 1960–85 period in a large number of developing countries, Temple and Johnson (1998) demonstrate that economists would have reached a better prediction of economic development had they accounted for the effect of social capital. In their article on the economic pay-off of social capital in a sample of market economies, Knack and Keefer (1997) found that indicators of trust and civic norm were significantly and positively associated with economic growth. They refute Putnam's finding that membership in formal groups is associated with economic performance but they state that a 10 percentage-point increase in trust results in a 0.8 percentage-point increase in growth. The effect they found results from a rising share of investment in GDP. In a recent paper, Beugelsdijk et al. (2002) have submitted the Knack and Keefer results to a series of robustness tests and have given critical comments on their findings. They found a lower growth effect of trust ranging between 0.4 and 0.8 percent. Moreover, the significance of the relationship is affected by the way investments are operationalised.

Perhaps of greater relevance to the European context is Beugelsdijk and van Schaik's study of the relationship between social capital and growth in 54 European regions (Beugelsdijk and van Schaik, 2001). Two major findings emerge from their research. The first is that – contrary to their later research (Beugelsdijk et al., 2002) – their measure of trust is found to have no significant effect on the growth rate across European regions. The second is that not only the existence of network relationships is associated with higher growth but also that the level of active involvement in these networks is beneficial for growth.

The social capital argument also implies that divided societies will have greater difficulty in coping with adverse economic shocks. This expectation finds support in Rodrik (1999) who provides econometric evidence showing that the economies which experienced the sharpest fall in growth rates in the 1970s are those with weak institutions and divided social ties. In relation to this, we can also point to the role of social partners as a form of social capital. For example, in the Netherlands, the social partners have been intensely involved in designing the Dutch socio-economic policy. This is often seen as the reason behind the Dutch economic success. Also, in a large number of other Member States, partnerships between the social partners and the governments have been built up (European Commission, 2002b).

More generally, there is an opportunity cost of not having (or having an insufficient level of) social protection. For example, in the absence of socialised health care, health insurance would have to be provided privately. This can turn out to be very costly and still leave many unprotected, as is clearly the case in the USA. It can be noted that social transfers enhance social cohesion and, therefore, reduce the risk of production disruption due to social conflicts. To some extent, Jordan's (1996) application of the theory of clubs as an explanation for social exclusion can be linked to the debate on social capital as social networks.

The opportunity cost of inadequate redistributive policies is not only inequity but also higher crime and social unrest, leading to higher private security and insurance costs. Hence, an adequate level of social provisions is expected to contribute to social peace. Because social conflicts disrupt employment, destroy infrastructure and deter investment, their prevention – through the benefit system – is beneficial for investments and productivity. Social cohesion is expected to have a positive effect on the creation of prosperity (Begg and Berghman, 2001). In this sense, social transfers contribute positively to the social climate. When the social climate is good, enterprises can go about their business without concern for possible disruptions. Kennedy et al. (1998) provide some evidence for the relationship among inequality, social capital and social peace. The authors, using data for 39 US states, come to the conclusion that income inequality correlates strongly with violent firearm criminality and social capital indicators such as per capita group membership and lack of social trust. Social capital variables also correlate strongly with violent firearm criminality. The authors also suggest that the effect of inequality on criminality is partly mediated by social capital.

Recent trends towards individualisation have substantially increased the risk of family instability and single parenthood. These demographic processes are not without consequence for the general well-being of, in particular, single mothers and their children. This is especially true because the primary sphere of redistribution and welfare is the household, that is the most basic social network. Social assistance is one way of preserving well-being. It mends the problems of a social protection system that is not fully equipped to deal with the changing reality of society.

Although the relationships between social capital and economic performance, on the one hand, and between social policy and social capital, on the other hand, needs further investigation, what the argumentation above shows is that there is but a thin line between social and economic or employment objectives.

3.4 THE ECONOMIC ROLE OF CENTRAL AND DECENTRAL AUTHORITIES

3.4.1 Subsidiarity and Fiscal Federalism

At present, the EU Member States are being pressured due to two developments. First, Member States are yielding power to the European Community as a result of the European integration process. Secondly, within the Member States, there is a process of decentralisation such that functions of the central public authorities are being transferred to local governments or the market.[16] In both these processes, there is the problem of choosing a frame of reference – that is Europe, the Member States, the decentral collectivities, the market – for the economic function generally performed by the State.

Theories of fiscal federalism provide some insight into whether, in a federal setting, the central authority – or rather the decentral entities – can perform the allocative, stabilisation and redistributive functions. The principle of subsidiarity assumes a significant role in economic theories of fiscal federalism. In this context, it means that what can be achieved efficiently by sub-central entities should not be done by higher levels of government. Subsidiarity prioritises policy or system competition among decentral entities. Although the EU is not a federation *senso stricto* (there is no central EU government, for example) it can be thought of in terms of a federal construction in which sub-central entities – the Member States – relate to a central authority – Europe and its institutions. Therefore, the implications from fiscal federalism literature do apply to the EU framework. In this section, we evaluate the relevance of the findings for the European context, especially in the field of redistribution and minimum protection. We argue that the choice of the preferred frame of reference should not solely be guided by efficiency considerations. Concern for equity should also be taken into account.

3.4.2　Fiscal Policy and the Stabilisation of Economic Shocks

The stabilisation function relates to the internal and external economic equilibrium. It implies control of monetary policy, prices (inflation), growth, the balance of payments, and so on. Although the economic conditions may differ among sub-central areas, there is little support in fiscal federalism literature to allow macroeconomic stabilisation policies to vary among these regions. Because of the obvious side-effects of such policies, the use of stabilisation instruments requires centralisation. If, for example, the decentral authorities were to have the power to create their own money, there would be an incentive for expansionary monetary policy that would induce inflation. If decentral authorities were able to run budget deficits in order to absorb adverse economic shocks, there would be spillover effects into other areas, especially when the propensity to import is large. This is particularly true when economies are open – as within the EMU – so that the expenditure multiplier would be rather small (see Oates, 1972: 5). As Gourinchas (1997) argues, federal fiscal policy acts as an automatic stabiliser in the presence of asymmetric shocks. Lee (1998) argues that, on the one hand, local redistribution responds best to the local demand while, on the other hand, a centralised system of redistribution is superior when economic shocks are asymmetric. This is all the more true when local jurisdictions have fewer possibilities of correcting imbalances by borrowing or running budget deficits. Similarly, Sinn (1993) argues that, on the one hand, interregional social transfers are a means of promoting social peace in Europe and thus contributing to the full exploitation of the economies of scale in a large EU market. On the other hand, he points out that such transfers work as an insurance mechanism because today's wealthy regions might need the poor regions' support when the roles are reversed.

By agreeing to take part in the EMU, the Member States (or at least a number of them) have constrained themselves in the use of their monetary, budgetary and fiscal instruments. These nations have forfeited their main instruments for restoring competitiveness: that is the exchange rate and the possibility to run budget deficits. In the longer run, it is expected that the efficiency gains of the single market will be favourable to employment and economic activity.[17] This, in turn, should benefit social security. Nevertheless, it is uncertain whether or not these benefits will be equally distributed among groups of individuals and among countries within the EU (Begg and Nectoux, 1995). Since there are no redistribution mechanisms at the European level (with the exception of the Structural Fund and the Social Fund which have only limited budgets), the future of social security and social integration are at stake.

From an economic point of view, the advantages of the EMU are not equal among Member States. Convergence of interest rates, inflation and wages leads to an increase of real labour costs. This has a negative effect on productivity in the economically weak regions, thereby increasing unemployment in the short run. For the moment, it might be too much to require compensation mechanisms among nations through solidarity mechanisms. However, with the potential of increased labour market mobility and new social risks, the need to co-ordinate the Member States' social policies is becoming more pressing. Integrating social and employment policy further at the European level is a guarantee for a strong Europe.

When the EMU is fully brought into operation, its members will only be able to respond to economic shocks through a limited set of instruments: that is in and out migration of production factors, increased labour market flexibility or variations in the cost of production factors. However, implementing any of these measures is not without problems. The use of migration as a stabilisation instrument is debatable and politically sensitive. Moreover, migration flows are difficult to steer. Given that in open economies, such as in the EU, countries are price-takers, it is impossible for them to significantly alter the return rate of – highly mobile – capital through changes in capital taxation. Restoring competitiveness by increasing wage flexibility also has its problems. Because wages are sticky, adjustments will be slow and probably insufficient to correct a temporary disequilibrium. Labour costs can, however, also be made flexible through changes in taxes and social security premiums. This will, however, inevitably lead to a sobering of public provisions and open the possibility for social dumping (see Chapter 4). Because price and wage rates comparisons will become easier within the EMU, labour mobility is likely to increase in reaction to wage differentials. The wage, however, is not the sole aspect of labour costs.

Fringe benefits also play a part and can be at stake when competition increases. Although labour market flexibilisation potentially improves allocative efficiency – and therefore function as a stabilisation instrument – flexibilisation also increases work insecurity. However, using labour market flexibilisation as a stabilisation instrument has its limits too. This is particularly the case when the labour market is tight.[18] In the following, we concentrate on the distributive and allocative effects of wages and taxes, as well as the effect of migration.

3.5   REDISTRIBUTION AND ALLOCATION IN THEORIES OF FISCAL FEDERALISM

Factor mobility in response to wage or fiscal differentials plays an important role in models of fiscal federalism dealing with the desirability and sustainability of decentral redistribution policy. In discussing the interplay between allocation and redistribution in a federal setting – and referring to the above allocative efficiency argument for social protection (see Table 3.6) – we pay attention to the differences in preferences for redistribution and income externalities among decentralised levels of government. Factor mobility, with its impact on social tourism and social dumping remains, however, one of the major issues in the literature of fiscal federalism.

3.5.1   Factor Allocation in an Economic Union

From a macroeconomic point of view, the Hecksher–Ohlin model predicts that economic integration is conducive to an alignment of unit production costs, at least in the exposed sector. Either free trade or free migration will lead to the international equalisation of factor costs and an efficient allocation of production factors. Similarly, Tiebout (1956) associates government activity in a multi-level government to market mechanisms. A diversity of local governments – with their own sets of public services – enables individuals to choose the location that best suits their tastes and preferences. If citizens (and investors) are dissatisfied with the provision of local public goods, they will 'vote with their feet' and migrate to another sub-central entity. This process will lead to an efficient allocation of factors, just as the invisible hand leads to an efficient allocation of resources on the market. However, the Tiebout model must be qualified since it rests on a number of unrealistic hypotheses. There is, for example, no full competition among decentral communities, a limited number of communities, no free access to the creation of new communities and the decisions concerning the production of public goods involves more than pure profit (it is also the result of a political process). The aforementioned allocative efficiency gain due to mobility of labour and capital does not always hold. As Boadway and Wildasin (1984) show, this inter-local mobility – induced by tax differentials or variations in the level of public goods – might not be desirable from a collective point of view. Inefficient labour migration will result when total local expenditure is on pure public goods, financed by residence-based taxes, or on private-type public goods, financed by source-based taxes. By the same token, mobility of capital is expected to result in tax competition among local jurisdictions. Ultimately, it will lead to zero taxes on capital, which implies either a reduction of public expenditure or an increase in the taxation of other production factors, neither of which is an optimal outcome.

Adverse selection also accounts for the inefficiency of sub-central redistribution. Basically, allowing for policy competition in fields where governments first stepped in to correct market failures is just as likely to result in those same failures (Sinn, 1997). Redistribution and insurance are two sides of the same coin. Policy competition in the area of redistribution is equivalent to the insured choosing their insurance company ex post (Sinn, 1993). The market breaks down because the rich or skilled choose the nightwatchmen State while the poor or unskilled choose universal coverage. In the presence of mobile production factors, mobility is likely to result in a sorting effect making redistribution policy impossible. Wildasin (1997), however, argues that an integrated labour market with free mobility works as an insurance against income risk, so mobility ensures equalisation of factor income and makes redistribution redundant.

3.5.2 Factor Mobility

Factor mobility plays an important role in the models of fiscal federalism. Fiscally induced labour mobility is shown to decrease welfare because fiscal differentials trigger mobility that does not follow from factor price differentials. Moreover, factor mobility is conducive to a reduction of the tax base (due to out migration) and an increase in the tax burden for the immobile production factor.

Mobile labour
Models show that, when factors of production are assumed to be immobile – or that mobility is very costly and sub-central areas have different tastes – decentralisation of the redistributive function is most efficient (Pauly, 1973).[19] Autonomous governments can determine their redistributive policy according to what they consider to be an acceptable distribution of welfare.

However, the situation changes when production factors are assumed to be mobile. From a macroeconomic point of view, economic integration leads – in the exposed sector – to the alignment of unitary costs of production among nations. From a microeconomic point of view, the integration process leads to an increased mobility of production factors. Indeed, production factors will be responsive to fiscal differentials. Labourers will locate themselves in the sub-central area where their utility (or net income) is maximised and capital will locate itself where its returns are maximised. In general, labour and firms will migrate to the areas where they maximise their fiscal residuum (the net fiscal benefit). Jurisdictions will try to keep their mobile factors of production and attract industry by downward competition on taxation (social dumping). This will lead to a deficient tax base and an inequitable tax burden.

Suppose, for example, that the world consisted of several regions and that there were two groups of workers, the skilled and the unskilled, in each region. In the absence of mobility, each region could carry out its own redistributive policy and operate transfers from the skilled to the unskilled up to their level of choice (the level that maximises welfare). If the mobility of the skilled workers were introduced, such an outcome would no longer be possible. The skilled, who were richer and had to pay for the cash transfers to the unskilled – who are poorer – would now have the possibility to migrate and locate themselves in the region where their after-tax income is maximised. We could expect them to migrate to regions where taxes are lower. Unskilled labourers could also maximise their after-tax income by moving to regions where redistribution is higher than in their region of origin (social tourism). In a small-country setting, it can be concluded that the redistributive tax has no effect on the net income of the skilled workers, but that it results in inefficiency costs supported by unskilled workers.

Musgrave (1959) and Oates (1972) argue that the central government should have the final say in matters of redistributive policy. If not, there might be incentives for the poor to migrate to regions with more redistribution and for the rich to migrate to regions with less redistribution and lower taxation. It is interesting to note, in this respect, that the English Poor Laws were originally designed with a no-mobility clause, implying that the benefit could only be paid to the residents within their own parishes. This was done in order to avoid undesirable migration flows. Buchanan (1950) also points to the fact that, even if the various jurisdictions were to follow the same redistribution policy, there would still be incentives for the poor and the rich to migrate to countries with a greater proportion of rich because the fiscal residuum in these countries is higher. For an identical level of public expenditure, taxes can be lower in the region with the highest income per capita than in the region with the lowest income per capita. This calls for compensating mechanisms. Unless fiscal policy is distributionally neutral (lump sum) – which is generally not the case – there is a potential for migration flows which undermines national redistribution policies. High fiscal pressure would result in the segregation of rich and poor.

Mobile capital

As capital is generally more mobile than labour, it will tend to be even more responsive to fiscal differentials among regions and render the redistributive policy through capital taxation even less sustainable. The mobility of production factors across sub-central entities hampers the redistributive policies of national authorities. Not only the actual mobility of production factors has this effect, but the mere fear for mobility has the same consequence. Because they fear mobility, the authorities will be reluctant to establish a redistribution scheme that is more generous than that of their neighbours.

Gabszewicz and van Ypersele (1996) and Lejour (1995) have shown that competition in the capital market leads to under-provision of social protection compared to the optimal level under autarky (see also Cremer et al., 1995; Oates, 2001). It therefore follows that there will be an incentive to diminish taxation for the most mobile production factors in order to keep them within one's own economic system. This is even more salient for countries with high debt levels, since they rely heavily on taxation to finance this debt. Within an integrated economy, an equilibrium can only be achieved if the optimal levels of fiscal pressure and redistribution are decided upon, or co-ordinated, by a higher authority that takes into account the costs and benefits in the sub-central areas. Redistribution then calls for central intervention – or a co-operative solution – in order to internalise these externalities. Cremer and Pestieau (1996) demonstrate the possibility of such a co-operative solution within a federal setting.

3.5.3 Relevance of the Mobility Argument for Europe

Although a number of US studies support the hypothesis that there is an effect of welfare differentials on geographic mobility – and that this potentially depresses the level of assistance benefits – they are not in agreement on the size and significance of the effect.[20] The results are inconclusive concerning the expected depressing effect of welfare migration on social security benefits. Wildasin (1989) suggests that there are potentially large welfare losses due to fiscal competition. Nord (1998) demonstrates that in the USA mobility of the working-age poor turns out to be at least as high as that of the non-poor, but that it also reinforces existing spatial concentration of poverty. Regions with large proportions of low-wage jobs attract the poor.

But is this assumed mobility of production factors realistic in the European context? Here, we need to distinguish among labour mobility, mobility of idle labour force and mobility of capital.

Capital is the most mobile of all production factors. Industrial activity can relatively easily – but at some cost – be relocated to regions where productivity is higher and production costs lower. In the open economy of the EU, we can expect that fiscal competition among the Member States will have an impact on the localisation of capital.

Although cross-country mobility of labour induced by tax differentials does take place in Europe, it occurs at such a low rate that it does not seem to threaten the redistributive policy of the Member States. Aside from information problems, the fiscal gain obtained from moving to a region with lower taxation does not always make up for the costs of moving. Cultural and linguistic differences, as well as the psychological toll associated with migration, may impede labour mobility. In the long run, however, when the monetary and economic union are a step further, information on wage and taxation rates will be cheaper and easier to obtain. This might stimulate migration streams.

The mobility of the idle labour force (the welfare recipients) is seen as a threat to the redistribution policy of the Member States. However, the mobility of this group is generally quite low. While workers are granted the right of residence when moving to another Member State, they are generally denied residence when unemployed.[21] In general, the right of residence will be denied to workers applying for social assistance. From the point of view of labour mobility, there do not seem to be any practical problems in carrying heterogeneous minimum protection policies within the Member States of the EU.

At first glance, the Pauly model of decentralised redistribution seems to best fit the European situation. However, according to Wellisch and Wildasin's review, immigration among EU countries appears to be quantitatively significant (Wellisch and Wildasin, 1996). They see five reasons for continued high rates of migration in Europe (see also Chapter 7):

- the demographic pressures due to rapid population growth in neighbouring regions;
- the favourable migration policy of some EU countries;
- the large income differentials between EU countries and neighbouring nations;
- the important risks of political and economic instability in Eastern Europe and North Africa;
- the enlargement of the EU or the extension of the right to move freely to citizens of non-EU countries.

EU enlargement

Given the lower average skill levels of the labourers in the central and eastern European acceding and candidate countries – and their expected receptivity to wage differentials – mobility is expected to increase.[22] These new low-skilled migrants will compete with low-skilled nationals which will depress wages at the lower end and exacerbate inequalities. There is evidence that migrants are indeed over-represented in blue-collar jobs compared to white-collar jobs (OECD, 2001: 173, 176). Furthermore, Lejour et al. (2001) using a general equilibrium model for the world economy show that, although the economic effects of the EU enlargement are positive, they are dominated, in some cases, by negative migration effects of workers with an average skills' level. This leads to – especially in Germany – a decrease of the low-wage/high-wage income differential and to a reduction of the GDP per capita. This negative migration effect also increases – and extends to other countries – when it is assumed that the migrants are exclusively low skilled.

Competitive markets generate considerable inequalities. Because the EU aims at stepping up growth, integrating markets and increasing efficiency, it also needs adequate redistributive policies. After all, one of the aims of the EU is to combat exclusion.

3.5.4 Redistribution: a Local Public Good?

The decentral supply of social security has an obvious advantage when tastes differ among the various regions. Local authorities are better informed – have easier and cheaper access to information – about the preferences of their residents with respect to the degree of redistribution they desire. When the income distribution enters the individual's utility function, it could be seen as a public good (see also Section 3.2). The efficiency of decentralised redistribution actually depends on whether one sees it as a *local* public good (Pauly, 1973) or not (Thurow, 1971). When the own locality's income distribution matters and there is no mobility, as in the Pauly model, a decentral system of redistribution is most efficient and maximises the locality's social welfare function (see also Wildasin, 1997). If these regional specificities were ignored and redistribution policy were centrally allocated, this would cause welfare losses. It would be inefficient, because in some regions, redistribution would be too low and in other regions too high. If, on the contrary, the overall distribution of income has priority, redistribution is a pure public good and a centralised redistribution system is optimal (Buchanan, 1950; Thurow, 1971; Brown and Oates, 1987). The well-being of the poor is of general concern and there are externalities associated with a decentralised system of redistribution which lead to lower than optimal welfare payments.

In summary, the larger the factor mobility the weaker the case for decentralised redistribution. However, the larger the differences in tastes the more efficient a decentralised system. It seems, however, that the dominant pattern in European countries is to organise minimum protection schemes at the national level (van Oorschot and Smolenaars, 1993). When preferences for redistribution differ among jurisdictions, neither a decentral nor a centralised system of redistribution is optimal when there is mobility. In such a world – that closely resembles the EU reality – optimality requires local redistribution mechanisms and federal subsidy or grant mechanisms to correct for externalities.

Models of fiscal federalism – which consider the maximisation of a single social welfare function – are too remote from the EU reality to draw useful conclusions concerning redistribution policies in Europe. Such models assume that the EU social model has already been shaped. In reality, Europe is in the process of doing so and a great deal of political effort is still needed. However, the use of a single welfare function is not essential in determining a role for the EU. As has been demonstrated, when Member States maximise their own welfare function, mobility of production factors results in suboptimal levels of redistribution. In an economic and monetary union, selective mobility is likely to impede Member States in their optimal redistributive policy. Some correcting mechanisms at the EU level are, therefore, required.

3.6   CONCLUSION AND DISCUSSION

Critics claim that while the welfare state enhances equality and reduces poverty, it has a negative effect on the level of public deficit, productivity, labour market participation, work incentives, economic growth and competitiveness and the rate of savings and investments. However, hardly any conclusive evidence has been produced yet (Atkinson, 1995, 1996, 1999). What is often forgotten is that, if one wants to measure the cost of the welfare state in terms of efficiency losses, one needs an alternative model to which these costs can be compared. If the alternative is the pure *laissez-faire*, one should not forget that the market embodies several failures. Moreover, a financial burden will always be the counterpart of the provision of the goods and services presently provided by the social protection system. Whether one chooses State or market provision, one must still pay for it. In the end, the latter might not be cheaper – both in financial and efficiency terms – and it carries the risk of social exclusion for those unable to pay.

It can be argued that social protection is far from an economic burden. It is a productive factor contributing to political stability and economic dynamics.

Social protection systems can potentially support lifelong learning and keep the workforce employed longer. On changing and dynamic labour markets – such as transitional labour markets with increased flexibility of the labour market, part-time work, non-linear careers (Schmid, 1998) – it contributes to the acceptance of new social and economic risks. With the rise of the knowledge-based society, some people will face new risks and uncertainties and may lack adequate skills to enter or re-enter the labour market. Social protection is then needed to compensate for these risks. However, it is becoming clear that it is in need of modernisation in order to be able to cope with newly emerging social and economic patterns – ageing, changing nature of work, changing in the gender balance in working life and co-ordination of national social security schemes for people moving within the EU (European Commission, 1997, 1999). Another issue relates to the changing size of economic units. According to the principle of subsidiarity, there is a large role to be played for intra-household transfers and mutual help within the household. With the advancement of individualisation, the decrease in the number of persons per household and the rising numbers of single parents, this type of welfare provision is under growing pressure. The recourse to public or private insurance mechanisms is due to increase.

The fact that markets present some failures does not imply that government intervention will, by definition, lead to an improvement. The government does not always have all the necessary information at its disposal. It is also possible that pressure groups or interest groups affect the policy outcome. Furthermore, an extensive bureaucracy can be a source of inefficiency. It is possible, as we have shown that public intervention can correct market imperfections, particularly in the field of social protection. In other words, we use these insights as an organisational framework. A full understanding of the matter requires an analysis of how the State, as an institution, works, which is beyond the scope of this research.

It should be noted that the potentially positive effects of social protection mentioned above depend on the details of the systems. The financing, the incentive structure within the system, as well as the efficiency of policy delivery will affect economic performance. Social protection has multiple functions. The regime type or the way social protection is designed to attain these objectives will determine the balance of the effects in terms of economic and social performance (see Chapter 4). From the point of view of subsidiarity, the labour market and the family are the primary institutions for maintaining one's standard of living. In the liberal tradition, the welfare state can only be subsidiary to these institutions. The family, because of intra-family transfers and mutual help, plays an important role as a risk-sharing institution. Parents care for their children and – at a later age – vice versa. Partners, through income pooling, also insure each other from income fluctuations. However, socio-demographic changes – such as increased individualisation and its effect on loosening family structure, and the rising number of singles and single-parent families – hinder this insurance function. The ageing of the population can also be mentioned here. The elderly have an effect on the public budget due to their increasing numbers relative to the active population. Moreover, there is an increased need for adequate income protection schemes because the elderly tend to be more risk-averse than the average population. Increased labour flexibility certainly contributes to allocative efficiency, but it also increases the income risk and weakens the labour market position of the lower skilled. Well-designed compensation mechanisms are required to help individuals absorb these shocks. A shift from a passive compensation policy in unemployment insurance to an active policy increases the productive effect of minimum protection schemes. From the point of view of positive subsidiarity – and in the wake of the knowledge-based society – an upgrading of human capital and employability, especially among the vulnerable workers with obsolete skills, would also increase this effect.

Nation states are not an island; they interact through numerous institutions. Fifteen European countries take part in the EU and a smaller number have, furthermore, accomplished the EMU. The EU construction has consequences for the social protection system of the Member States. When capital is highly mobile and households are ready to cross borders, Member States are constrained in their ability to deliver adequate levels of minimum protection. The two main risks arising under the pressure of mobility are social dumping through fiscal competition and social tourism. Fiscal competition in the EU has a disciplinary effect which is welcomed by those who fear Leviathan. However, the welfare state is a productive activity of governments. Moreover, fiscal competition among Member States leads to an opportunity cost. It would be more lucrative to invest in improving Europe's competitive position with the rest of the world and to increase Europe's share of the world market. There is a growing understanding that the EU is more than a mere market. Economic progress is certainly required to position the EU in the world economy and make it competitive. It is also certainly required to make the financing of social protection feasible, but a social market economy is certainly an option. As the EU Member States become increasingly integrated, income disparities among them become less ethically acceptable. It seems rather unlikely that in the short run social tourism will occur within the EU. However, when the free mobility of citizens is fully operationalised, the risk of social tourism becomes more realistic. Moreover, the enlargement of the EU is likely to lead to increased mobility, especially from low-skilled workers. The expectation is that this will exacerbate inequalities and obstruct the Member States' redistributive policies.

The need for a fine-tuning in the social field at the European level follows from the need to prevent distortive competition on the one hand, and to preserve the social character of the European model on the other hand. The EMU constrains the monetary, budgetary and fiscal policy of the Member States. Thus, the Member States have lost important instruments for adjusting their competitive positions. Social protection contributions and labour costs will presumably play a more prominent role in determining the competitive position of the member countries. They will pressure, on the one hand, the mere existence of the social protection system and, on the other hand, the social partners – with respect to labour costs. By the same token, social protection has the virtue of alleviating shocks that affect various parts of the EU. However, we lack such instruments at the EU level.

Using subsidiarity, a practical solution to avoid the downward spiral of fiscal competition is for the Member States to agree upon European minimum levels of social protection such as that a decent level of subsistence is guaranteed. Such a mechanism would make it possible to absorb macroeconomic shocks as well as the externalities of the redistribution mechanisms resulting from European market integration. Even in the absence of labour mobility among regions, some degree of convergence might be desirable. Indeed, in that case, factors cannot reallocate themselves so that they maximise their welfare and share in the economic gains of the EMU. Within the framework of total economic integration – constrained budget policy for the Member States and no independent monetary policy – extensive disparities in welfare among European regions will be unsustainable.

Co-ordination of taxes and benefits through collective agreements is required. It is feasible and is also superior to planned harmonisation (Cremer and Pestieau, 1996). It can also prevent Europe from relinquishing its social achievements when put under pressure. In that respect, the open method of co-ordination is a step in the right direction. From the point of view of positive subsidiarity, the EU has a facilitating role to play.

NOTES

1. Atkinson and Stiglitz (1980: 343) formulate the theorem as such: 'If households and firms act perfectly competitively, taking prices as parametric, there is a full set of markets, and there is perfect information, *then* a competitive equilibrium, if it exists, is Pareto-efficient.'
2. This is with reference to Beckerman's notion of 'poverty reduction efficiency' (Beckerman, 1979).
3. Note, however, that such questions of co-ordination are not solely to the interest of macroeconomists. A large body of literature has developed on the subject of co-ordination (vertical and horizontal; see Section 2.3.2) of activities within the firm. See, for example, Aoki (1990).

4. The core of his argument is that efficiency is not one of the primary objectives of the social welfare function. Efficiency is nothing but a rule determining whether or not – given a production frontier – the realisation of the objectives is optimal.
5. Some doubt that the distribution of utilities should be of any concern (Sen, 1992).
6. The first part is referred to as the 'difference principle'. The 'just savings principle' introduces an intergenerational aspect. The savings – money, but also productive capital accumulation – that a society makes should be appropriate for future generations least advantaged.
7. This interdependence of utility can also justify the use of a relative poverty threshold as the one used in the following chapters.
8. See also Gelissen (2002) for a recent study of public opinion and the welfare state.
9. See, for example, Headey et al. (1997, 2000) and Goodin et al. (1999) for international comparative research into the effect of social security transfers on long-term poverty and poverty transitions in Germany, the Netherlands, the UK and the USA.
10. Moral hazard occurs when one of the parties in a transaction can take actions that affect the value of the transaction by the other party and that this other party does not have those instruments at its disposal to monitor or enforce the transaction perfectly. Adverse selection occurs when one of the contracting parties to a transaction has relevant information that is not known by the other party.
11. Note again that public insurance still bears the risk associated with moral hazard.
12. Coase and Meade have suggested a market solution to the problem of externalities, respectively, through negotiation between the parties and merging of the activities of the parties. When none of these solutions is applicable possible solutions are regulation, imposition of a Pigovian tax/subsidy, or production at a higher level (see Barr, 1989: 62).
13. Public goods, such as national defence, are characterised by non-excludability and non-rivalry: nobody can be excluded from consuming the public good and the consumption by one more individual has no effect on the level of consumption by others.
14. See also Moffit (1992) for an extensive review of the incentive effects of the welfare system in the USA.
15. See Portes (1998) for a review of the sociological implications of social capital. Portes also points to some negative effects of social capital.
16. Note, however, that minimum protection schemes are organised at the national level in the large majority of EU countries (van Oorschot and Smolenaars, 1993).
17. Efficiency gains from international trade and efficient allocation are expected. In 1998, the Cecchini report expected an additional yearly GDP increase of 4 to 6 percent in the EU.
18. See Fouarge and Kerkhofs (2000) for evidence for the Netherlands.
19. Migration costs include the monetary, as well as the social and psychological, cost of migration.
20. See Brown and Oates (1987: 320–23) and Moffit (1992: 31–6) for a review.
21. Except for a limited period of three months in order to look for employment.
22. The acceding countries Cyprus, the Czech Republic, Estonia, Hungary, Latvia, Lithuania, Malta, Poland, the Slovak Republic, Slovenia have joined the EU as of May 1st, 2004. Bulgaria and Romania are candidate countries. They expect to join the EU by 2007.

4. European Welfare Regimes and Poverty

4.1 SUBSIDIARITY: THE GUIDING PRINCIPLE

Originally, redistribution from the rich to the poor and the prevention of poverty were not institutionalised. It generally occurred at the local level through the Church, local authorities and private initiatives. Intra-family transfers in this respect were also of primary importance. As time went on, part of the redistributive task was assumed by the State. As we discussed in the previous chapter, role distribution between the State and lower-plane entities – such as the market – is directed by a whole set of factors favouring either public or private governance. In this, subsidiarity is the governing principle: if actions can be undertaken by lower-level entities, they should do so. In the field of minimum protection, it implies that the primary responsibility lies with those entities closest to the individuals in need. In the first instance, therefore, self-help through the market or the family is to be preferred. Only if that fails is there a role for public authorities. As such, subsidiarity involves an efficiency test: the lowest level of authority is best suited for action; if that level fails the next level takes over suited. However, subsidiarity has a more positive interpretation which emphasises the facilitating role of higher entities.

Member States of the European Union (EU) are now engaging in a process of economic and monetary integration. In doing this, they have accepted some limitations of their powers and have, thereby, lost some key policy instruments for correcting adverse shocks. This is most apparent in the field of monetary and budgetary policy. As a consequence, it is feared that the pressure on social security budgets will be increased, impeding Member States in their battle against social exclusion and income poverty. The future role of the EU with respect to minimum protection is then brought into question.

Judging from the literature on fiscal federalism, there are reasons to believe that increasing economic integration will exert a downward pressure on social security budgets (Lejour, 1995). Therefore, if, for equity reasons, the level of minimum protection is of concern, co-ordination of the Member

States' policies is to be considered in order to avoid rolling back the welfare state. However, the possibility for top-down policy co-ordination or harmonisation in Europe is small and the prerogatives of the EU are few and subject to the test of subsidiarity.

In this chapter, we distil relevant research questions from the theoretical insights developed in the previous chapters and discuss them in the light of the economic and social efficiency of poverty alleviation and income redistribution (see below for an operationalisation). First, let us examine the potential role of the European Union in the field of minimum protection. We have formulated research questions relative to various hypothesised positions adopted by the EU in the field of minimum protection (Section 4.2). From the point of view of negative subsidiarity, it is first assumed that the EU makes no use of its prerogatives in the field of social security to harmonise or co-ordinate the social security systems of the Member States. It is also assumed that Member States oppose any EU involvement in this policy field. This situation leaves the door open for fiscal competition and its possible implications in terms of a race to the bottom. Suppose, however, that the EU does make use of its prerogatives in the field of minimum protection. In accordance with positive subsidiarity, the EU would then stimulate convergence of minimum protection systems or help facilitate co-ordination among Member States.

From the previous chapter, we conclude that public intervention in social security is closely related to social and economic efficiency. In other words, public authorities are best placed to foster societal equity objectives, but social protection also has a function as a macroeconomic stabilisator, as a creator of the requirements for a fertile economic environment – in terms of human capital formation, social peace, preventive health care, and so on – and as the facilitator of labour market flexibility. We ask whether or not market mechanisms are able to promote welfare. How much better than the market are the various welfare states in combating poverty and inequality (Section 4.3)? This discussion will be placed within the framework of welfare state regimes which, in themselves, are a way to operationalise subsidiarity.

4.2   EUROPE AND MINIMUM PROTECTION

4.2.1   The Way Ahead

EU Member States share common concerns. These include maintaining high rates of economic growth, stimulating competitiveness, reforming social protection schemes (especially in the face of future pension liabilities) and fighting social exclusion. In Chapter 1, we showed that the EU has competencies in the field of social protection and the combat of social exclusion. In particular, the Treaty of Amsterdam included the following objectives: the improvement of the standard of living and quality of life of those living in the European Community; economic and social cohesion; solidarity among Member States; the promotion of employment; the improvement of living and employment conditions; a proper level of social protection; social dialogue; the development of human capital to ensure a lasting high level of employment; the combat against exclusion (articles 2 and 136 of the Treaty of Amsterdam). The EU competencies to realise the above objectives must, however, first be put to the test of subsidiarity. In the present situation, as we stated earlier, the principle of subsidiarity is used by the Member States to oppose EU intervention. If the Member States continue along this line and leave no role for the EU in the field of social protection, a social Europe will not develop and social and economic efficiency indicators will differ among members, according to the type of social policy in the specific country (see Chapter 3, Table 3.2). However, the principle of subsidiarity can also be understood differently (Chapter 2). There are economic arguments why intervention at a higher plane in the field of social protection is sometimes justified (Chapter 3). In particular, the EU could take on a more proactive role and stimulate and encourage policy developments.

In the absence of co-ordination mechanisms, policy competition can be efficient and stimulating for economic activity, because it can induce authorities to conduct an efficient policy in their quest for competitive advantage. However, in some respects, policy competition can be quite inefficient. Fiscal competition potentially induces negative effects on the welfare state and income distribution. Moreover, there is also the problem that, in the presence of international mobility, the lack of co-operation among Member States might also lead to the dismantling of the welfare state. Social dumping may result in a process of convergence towards ever lower levels of social protection. Theories of fiscal federalism have taught us that the need for centralisation of social policy strongly depends on the assumptions concerning the international mobility of production factors. As far as labour is concerned, several processes are at work. Increasing migration increases labour supply, which has a depressing effect on wages and, ultimately, on the level of welfare benefits. Welfare migration has in itself a more direct negative effect on the level of welfare benefits. In the short term, the fear for large labour mobility within the EU is unwarranted. However, in the longer term – and as a consequence of the EU enlargement – it is to be expected that migration will increase. Nonetheless, estimates remain at a relatively low level: a migration potential of three to four million persons is expected (de Mooij, 2000). Empirical research shows that this has only a minor effect on the wages of nationals. However, the consequences of migration for income distribution are expected to be larger. There will be a pressure at the lower end of the labour market, either in the case of low-skilled labour or welfare migration, which will affect the distribution of income and poverty. This is clearly an undesirable outcome if the EU is to promote economic and social cohesion.

There are also other problems facing the future of Economic and Monetary Union (EMU). These relate to the existence of asymmetric shocks or – in the same vein – asymmetric responses to symmetric shocks, as well as the persistence of disparities across the EU Member States. Adjustment mechanisms might be needed to accompany the increased integration at the EU level, so that the euro does not come under increasing pressure. However, the EMU limits the possibility for corrective policy. Monetary, budgetary and fiscal policies within the Member States are constrained because of their EMU membership. Thus, the Member States have lost important instruments for adjusting their competitive positions. In the absence of European instruments for dealing with macroeconomic stability and social exclusion – and given the low degree of labour mobility (potentially an instrument to correct for disequilibrium) – social protection contributions, labour market flexibility and labour costs will play a more prominent role as corrective mechanisms and in determining the competitive position of the Member States. This will pressurise the social protection systems and social partners with respect to labour costs. In addition, social exclusion, by undermining the value systems and social cohesion, can hamper the competitive ability of the EU.

Assuming that the co-operation – through the open method of co-ordination – among EU countries leads them to agree on a number of targets in the field of poverty, we can compute the cost of reaching the targets. How are the costs affected by setting the targets at, for example: a 50 percent reduction of the poverty rate; a poverty rate not exceeding some pre-defined value; or even a complete reduction of poverty? The first empirical research question relates to such computation. What are the costs involved in achieving a commonly agreed upon poverty reduction target? This will be further discussed in Chapter 8.

4.2.2 Alternative Scenarios for Europe

Theoretical analysis concerning the possible involvement of the EU in redistributive policy has showed that there are arguments to be made for EU intervention. Although these are not that clear-cut, various hypotheses can be formulated in the field of social exclusion. Social exclusion has a broad meaning and encompasses aspects of unemployment, housing, health and life situation, as well as the lack of durables or income and the inability to take part in community life (Vleminckx and Berghman, 2001). This – necessarily limited – study will focus on the income aspect of social exclusion, that is income poverty and income inequality.

We distinguish three scenarios in the area of poverty, which we deal with in Chapter 7. The first one reflects the assumption that a race to the bottom is taking place among Member States. The second scenario assumes that, in the long run, EU convergence of social security systems will occur, that is convergence to the EU average. In the last scenario, it is assumed that Member States are on a path towards voluntary high-level co-ordination. In Figure 4.1 – representing the vertical and horizontal dimensions of subsidiarity – the scenarios are grouped with the Member States because they influence these policy options. In the case of harmonisation and imposed co-ordination, the EU would have the initiative; hence, these policy options are depicted at the EU pole. However, as we discussed previously, these are not very realistic options in the short term. The option of horizontal subsidiarity, where social partners at the EU level have initiative for action, is not covered in this study.

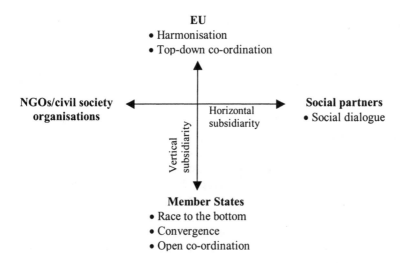

Figure 4.1   Vertical and horizontal subsidiarity and policy options in Europe

Race to the bottom
The first scenario – the doom scenario – is that Member States engage in a *race to the bottom* using some of the last instruments at their disposal to improve their competitiveness: taxes and social transfers. In other words, Member States might reduce wage costs, tax levels and social security

premiums in order to make labour cheaper. Thus, they would become interesting both for foreign workers and foreign investors, and their products would be more attractive for the international market. In the end, this process of social dumping would lead to a situation in which all countries set their wages, taxes and social premiums to the lowest common denominator. This process would stop when spending has reached the level of the lowest spender in the community. Only then are there no more incentives for mobility of production factors.[1] This doom scenario has clear implications for poverty and income distribution for the working-age population both within and among Member States. If tax and premium revenue are lower, only lower social transfers can be financed. If there is direct competition on wages, diminished wages will obviously also affect poverty. In our analyses, we examine only the first-order effects of this scenario since we do not account for behavioural effects (see Section 7.2). Instrumentation takes place with respect to replacement income (unemployment benefits, unemployment assistance and social assistance) within the working-age population, on the one hand, and household wage income, on the other hand.

The second research question to be dealt with relates to the above scenario. What are the implications for poverty of the working-age population of a race to the bottom on replacement income? What are the consequences of cutbacks in replacement income for the income distribution within and among EU Member States? With respect to wages, we ask: what are the implications of a race to the bottom – leading to a direct reduction of wage income – for poverty of the working-age population of the EU Member States? What are the consequences of wage cuts for income distribution within and among EU Member States?

Using data for European countries, we simulate a situation in which replacement income in percentage of median wage is equal to the lowest common denominator throughout Europe. For the simulations on wages, we assume that they are adjusted downwards to the lowest common denominator. We then proceed to the first-order simulation, determining the effect – in terms of poverty increase and increase in inequality – of such an alignment of replacement incomes. We expect this scenario will show an exacerbation of poverty and inequality in Europe. This scenario corresponds to a situation of negative subsidiarity at the EU level.

Mean convergence
It would be less radical and probably more realistic to assume that competition leads Member States to set minimum replacement incomes that are, relative to gross wages, equal to the EU average. This *EU-convergence scenario* implies cutbacks in the countries with relatively generous replacement incomes, but increases in social security spending in the

countries with below average replacement incomes. The corresponding changes are simulated on wages. The third research question applies to this scenario. What are the effects of a mean convergence of replacement income in EU Member States on poverty and inequality among the working-age population? And with respect to wages: what are the effects on poverty and inequality among the working-age population of a mean convergence of wage income within EU Member States?

This scenario will be instrumented by first computing the average ratio of replacement income to median gross wage throughout Europe. We simulate a net income reduction proportional to the difference between the national ratio and the overall EU ratio in countries where replacement income is more generous than average – and vice versa for countries with below average replacement incomes. Poverty and inequality indices will be measured according to this new, fictitious, income distribution. Similar procedures are applied to wages, where they adjust downwards if they are higher than average, or upwards if they are lower.

High-level convergence
Ultimately, one can imagine that the relatively high level of welfare in Europe – in comparison with other trade partners – is perceived as a real asset to be preserved. Taking the open co-ordination scenario seriously, one could suppose that under the leadership of a group of countries with well-developed welfare state arrangements, Member States (or at least some of them) agree to set a common minimum level that is equal, in terms of purchasing power, across nations but higher than in the two scenarios described above. This scenario could be referred to as the *California effect scenario*. This refers to the effect the stringent environmental legislation in the state of California has had in terms of upgrading of legislation in other US states. From this, one can assume that, in the process of economic integration, productivity in European countries will converge up to high levels. This will affect the terms of employment, which we measure here only in terms of the wage level. With regard to this hypothesised California effect, the fourth empirical research question is: what are the consequences – in terms of poverty and inequality – of a genuine social Europe involving relatively high levels of replacement income? As far as wages are concerned, what are the consequences – in terms of poverty and inequality – of a high level converge of productivity, involving relatively high wages?

This scenario assumes convergence towards high levels of replacement rate. In practical terms, this involves simulating an increase in replacement income in all countries with the exception of the one with the highest replacement rate. The procedure is similar to that in the other scenarios. First, the level of replacement income relative to gross wages is determined.

Assuming the country – or the group of countries – with the highest ratio exercises positive externalities in terms of upgrading replacement incomes in the other countries, we simulate such an increase. We expect this scenario will have an income-equalising effect both within and among Member States. It should be noted that this scenario could be placed within the framework of positive subsidiarity. We assume that initiatives are being taken – with the support of the EU – to integrate the systems.

4.3　WELFARE REGIMES AND POVERTY

One of the major spheres of government intervention is welfare. Specifically, the welfare state fulfils an important role in the prevention of poverty and inequality. In economic theory, inequality and poverty aversion may result from equity considerations through an altruistic feeling that it is unfair to suffer from poverty in a world of affluence. Concern for poverty can also result from efficiency considerations whenever information is imperfect or market provision fails. In that case, it relates to the belief that poverty impedes the efficient functioning of the market and society, and that it involves the diversion of resources to harmful social consequences. In this section, we discuss the role Member States' public authorities play in the field of income protection and we investigate the role they allocate to the market. We then derive research questions relating to the economic and social effectivity of public transfers in reducing poverty and inequality.

Answering these questions requires comparative research across nations so that the relative effectivity of these transfers can be quantified and compared. Welfare state arrangements do not stand alone and can be fitted into the stylised models discussed below. Although these models are a simplification of reality – for they do not account for the full diversity of the institutional set-up, policy design and functioning of the welfare states – they are a useful tool in discussing international comparisons. Because the countries under study are illustrative of specific types of welfare arrangements, we are able to draw general conclusions from the cases under scrutiny. However, more importantly, the distinction among welfare state regimes refers to the allocation of welfare production at the level of the household, the market and the State (Esping-Andersen, 1999: 73). That is why we chose to operationalise the principle of subsidiarity by using welfare state typologies.

Most typologies of welfare arrangements, as they are found in the literature, are based on an analysis of the role distribution among the State, the market and the household or family. In general, a distinction can be made between welfare state arrangement models where public authorities play a major role in the provision of welfare while the role of the market is minor, and that in which the market is omnipresent while the role of the State is kept to a minimum. Between these two extremes, there are a host of variants. Without reviewing the very rich literature on welfare state typologies, we will briefly discuss three widely used typologies that are particularly interesting from the point of view of role distribution among the State, the market and the household.[2] These are the traditional distinctions among the Beveridgian and Bismarkian models, the typology suggested by Titmuss (1974), and the welfare regime classification by Esping-Andersen (1990, 1996, 1999). In particular, Esping-Andersen's concept of de-commodification – see Section 4.3.1 – provides an adequate way to operationalise the degree of State and market involvement (Esping-Andersen, 1990). We will discuss what the implications of the models are in terms of income redistribution and poverty.

4.3.1 Welfare State Design and Expected Effects on Poverty

Probably the most basic distinction to be made in terms of welfare state models is that between the Bismarkian and the Beveridgian models. The Bismarkian approach, developed at the end of the 1880s, typically represents the corporatist approach to welfare state arrangements. It guarantees social and economic status through selective labour-income related benefits. These Bismarkian social security schemes are based on social insurance principles (Roebroek, 1993: 36). The Beveridgian approach, initiated at the time of the Second World War, can be defined as universal. Its aim is to provide a minimum guaranteed income for all residents. In principle, these benefits are not related to past income. In consolidating welfare state arrangements in Europe throughout the 20th century, countries have started to mix elements from both models so that neither of these two models now exist in their pure forms. Welfare states arrangements have become mixed as the increasing knowledge concerning the effectivity of policy orientation drives countries to adopt one another's policy instruments. Thus, we see that the Beveridge– Bismark dichotomy has lost its relevance. Nevertheless, welfare states still appear to come in types. Across nations, a number of common traits and institutional designs can be distinguished.

   Titmuss (1974) makes a theoretical distinction among three models of social policy to reduce inequality. In the first model, the *residual welfare model of social policy*, it is assumed that the needs of the individual are better met by the private market and the family. Authorities operating at a higher level should only come into action when these channels fail. This model is in line with the negative definition of subsidiarity. The second model, the *industrial achievement–performance model of social policy*, allows social welfare tools to play a role. The model 'holds that social needs should be met on the basis of merit, work performance and productivity' (Titmuss, 1974:

31). This model shows much similarity with the Bismarkian–corporatist approach to social welfare, in that it implies a selective benefit system in which benefits are highly income-related: one has to deserve income support, through paid work, in order to get it. This model is primarily based on the Protestant principle of subsidiarity (see Chapter 2). In the last model, the *institutional redistributive model of social policy*, social welfare is seen as an integrated institution in society. The State is seen as a provider of universal services. This model closely resembles the idea of positive subsidiarity.

Esping-Andersen (1990) also distinguishes three different models of welfare state regimes: the liberal, the corporatist and the social democratic. These regimes are characterised by the degree of de-commodification of the welfare states as well as the social stratification and solidarity. This index of de-commodification incorporates information on the generosity of the benefits, the qualifying conditions and the individual share in the funding of the benefit, that is the degree to which beneficiaries have contributed financially to the type of benefit they receive. The more generous the benefits are and the less beneficiaries have had to contribute to their own benefit, the larger the de-commodification index will be. This indicates a high degree of socialism in the welfare system. Before discussing the implications of these regimes for income redistribution and poverty, let us first provide a brief definition. In the *liberal welfare regime*, individuals – the most decentral level – are assigned the responsibility for their own welfare, leaving the State to be nothing other than a night-watchman. In this sense, the liberal welfare regime parallels Titmuss' residual welfare model of social policy. The *conservative–corporatist welfare regime* aims at preserving traditional values. The principle of subsidiarity has played a major role in this regime type. Individuals organised into social units – the family or corporation – are responsible for their own welfare. The granting of social rights is generally not contested, but these are linked to class and status. This corporatist welfare regime is essentially identical to Titmuss' industrial achievement–performance model. Of the three regimes, the *social-democratic welfare regime* is the one that best promotes the principle of universality and the de-commodification of social rights. Within this regime, as in Titmuss' institutional redistributive model of social policy, the State is seen as the major provider of welfare. Welfare states are, of course, unique in terms of institutional set-up, policy design and function but, as suggested by Esping-Andersen, they also cluster around these three ideal typical distinct regime types (see also Goodin et al., 1999).

Welfare regimes and redistribution
Equality of opportunity is a fundamental value underlying the liberal welfare regime. This equality is believed to be best achieved through the working of

the market. Therefore, the well-functioning market economy is perceived as primordial and in order to preserve it, the State must interfere as little as possible with the economy. Individuals are expected to finance their own insurance on the market, and the State will only interfere if this fails. Although a safety net may exist – based on universalistic principles – it will generally offer low and means-tested benefits targeting those in great need. Moreover, an important distinction is made between the deserving and non-deserving poor. Only those in financial distress through no fault of their own – and who are willing to work – will be given income support. Those unwilling to take part in the production process will not qualify for welfare provision. The liberal regime stimulates labour market participation. Minimum wages, if any, are, therefore, kept at a low level. Work incentives are furthermore preserved by relatively high labour incomes and low tax rates. This regime, therefore, relies on a trickle-down effect by which income growth of the well off will, ultimately, benefit those less well off.

Under the corporatist principle of subsidiarity, the responsibility for one's own welfare is to be carried by the individual him or herself and the social group – the primary social group is the family – to which that person belongs. By doing this, the value of social cohesion is supported. The provision of welfare is strongly based on the concept of a male breadwinner in the household who supports the rest of his family. The basis for solidarity is, therefore, strongly status-oriented and selective. Risks are pooled according to status membership and the benefits' levels are strongly linked to past income. In such a setting, social protection preserves the existing social differences. In the corporatist welfare regime, the State takes on an intermediary role: it acts in order to facilitate and stimulate insurance schemes within social groups. However, it also takes on the organisation of the residual risk pool. The minimum wage is generally high but, while labour market participation of male household heads is stimulated, female labour participation is discouraged.

Within the social democratic welfare regime, role distribution between the individual and the State favours the latter. The State is assigned a dominant role in terms of welfare provision for the citizens. Instruments of preference are: the guarantee of a minimum standard of living, the provision of full citizenship and the prevention of social exclusion (Arts and Gelissen, 2001). The fundamental value advocated by the social-democratic welfare regime is that of social equality. Contrary to the liberal welfare regime, citizens are highly de-commodified; they are not – or only to a small extent – dependent on market mechanisms for their welfare. However, because the costs of universal welfare provisions with relatively generous benefits are high, the system also promotes and facilitates full employment both for men and women. Although the minimum wage is high, wage moderation is applicable at higher income levels (Wildeboer Schut et al., 2000).

Expectations with respect to poverty and inequality

Given the residual role of the State in liberal welfare regimes and the stress put on labour incentives and the working of the market, income inequalities are expected to be large and income redistribution is expected to be low. Although the regime aims at the alleviation of poverty among the (deserving) needy through targeted transfers, replacement rates are expected to be low, in order to preserve incentives. Therefore, liberal regimes are expected to do a poor job at preventing poverty. Over the longer run, as a consequence of the more flexible, less regulated labour market, income mobility is expected to be large. Changes in the labour market are expected to strongly affect the income position of individuals. Finally, due to the low level of the safety net, temporary income fluctuations are expected to be large.

Because benefits, in the corporatist regime type, are linked to past income and past contribution record, the redistributive impact of social security is expected to be small. Moreover, by this system of mutual aid, according to the principle of subsidiarity, the risk pools are limited to the social–occupational group, so that the redistributive impact is also expected to be limited to these groups. Because little priority is given to the prevention of poverty and the terms for acquiring replacement income are rather strict – in terms of work history and paid premium – poverty is expected to exist. The corporatist setting is expected to result in a dichotomy between the rich (working) and the poor (not working). Since the objective of the system is to maintain the established social order, redistributive effects are also expected to be small in the long run. For the same reason, temporary income fluctuations will be small.

Within social-democratic regimes, the pursuit of equality of outcome through a universal setting will lead to low levels of inequality and a high level of income redistribution. By the same token one can expect labour market changes to affect people's income position, albeit to a lesser extent than would be the case in a liberal setting. Given that the system intends to shift the balance of trade in favour of the poor, the level of poverty is expected to be low. In the longer run, redistributive effects are expected to be large; larger than in the two other models. Income fluctuations through time are expected to be low.

4.3.2   Three Types of Welfare Regimes or More?

Esping-Anderson's typology has been criticised for his neglect of the southern model of the welfare state, his mis-classification of the antipodean welfare regime – Australia and New Zealand – as liberal welfare states, his misconception of the East-Asian model and his neglect of the gender perspective in welfare arrangements (Pierson, 1998; Arts and Gelissen, 2001; Gelissen, 2002). Because our primary focus here is European welfare states, we only examine the first criticism, that is the omission of the southern welfare model. Several authors believe that the southern countries belong to a different welfare regime type. This is characterised by an immature and selective clientelistic social security system granting low benefits and lacking a well-articulated system of guaranteed minimum benefits (Leibfried, 1992; Ferrera, 1996; Bonoli, 1997). In this southern model, welfare obligations are carried out at the family level. Although, in his later work, Esping-Andersen (1996) recognised that the southern countries share some common Catholic and familial traditions, his opinion is that they do not form a specific type of welfare regime. They were, in his view, merely underdeveloped species of the traditional corporatist type (see Gelissen, 2002). With no further elaboration, we recognise that European countries display common traits and that they can be grouped together in distinct welfare models. The distinction among welfare regimes is important because institutional arrangements have a direct effect on social exclusion and the effort to combat it.

The role distribution implied by the principle of subsidiarity – and its operationalisation in terms of welfare regimes – can be summarised in Figure 4.2. When the prime responsibility for the individual's welfare is on the individuals themselves, we speak of the liberal social welfare regime. When the primary responsibility is on the social group or public authorities, we then speak of the conservative–corporatist or social-democratic welfare regime, respectively. The southern welfare regime strongly relies on traditional family values for guaranteeing the welfare of individuals.

Individual/Market	Family	Social group	Public authorities
Liberal	Southern	Corporatist	Social democratic

Figure 4.2   Subsidiarity/primary responsibility and welfare regimes

4.3.3   The Real World

The welfare regimes, as sketched in the previous section, and the interrelations among the individual, the family, the social groups, the market and the public authorities, are basically ideal types. However, real life welfare states are very likely to exist in hybrid forms: while parts of the system follow one approach, other parts might follow a different one. Moreover, it would be wrong to assume that membership in a regime type might not change over time.[3] Nevertheless, it is sensible to categorise countries according to the type of welfare regime they follow. We are, to a large extent, dependent on the datasets at our disposal for the empirical assessment of our research questions. Our approach – using micro-data – offers a different, valuable, perspective than one based on macro-data, since it permits us to estimate accurately the outcomes of the institutional arrangements on social and economic indicators. The impact of policy regimes on social and economic performance can be assessed more accurately when making use of the panel character of the data at our disposal. Indeed, panel data allow us to follow people over time and keep track of their socio-economic fate. By doing this, we can gain insight into the long-term and dynamic effects of welfare state institutions. In Europe, three panels – for the Netherlands, Germany and Great Britain – have been running for a period of time long enough to be able to carry the longitudinal analysis of the type we want to undertake in Chapters 5 and 6. These countries can be used as illustrations of the welfare regimes in Esping-Andersen's typology. It must be said at the outset that such country classification is subject to debate. In fact, no country fits perfectly into one of these types, nor are regime types stable features of a country's socio-economic policy over time. Nevertheless, as we will show, such a typology is found to be a useful analytical tool.

The least problematic case is, most likely, Germany because it is generally recognised that the German welfare state is a predominantly corporatist regime. In this typology, Great Britain can – to some extent and some 'good will' – be classified as a liberal regime. Great Britain cannot be regarded as a prototype – like the US model – of the liberal regime, but it shares some key features of the archetype.[4] The position of the Netherlands is somewhat more ambiguous. The Netherlands does not fit squarely into one of the distinguished welfare regimes. While some – including Esping-Andersen himself – see the Netherlands as social democratic, others consider the Dutch regime to be conservative–corporatist or even liberal (Gelissen, 2002). In a recent empirical study of 11 welfare states Wildeboer Schut et al. (2000) confirm Esping-Andersen's typology as consisting of a liberal, a conservative and a social-democratic cluster of countries. However, they also conclude that the Netherlands cannot clearly be assigned to one of these clusters (Wildeboer Schut et al., 2000: 31–2, 154–5). The Netherlands has traits common to both corporatist and social-democratic welfare regimes. One typical corporatist feature is the manner in which social partners have been involved in designing the Dutch socio-economic policy. This is often seen as the reason behind the Dutch economic success. The universal coverage and high replacement rates, however, are typical features of the socio-democratic-regime type. Compared to other countries in the corporatist cluster, it is the least corporatist country. In the same vein, compared to other countries in the social-democratic cluster, the Dutch regime is the least social democratic

(Wildeboer Schut et al., 2000: 20). Between corporatist and social democratic, the Dutch regime is more of the latter than the former. Following Goodin et al. (1999) and bearing in mind the above discussion, we consider the Dutch social protection system to represent the social-democratic type. Note that in Chapter 7, use is made of the European Community Household Panel (ECHP), allowing us to cluster EU countries among the four regime types distinguished above.

4.3.4 Poverty Reduction and Welfare Design

In general, all social insurance systems within the EU Member States cover similar risks. However, the level and the duration of benefits and the eligibility rules differ largely among Member States. This leads to significant variations in the level of expenditure on social protection among them. There is also a great difference among Member States with respect to the preservation of incentives and distributive efficiency. Countries in the social-democratic tradition (Sweden, Finland, Denmark and the Netherlands) are characterised by high activity rates, high levels of spending on social protection, high replacement rates and low inequalities (see Table 4.1). Countries in the conservative–corporatist tradition (Germany, Austria, Belgium, Luxembourg and France) tend to be characterised by moderate participation and unemployment rates, average replacement rates and poverty incidence. Anglo-Saxon, liberal countries (the UK and Ireland) combine high activity rates with low unemployment. Replacement rates, as well as social expenditures in percentage of GDP, are low. Inequality and poverty are consequently high. The countries in the southern regime (Italy, Greece, Portugal and Spain) share relatively low rates of activity and high rates of unemployment, especially long-term unemployment. Although replacement rates may be high in some cases, they tend to be selective and applicable only under restrictive conditions. Social protection expenditure is low while poverty rates and inequality are high. Below, we point out the institutional differences underlying the dissimilarities in social and economic indicators in the EU.

From the point of view of work incentives, there are some interesting differences among the Netherlands, Germany and the UK. Upon examining the replacement rates from unemployment benefits for the average production worker (OECD, 1998), it turns out that on average they are highest in the Netherlands, followed by Germany, and lowest in the UK. For singles and single-income couples, this results in the lowest income differential when out of employment in the Netherlands and the highest in the UK. The differences between the Netherlands and Germany are rather small. We can, therefore, expect that the effect on the poverty risk of losing employment would be larger in Great Britain than in the Netherlands or Germany. However, one can conclude from the Organisation for Economic Co-operation and Development (OECD) data that the expected income increase for single-income couples gaining employment is 49 percent in the UK compared to 22 to 25 percent, respectively, in the Netherlands and Germany. Labour market participation seems to offer larger incentives to leave poverty in the UK than in the other two countries. After a long term of unemployment, however, the difference among the countries appears to diminish. For a single-income couple with children, the prospective income increase equals 26, 28 and 31 percent, respectively, in Germany, the Netherlands and the UK (OECD, 1998).

Table 4.1   Key economic and social indicators for European countries

	A	B	DK	D	EL	E	F	FIN	I	IRL	L	NL	P	S	UK
GDP/head[a]	23.5	23.4	25.0	22.7	14.2	17.3	20.9	21.4	21.2	24.1	38.8	23.8	16.1	21.6	21.6
Growth[b]	2.1	2.5	1.7	1.6	3.5	3.7	2.9	4.0	1.4	9.8	7.5	3.6	2.9	3.8	2.1
Activity rate[c]	67	57	75	64	55	50	60	63	51	60	60	69	67	69	70
Unemployment rate[d]	5	10	5	9	12	19	12	11	12	8	3	4	5	8	6
Long-term unemployment rate[e]	2	6	1	5	6	10	5	4	9	6	1	2	2	4	2
Replacement rate[f]	66	71	83	75	–	73	82	83	42	57	88	83	83	81	68
GDP share of social protection[g]	30	30	34	31	23	22	31	32	25	19	26	31	22	35	28
Average tax rate[h]	3.3	11.9	36.2	7.9	0.5	5.6	1.7	23.3	12.9	15.7	–	9.5	1.9	28.5	15.0
Social security contributions[i]	17.5	13.1	2.6	18.3	15.8	6.1	18.4	6.2	10.0	8.8	12.5	28.6	11.0	1.0	7.6
Poverty rate[j]	13	17	12	16	21	18	16	–	19	18	12	12	22	–	19
Inequality[k]	26	28	23	28	34	33	29	–	33	33	28	30	37	–	34

Notes:
a) GDP per head in Purchasing Power Standard in thousand, 1999.
b) Real GDP growth rate, 1998–9.
c) Number of employed persons in percentage of population, aged 16 to 94, 1998.
d) Number of unemployed in percentage of active population, 1998.
e) Number of unemployed for 12 months or more in percentage of active population, 1998.
f) Net replacement rate after tax, average for various family types, 1995.
g) Social protection expenditure in percentage of GDP, 1998.
h) Personal income tax at the level of an average production worker, two-child families, 1993.
i) Employees' social security contributions at the income level of an average production worker, two-child families, 1993.
j) Percentage of persons with income below 60 percent of median standardised income, 1995.
k) Gini coefficient multiplied by 100, 1995.

Sources: a, b, c, d, e: Eurostat, 2000c; f, g: Ferrera et al., 2000; h, i: OECD, 1994; j, k: Eurostat, 2000a.

How redistributive the welfare regimes are – and how well they prevent poverty – is an empirical question that will be investigated throughout the next chapters. We discuss our empirical results in the framework of welfare regimes. Earlier, Goodin et al. presented what they called a 'first cut ... at the analysis of alternative welfare regimes as viewed through the lens of panel data' (Goodin et al., 1999: 17). Although we do not aim at reproducing the results presented by Goodin et al. (1999), sections of the analyses here can be seen as complementary to those presented there. The novelty is both in the methods used here and the fact that we use British data. However, contrary to Goodin et al., but unless otherwise mentioned, the population under scrutiny is not only that of working age.

The research questions developed below relate to the evaluation of the social and economic efficiency of welfare regimes. Does the market manage to prevent large inequalities and poverty? How efficient are social transfers at reducing poverty and inequality? Do welfare regimes preserve incentives in that they promote mobility and do not impede income growth? These research questions relate to short-, medium- and long-term economic and social efficiency.

Short-term social and economic efficiency

The fifth research question refers to the measurement of social efficiency of welfare state arrangements in terms of inequality and poverty. It involves a comparison of outcome indicators for three archetypes of the social democratic (the Netherlands), corporatist (Germany) and liberal (Great Britain) approach to welfare state arrangements: what is the extent of poverty and inequality in the Netherlands, Germany and Great Britain? Who are the groups most affected by poverty?

For the investigation of *social efficiency*, we make use of inequality and poverty indices that are computed on income data (see Chapter 5). People are poor when their income is lower than some pre-defined percentage of median income. Using cross-tabulation of key socio-economic variables and poverty status, we disclose the groups most affected by poverty. With econometric models, we analyse in greater detail the degree to which these socio-economic variables affect the probability of being poor. *Economic efficiency* is evaluated by looking at the effect of the economic status of the individuals and other persons in the household on the poverty risk. Economic efficiency is also judged by comparing income levels across population groups (employed versus unemployed).

We expect the Netherlands, with its more egalitarian welfare setting, to display the lowest poverty and inequality rates, followed by Germany and Great Britain. From previous research, it is well known that unemployed, single parents and the elderly are more prone to poverty. We expect the poverty incidence in these groups to be larger in Great Britain than in the two other countries. With respect to economic efficiency, we expect the effect of economic status (employed or unemployed and for how many hours) to be more important in Great Britain, which puts more stress on market mechanisms, than in Germany and the Netherlands. Of these two factors, we expect labour market status to be a stronger determinant of the poverty risk in a breadwinner regime such as Germany than in the Netherlands.

The sixth research question is concerned with the redistributive impact of welfare state arrangements. We compare the results of the previous research question to those of a situation in which no transfers take place: what is the effectivity of public transfers in reducing poverty and inequality? Can public transfers be socially and economically efficient?

Following Beckerman (1979), pre-transfer inequality and poverty measures are computed. They represent the situation in which only the market forces are at work, without intervention from the public sector. These computations are taken as illustrations of the distributive outcome that would result from the working of the market and are compared to post-transfer measures in order to assess the *social efficiency* – that is the degree of income redistribution – of redistributive systems. We return to the way we measure redistribution as well as on the shortcomings of the approach followed in Chapter 5 (Section 5.3).

The discussion in Chapter 3 showed that a trade-off might exists between social and economic efficiency. *Economic efficiency* is assessed by comparing the level of income before and after transfers. The smaller the difference, the stronger the incentives structure.

Medium- and long-term social and economic efficiency

The new reality of poverty is that economic mobility is increasing. Hence, although large numbers are found to be persistently poor – 7 percent of the EU population lives in persistent poverty (Mejer and Linden, 2000) – the year-to-year income mobility and transitions in and out of poverty are substantial (Maître and Nolan, 1999). These high mobility rates, combined with high rates of persistent poverty and the high degree of polarisation between the poor and the non-poor make the traditional dichotomy between the groups of insiders (those who are never poor) and outsiders (those who are persistently poor) increasingly relevant to scientific research. There is also growing concern that social protection and labour market policy is not as integrated as it should be. In a dynamic labour market, transitions from social security dependency to work must be improved. Therefore, research must go beyond mere cross-sectional benchmarking and trend analysis, and account for the 'time nature' of poverty and economic mobility (Jenkins, 2000). Traditional research methods should make way for an approach which takes the increasing economic mobility into account (see Chapter 6). Using panel data, it is possible to account for this new reality and to estimate the dynamic effects of welfare regimes. It would be interesting to investigate whether Kuznets's idea that, in the long term, inequalities will decrease in the process of economic growth (in the downward part of the inverted U-shaped relationship between growth and inequality) applies in modern welfare states. More precisely, it would be interesting to see whether the income positions at the lower end of the income distribution are improving through the trickle-down effect. Our seventh research question will then be: what is the medium- and long-term performance of welfare states in terms of reducing poverty? How successful are welfare states in triggering exits from poverty? Can this be achieved without hurting economic efficiency in the longer run?

We determine if a welfare state succeeds in preventing medium- and long-term poverty, in which case it would be *socially efficient*. This research question is handled using several methods. First, we aggregate individual incomes over the years and apply poverty and inequality measures to this 'longitudinal income'. Secondly, we construct spells of poverty and compute exit rates from such spells. Finally, we define poverty profiles that make a distinction between transient and persistent poverty (see also Walker, 1994). A question to address is whether public transfers contribute to the reduction of the length of poverty spells or whether the major part is done by the market. We expect medium- and long-term poverty and inequality to be lowest in the Netherlands, next lowest in Germany and highest in Great Britain. Again, this expectation is based on the belief that a social-democratic regime type performs better at redistributing income and poverty than the other two. The liberal regime tends to provide low coverage – especially in the long term – so it is expected to perform the worst.

From an economic perspective, a positive role for social protection could be defined as the preservation of incentives to work. Long-term *economic efficiency* is assessed by investigating whether labour market mechanisms still accomplish their tasks in terms of preventing long-term poverty. Economic efficiency is also assessed in terms of the extent to which poverty transitions are more or less associated with labour market transitions. We apply econometric models to explain (long-term) poverty entries and exits. A welfare state will be more efficient from an economic point of view when exits from poverty, or income increases, are due to labour market changes rather than to public transfers. Labour market events are expected to have a large effect on one's poverty status

The increased internationalisation of economies, the move towards the knowledge-based society and the dissolution of traditional family ties are all developments that have consequences for social exclusion. Because economic systems increasingly engage in international trade, especially within the European context, they are increasingly exposed to imported economic shocks. An economic downturn in a neighbouring country will therefore have repercussions for national income distribution. Moreover, in the knowledge-based society, there is an increased risk of social exclusion for those unable to keep themselves employable. As outlined in Section 4.2, the Member States now have less manoeuvrability in their use of stabilisation instruments. One can, therefore, question how employment shocks affect income distribution and long-term poverty. Income security and basic care are, to a great extent, supplied by the family. The increased rate of dissolution of family structure, therefore, has potentially major consequences for the design of welfare systems. This is because new risks of social exclusion and poverty are created. The eighth and last research question relates to the measurement of the extent of persistent poverty in various Member States. It also investigates, in greater detail, how labour market and family composition shocks affect income in a longitudinal setting, and how such shocks are absorbed by the various welfare state arrangements. The research question is, therefore, the following: what is the extent of persistent poverty? How is persistent poverty affected by shocks in the labour market and within family structure? How are these shocks absorbed in the various welfare state systems?

Persistent poverty is expected to be lowest in the Netherlands because of its universalistic approach to social protection, next lowest in Germany and highest in Great Britain. Our conjecture is that a status-oriented welfare regime, such as Germany, is best able to absorb temporary income shocks. Such shocks are likely to be large in Great Britain, where market mechanisms play a more important role. For this reason, too, household and employment shocks on income are expected to be larger in Great Britain.

4.4   CONCLUSION

The European integration process restrains the way Member States can operate independently from one another. Even in the sphere of social protection, the Member States will come under increasing pressure to co-operate. In Chapter 7, three scenarios are investigated regarding possible outcomes of the co-operation process among Member States and the effect on poverty. The data used in Chapter 7 are from the European Community Household Panel. Only the first-order effects are taken into account. Second order effects of the scenarios considered in terms of their effect on labour market behaviour remain outside the scope of the chapter.

The chapters to follow analyse indicators of inequality and poverty, as well as economic dynamics, in a number of EU Member States. The countries can be grouped with regard to the welfare regime they represent: liberal, universal or corporatist. Chapter 5 deals with the social and economic efficiency of redistributive systems. The interaction between medium- and long-term poverty and economic mobility within these welfare regimes is addressed in Chapter 6. In that chapter, we also briefly discuss model estimates of the effect of household and labour market shocks on permanent income and poverty. In these chapters, use is made of panel data for the Netherlands (social-democratic welfare state), Germany (corporatist welfare state) and Great Britain (liberal model). We show that these welfare regimes display different outcomes in terms of social and economic efficiency. However, social efficiency gains are not always at the cost of economic efficiency.

NOTES

1. In fact there is no reason why this process would end at that stage since lowering spending even further would improve the competitive position of the nation. Therefore, this process could well continue until spending on social protection is reduced to zero.
2. See Gelissen (2002) for a review of the literature.
3. For example, in France, the Bismarkian model as the unique model of social protection lost ground due to the Juppé Plan (Bouget, 1998). France has adopted different models for the various sectors of social security. In family and health care, the principles of citizenship and universality have gradually become the leading principles. For labour market-related benefits, the Bismarkian model still applies, while attempts to privatise supplementary pensions have been made.
4. For example, replacement rates in the UK will generally be much higher than other 'residual' welfare states. Furthermore, using principal component analysis by alterning least squares (PRINCALS) on 58 indicators relating to the labour market and the tax and benefit system, Wildeboer Schut et al. (2000) show that the UK in the least residual welfare state of all countries in the liberal cluster.

5. Income Redistribution and Poverty in Three European Welfare States

5.1 INTRODUCTION

The first empirical task we undertake in this book is to investigate the social and economic efficiency of redistributive policies in Europe. On the one hand, from the point of view of subsidiarity, we investigate whether market and family mechanisms work well as instruments to keep people out of poverty. On the other hand, we evaluate the extent to which redistribution through public transfers is effective in keeping poverty and inequality low. In order to control for the possible effects of the institutional setting, we decided in the previous chapter to study three European countries: the Netherlands, Germany and Great Britain. These countries each have a different social policy logic: social democratic, corporatist and liberal, respectively. We report here on income distribution and poverty incidence in these three countries. Apart from analysing the distribution of income, we quantify the impact of redistributive policy by their governments. Cross-sectional results and trends for the 1980s and the 1990s are reported. To keep track of a possible equity–efficiency trade-off, we also present data on income and income growth. Efficiency is also examined from the point of view of labour market incentives, that is the effect of labour market participation on the poverty risk.

The data used are briefly presented in Section 5.2. In this study, we focus on income as an indicator of well-being. The concept of income used is explained in Section 5.3 and its evolution over time is depicted in Section 5.4. The distribution of income is analysed in Section 5.5. In Section 5.6, we shift to the measurement of poverty. In Section 5.7 we describe the incidence of poverty and its determinants. Section 5.8 concludes this chapter.

5.2 THE DATA

Many international comparisons of poverty and inequality have been based on the analysis of annual cross-sectional data. The most well-known and comprehensive dataset is probably the Luxembourg Income Study (LIS), which has been used in a great deal of empirical studies.[1] In this study, we use panel data for three EU countries: the Netherlands, Germany and Great Britain. This means that the same respondents were interviewed at regular intervals. With each 'wave' of data collection – that is each year – the same people were interviewed, following similar routines and questionnaires. However, this does not exclude new samples from being added in order to compensate for the drop-out (attrition), whether selective or not, of panel members. The advantage of panel data is that – besides allowing for cross-sectional and trends analysis – they make it possible to monitor changes in the observed variables (household composition, labour market status, health, attitudes, income, and so on) at the individual level. The datasets used include the interviewed persons and their children.

The data for the Netherlands are from the Dutch Socio-Economic Panel (SEP) and were made accessible by Statistics Netherlands (CBS). This panel has been operating since 1984. Initially, interviews were carried out twice a year – in April and October – but in 1990 it was decided to switch to annual interviews. Previous to 1990, respondents were asked to report their net personal incomes for the month before interview. These data were multiplied by 12 to produce a yearly income. From 1990 onwards, however, respondents were asked for their gross income in the previous year. Paid taxes were estimated and subtracted in order to produce a net yearly income. This change in income measurement slightly increased the inequality of the distribution of household income. Therefore, a regression model was estimated in order to correct the income data, as explained in Fouarge (2002: 222–3). As in the two other datasets, household income was obtained by adding the individual incomes of those living in the same household. The Dutch income data at our disposal cover the 10-year period 1985–94. For a description of the Dutch data, see CBS (1991) and Lemmens (1992).

The German data are from the German Socio-Economic Panel (GSOEP), as made available through the PSID–GSOEP equivalent file, provided by the German Institute for Economic Research (DIW). Wagner et al. (1993) and Burkhauser et al. (1999) provide a description of the German data. The panel, which started in 1984 in West Germany, was extended after reunification, in 1990, to cover the whole of Germany. The 1986–96 waves of the data that were used contain retrospective income data for the year previous to interview. This means that use is made of net household income data for Germany from 1985 to 1995.[2]

The British data are from the British Household Panel Survey (BHPS). The data were made available by the Data Archive at Essex University (see Taylor et al., 1999).[3] In the BHPS, respondents were asked to report their gross income. The gross income variables refer to the period of one year previous to August of the current year, the date of interview. Gross incomes have been converted into net incomes, which are supplied as a supplement to the BHPS data (cf. Bardasi et al., 1999). Net household income for Great Britain from 1991 to 1997 have been used.

Using these data, a comparable longitudinal data file was constructed for all three countries (details on the sample sizes are presented in Appendix 2). This makes cross-sectional, as well as longitudinal comparisons possible. This means that a 10-year comparable dataset for Germany and the Netherlands is available – with income data for the years 1985–94 – and a five-year comparable dataset for all three countries, covering the years 1991– 5 (1990–94 for the Netherlands).

In cross-sectional studies, the household is the usual unit of analysis. However, because households change over time – due to marriage, separation, children born or leaving home – this does not make it an appropriate unit of analysis for panel studies (see Duncan and Hill, 1985; Jenkins, 2000). All analyses are, therefore, carried out at the individual level, although the household remains the unit of observation. It is assumed that individuals within the same household share a number of common characteristics. Characteristics of the household – that is composition and income – were assigned to every person, including the children, within the same household. With respect to household income, it is thereby assumed that income is equally shared within the household and that, if household income is found to be below the poverty line, all household members are poor. It could, however, be the case that income is not equally shared within the household. Yet, the data at our disposal are not sufficient to test this assumption. Socio-economic characteristics of the household head – his or her age, gender, economic activity, and so on – are matched to every person within the household. Many analyses of the poverty risk will be made with respect to socio-economic characteristics of the household head. This procedure will possibly wrongly classify some households; for example, when a poor household's head is unemployed but the other adults in the household are employed. For this reason, a number of labour market variables have been constructed at the household level: number of employed adults and number of hours worked by all adults (see Section 5.4.1).

The data are first weighted on a cross-sectional basis to make them representative for the population of the particular country at a particular time. However, longitudinal results have been weighted with a longitudinal weight in order to correct for a possible selective drop-out (see Fouarge, 2002: 227).

Comparing levels of income inequality and poverty across countries can be controversial for a number of reasons. Comparing trends and dynamics, however, is less controversial. Although we will spend some time describing the level of income inequality and poverty across welfare states, we are more interested in dynamic aspects and the question of how some countries succeed better than others in reducing inequality and preventing poverty. Poverty dynamics will be discussed in Chapter 6.

International comparisons are more reliable when similar definitions and operationalisation are used, as we have done here. International comparisons through time also improve in quality when similar periods of time are scrutinised, covering similar stages of the business cycle. This will have to be kept in mind, especially since the British business cycle runs ahead of the German and Dutch ones. However, the period used for the comparison of the three countries includes the economic upturn that followed the downturn at the start of the 1990s.

5.3 INCOME AND REDISTRIBUTION

5.3.1 Income Concept

One of the issues we are dealing with is the redistributive impact of welfare state arrangements. A number of income concepts are used in this study. Traditionally, a distinction is made between primary and secondary income distribution. Primary income distribution results from the production process: the price formation process on the labour market. It depends on the skills of individuals and on the value of these skills on the labour market, as well as the capital endowment of individuals. Primary income equals gross wages, income from investments and private transfers. The distribution of primary income is affected by public authorities both directly, through regulations – for example, minimum wage regulations – and indirectly, through the educational system (affecting the skills of individuals) and because it feeds labour demand (governments employ large proportions of the labour force). However, public authorities also levy taxes and social security premiums on primary income. From these taxes, they finance a wide range of activities, including the building of roads and hospitals, the educational system and social security transfers. The subtraction of taxes and social security premiums from primary income and the addition of social security transfers lead to disposable income, which is also referred to as post-government income. We take this as an indicator of the welfare level of households and individuals. We look at the share of social security transfers in disposable income and examine the extent to which these transfers reduce inequality and poverty. We define pre-transfer (or pre-government) income as post-government income minus social security transfers.[4] The relationship among the income concepts used in this study is illustrated in Figure 5.1.

Note that no attempt has been made here to measure one's 'full income'.

Full income is generally defined as the sum total of monetary and non-monetary income. Non-monetary income is comprised of in-kind income, non-cash transfers, imputed rent for owner-occupied housing, the value of assets and the value of leisure. Because of the measurement problems and data requirements involved with the estimation of full income, we focus here solely on monetary income. For poverty studies with a focus on assets and wealth holdings, see Wolff (1990), Rendall and Speare (1993) and Van den Bosch (2001) for an application on Belgian data. Smeeding et al. (1993) incorporate non-cash subsidies in their study of poverty in seven industrialised countries.

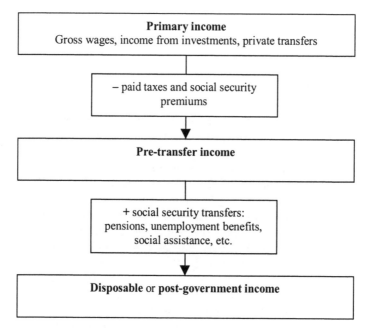

Figure 5.1   Primary, pre- and post-government income

5.3.2   Equivalence Scales

Households that vary in size or composition also have varying needs. Hence, the total household income of a given household type is not straightforwardly comparable to that of another household. One way of comparing income levels across household types is to use equivalised income. This means that income is corrected for differences in household size, composition, region of habitation, and so on. An equivalence scale can be seen as a vector of the level of resources, each associated with a household type, rendering the households an equal level of welfare. Equivalence scales are used to make different household types comparable. Hence, this permits us to make welfare comparisons such as: an income x for the family type i is equivalent to y for family type j. Such equivalencies are applied to control for economies of scale through income pooling within the household, as well as for the different needs of households with varying structures.

The choice of an equivalence scale reflects assumptions as to the economies of scale of household size, the consumption requirements of the household, as well as its home production capacity. Usually, equivalence scales are defined according to household size, the age of the household members and the position within the household (head, partner, child, and so on). There is no consensus about the equivalence scale to be used, but the choice of one is likely to affect the level of income, inequality and poverty (see Buhmann et al., 1988; Coulter et al., 1992). However, unless the population under scrutiny is going through major demographic changes, it is not likely to affect the assessment of changes and trends in income, inequality and poverty. A large body of literature has been devoted to the question of equivalence scales and their effect on measures of welfare, inequality and poverty.[5] The scale used here is the so-called modified OECD equivalence scale. It accounts for the total household size and the age of household members. A weight of 1 is attributed to the first adult, a weight of 0.5 to every other person aged 14 and older and a weight of 0.3 to every person aged younger than 14. Hence, additional adults in the household are considered to need half as much as the first adult, while children are assumed to need 30 percent as much income as an adult. The equivalence factors were first suggested by Hagenaars et al. (1994) and this scale has now become the standard in the EU (Atkinson et al., 2002).

5.3.3 Assessing the Redistributive Impact of Public Transfers

Beckerman (1979) suggests a framework in which to view the redistributive effects of income transfers (see also Creedy, 1996). He distinguishes three measures of efficiency of social transfers: vertical expenditure efficiency (the proportion of transfers going to people who were poor before the transfers were made), spillover (the proportion of transfers that have taken households above the poverty line) and the poverty reduction efficiency (the proportion of transfers targeted towards the reduction of poverty). Here, we use a more simple framework and measure the redistributive effect of public transfers as the proportional decrease in pre-government inequality or poverty (see Box 5.1):

$$redistribution = 1 - \frac{post - government\ poverty/inequality}{pre - government\ poverty/inequality} * 100\%$$

BOX 5.1   The measurement of redistribution

To assess the impact of welfare state arrangements on income distribution, we decompose the redistributive effect of social protection into two steps. The first one is the redistributive effect of taxes and social contributions levied on primary income. The second step relates to the redistributive effect of social transfers. For some measure of inequality I computed on a population n with post-government income distribution y, which equals primary income (m) minus taxes and social contributions (t) plus net social transfers (b), the redistributive effect taxes equals (see also Kakwani, 1986):

$$I(m;n) - I(m-t;n) = \delta_t.$$

The redistributive effect of social transfers is obtained from:

$$I(m-t;n) - I(m-t+b;n) = I(y-b;n) - I(y;n) = \delta_b.$$

The total redistributive effect of social policy is estimated by:

$$I(y-b+t;n) - I(y;n) = \delta = \delta_t + \delta_b,$$

or, in proportion of primary income inequality:

$$\frac{\delta}{I(m;n)} = \frac{\delta_t}{I(m;n)} + \frac{\delta_b}{I(m;n)}.$$

A larger δ indicates that a welfare regime is more redistributive. The δs can be expressed in percentages of primary income inequality. The same method will be applied to poverty measures to assess the poverty reduction effect of social transfers.

Of course, this is just a crude estimator of the true redistributive effect of social protection. In the absence of public policy, the distribution of primary income would probably be different (higher) and actors would behave differently (we will return to this in Section 7.2). It follows from neoclassical economic theory that high levels of social transfers cause disincentive effects on the labour market since the net marginal hourly wage – or gain for working an additional hour – is equivalently lower. It is also probably true that social transfers and taxation negatively affect the propensity to save and the willingness to invest in financial assets or the acquisition of human capital. When social security supplements income in case of unemployment, individuals are less inclined to build financial reserves through savings. Similarly, individuals might be less inclined to invest in human capital to keep up their market value when they know they can fall back on assistance and unemployment benefits. Finally, as mentioned in Chapter 3, social transfers are likely to affect the risk-taking behaviour of individuals and, therefore, the income distribution (Sinn, 1996). All in all, it is possible that the redistributive effect of social policy is overestimated. Our analyses should be supplemented by a careful modelling of the interactions between taxation, social security and labour market behaviour (see, for example, Gelauff and Graafland, 1994). However, such an approach is beyond the scope of this book.

5.4   TRENDS IN INCOME AND SOCIAL TRANSFERS

5.4.1   Trends in Income

Income is a quantity that is of interest for economic analysis. In particular, the *level* of income is often taken as an indicator for the level of welfare. Its *growth rate* can be seen as an indicator of economic efficiency. In Figure 5.2, median equivalised household income is presented for the period 1985–97. Germany is found to have the highest level of income over the years. Great Britain has the next highest median income and the Netherlands the lowest. However, the differences among these three welfare states are not very large. The position of the Netherlands is somewhat surprising, given that Dutch GDP per capita is around 25 percent higher than in Great Britain. However, our data are similar to computations based on the European Community Household Panel (ECHP) (Eurostat, 2000a: 107).

Throughout the 1980s, Dutch and German median income followed a similar trend, with an average growth rate of around 3 percent per year. The development during the 1990s differs for a variety of reasons. Although the sharp drop in real income in Germany in 1991 could be attributed to the inclusion of the East-German sample, the general decrease in real income during that time is also found when looking at median income – with a slight recovery in 1995 – of West-Germans alone. This trend can be attributed to the cost of German reunification and the slow economic growth due to the recession in the early 1990s. It was, in particular, the non-elderly singles, single parents and couples with children who saw their income positions deteriorate between 1991 and 1995.

The decrease in the Dutch income between 1989 and 1990 can, to some extent, be attributed to the change in the way income was measured in the Dutch survey (Fouarge, 2002: 222–4). The 1993 decrease in real income is attributed to the economic downturn in that year in the Netherlands. On the whole, median income increased with some 4 percent between 1991 and 1995. All household types saw their income positions improve during that period, but the non-elderly singles and couples with children improved more than average. Median income in Great Britain increased by 5 percent between

1991 and 1995. After 1995, the growth rate was even larger. The increase was largest among the elderly and single parents. Nonetheless, as we see in Section 5.7.2, their income position is still far from enviable.

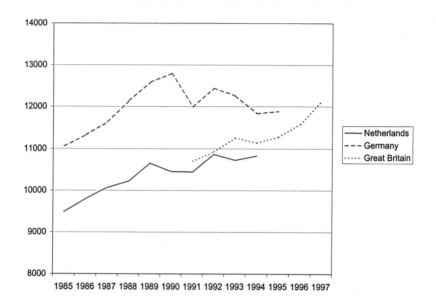

Sources: SEP; GSOEP; BHPS.

Figure 5.2   Trends in real median standardised income, 1995 prices and Euro Purchasing Power Standard (PPS)

We complement this description of the overall income level, and changes therein, by looking at income across a number of subgroups. A distinction is made by household type, employment status and labour market attachment of the household. First, we distinguish among household types. From the point of view of economic subsidiarity, larger households are expected to be better able to internalise income risk and household members to better provide for their mutual welfare.

Secondly, from an economic perspective the labour market status is expected to be a major determinant of people's welfare. Apart from the employment status of the individual, we consider the employment status of the head of the household. The category 'not employed' consists of people in a household where the head is unemployed, disabled, houseman or housewife, student, and so on. From the point of view of labour market incentives, small differences in income among people in gainful employment and those out of employment indicate the possible existence of disincentive effects.

Thirdly, the labour market attachment of the household is also expected to be a strong determinant of people's welfare. The degree of labour market attachment of the household is defined as the total number of hours worked by all household members divided by the potential number of hours worked for the household on a weekly basis (number of adults of working age times 38 hours). The variable, therefore, measures the level of labour supply by the household. It can also be interpreted as measuring the degree of labour market attachment by the household. If all adults work full time, the indicator of 'use of work potential' will be 100 percent. If, in a two-adult household, one of the adults works full time and the partner does not work at all, the 'use of work potential' will be 50 percent. It will also be 50 percent if both work part time.

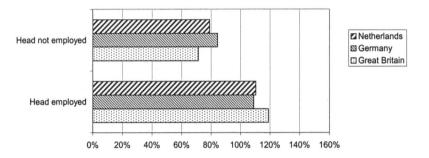

Note: Dutch data are for 1994.

Sources: SEP; GSOEP; BHPS.

Figure 5.3   Median equivalised household income by employment status of the household (indexed, average = 100 percent), 1995

In all countries, living in a household where the head is unemployed leads to a lower income (Figure 5.3). However, the difference is much more pronounced in Great Britain. This implies that the British have stronger incentives to work than the Dutch and Germans.

A similar picture is found when looking at the degree of labour market attachment of the household (Figure 5.4). Persons living in households making full use of the work potential are significantly better off than those who do not. Increasing the use of the work potential always pays off in terms of income, except in the Netherlands and Germany, for an increase at low

levels. This finding points to possible disincentive effects in these two
countries of holding small – marginal – jobs.

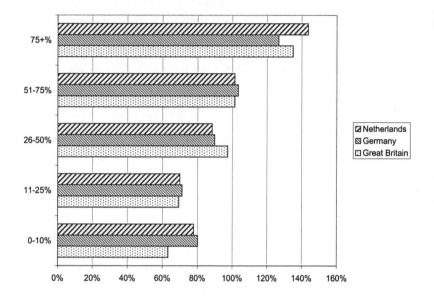

Note: Dutch data are for 1994.

Sources: SEP; GSOEP; BHPS.

*Figure 5.4   Median equivalised household income by use of work potential
in the household (indexed, average = 100 percent), 1995*

Examining income across household types shows that single parents have
a very poor income position in all three countries, though this is slightly less
so in the Netherlands (Figure 5.5). The income position of single elderly is
also relatively poor, especially in Great Britain. In all three countries, couples
without children have the best income position, especially in Great Britain.

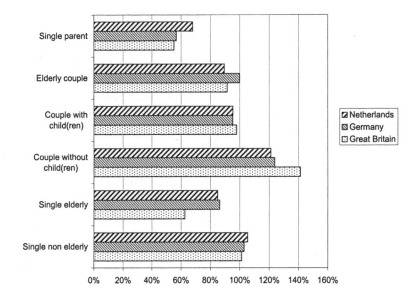

Note: *Dutch data are for 1994.*

Sources: SEP; GSOEP; BHPS.

Figure 5.5 Median equivalised household income by household type (indexed, average = 100 percent), 1995

5.4.2 Social Transfers

In modern welfare states, social security transfers make up a large part of one's income. As Table 5.1 shows, approximately 30 percent of household income can be attributed to social security transfers. However, social security income represents a higher proportion of total household income in the Netherlands than in Germany and Great Britain. The share of social transfers in the ECHP and the share of social protection expenditure of the Gross Domestic Product (GDP) are given in the last two rows of the table and show some differences in the ranking of the countries compared to our calculations. In particular, the share in Great Britain compared to Germany differs somewhat from what one would expect on the basis of macro-data. Considering the share of expenditure as a percentage of the GDP, the Netherlands and Germany have a similar level of spending while Great Britain's level is three percentage points lower. Our data do not quite reflect these differences. The data from the ECHP tend to slightly underestimate the share of social transfers in total household income. This might, however, be due to differences in definition.

Table 5.1   Share of protection transfers in total household income, the Netherlands (1994), Germany (1995) and Great Britain (1995)

	Netherlands	Germany	Great Britain
Total[a]	33	30	30
Household type[a]			
Single non-elderly	32	19	18
Single elderly	95	93	85
Couple without children	23	19	12
Couple with children	17	12	16
Elderly couple	88	84	63
Single parent	73	40	59
Other	48	37	29
Labour market status of head[a]			
Head employed	11	9	8
Head not employed	75	72	63
Use of employment potential[a]			
0–10%	88	86	76
11–25%	47	46	48
26–50%	20	21	20
51–75%	12	11	12
75+%	7	4	6
Share of social transfers (ECHP)[b]	28	26	24
Social protection % GDP[c]	31	31	28

Sources: a) SEP; GSOEP; BHPS; b) ECHP, numbers for 1994 (Eurostat, 2000a: 107); c) Eurostat (2000a), numbers are for 1996.

In all countries, the elderly, whether singles or couples, tend to be largely dependent on social transfers. To a lesser extent, this is also the case for single parents. Nonetheless, social transfers in Germany make up a smaller proportion of the single parent's income than in Great Britain and the Netherlands. With regard to the labour market status of the head of the household and the household attachment to the labour market, the results are very similar across welfare states: increased employment leads to a reduced dependency on social transfers. The only difference between the countries is found for households with little attachment to the labour market. For those households, social security transfers make up the lowest proportion of household income in Great Britain and the highest in the Netherlands. This is indicative of the liberal and social-democratic feature of the British and Dutch welfare systems, respectively.

While the share of social transfer income in Germany was rather stable during the 1980s, it increased slightly through the process of German reunification (see Figure 5.6). In the Netherlands, however, the proportion of social security income in household income decreased towards the end of the 1980s, possibly as a consequence of social security reforms in 1987. It cannot be ruled out that the increase in the share of social transfer income between 1989 and 1991 resulted from the change in the way income was measured in the Dutch data. Indeed, no major changes in the national social security setting took place during that period. Therefore, the slight increase (three percentage points) between these two dates should be taken with caution. In any case, the share of social security income seems to have stabilised at around 32–3 percent in the 1990s.

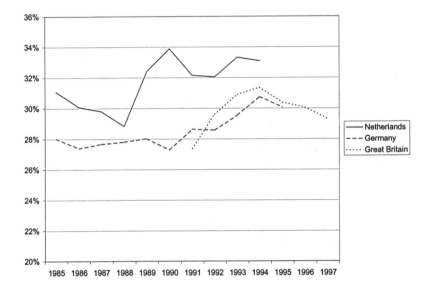

Sources: SEP; GSOEP; BHPS.

Figure 5.6   Share of social protection transfers in total income

Starting from a relatively low share of social security income in 1991, Great Britain caught up with Germany and the Netherlands between 1991 and 1994. These findings match the increase in social security spending as a percentage of the GDP observed over the same period in Great Britain (Eurostat, 2000b).

5.5   THE DISTRIBUTION OF INCOME

Now that we have depicted the income position across various household types and have described trends in the evolution of household income, let us now turn to distributional issues. The first empirical exercise consists of comparing income distribution data at various times and among welfare regimes. The second one is to measure the redistributive impact of social security transfers across nations. The intellectual challenge is to see whether the hypotheses formulated in Chapter 4 – with respect to the redistributive effect of welfare regimes – are verified in our data.

The inequality indices used in this section are the P75/25 ratio, the relative mean deviation (*M*; also known as the Robin Hood index), the Gini (*G*) and Theil (*T*) coefficients. These inequality measures are briefly explained in Appendix 3.

5.5.1   Inequality and Redistribution

The largest part of income inequalities is generated on the market. People's market income can diverge widely because some have paid employment while others are unemployed or because some have access to capital income and others do not. Even when employed, income will diverge due to differences in ability and skills, and their associated productivity differentials. Relative scarcity of skills – as well as possible discrimination – is also likely to play a role. When computing the inequality measures using the three panels, it appears that Germany and the Netherlands display a similar pattern of post-government inequality (see Table 5.2). Inequality in Great Britain, however, appears to be larger. Although Great Britain is found to be a relatively wealthy nation in terms of median income, inequality is nested at a higher level than in the Netherlands and Germany. This is in accordance with the expectation formulated in the previous chapter. Pre-transfer inequality turns out to be lowest in Germany and highest in the Netherlands, according to almost all the inequality measures reported in the table. Also, the Dutch and the German social transfer systems seem to do a much better job at redistributing income than the British system – which again is in line with the expectations (Chapter 4).

One attractive feature of the Theil coefficient is its additive decomposability by subgroup (see Appendix 3). Hence, total inequality can be expressed as the sum of between- and within-group inequality. In this section, we use this feature to show how inequality in subgroups accounts for total inequality in the mid-1990s. We decompose total inequality by household type and the household use of work potential. Across household types, inequality in the Netherlands is rather low. Therefore, the proportion of between-group inequality in total inequality is lowest in the Netherlands (Table 5.3). Between household types, inequality accounts for a larger part of total inequality in Germany, but even more so in Great Britain. Looking at the decomposition according to the use of employment potential of the household members, both the Netherlands and Great Britain appear to differentiate equally between groups, while the degree of differentiation in Germany is lower. Relatively speaking, the strongly redistributive Dutch welfare regime still appears to have strong financial incentives embedded in it.

Table 5.2   Inequality and redistribution, the Netherlands (1994), Germany (1995) and Great Britain (1995)

	P75/P25	Robin Hood	Gini	Theil
Netherlands				
Primary income	10.749	0.340	0.480	0.442
Pre-transfer income	8.009	0.330	0.465	0.416
Post-government income	1.847	0.198	0.285	0.147
Redistribution	77	40	39	65
Germany				
Primary income	5.956	0.342	0.479	0.430
Pre-transfer income	5.006	0.323	0.452	0.391
Post-government income	1.816	0.192	0.278	0.140
Redistribution	64	41	39	64
Great Britain				
Primary income	8.634	0.364	0.505	0.469
Pre-transfer income	5.319	0.331	0.462	0.382
Post-government income	2.133	0.225	0.318	0.179
Redistribution	60	32	31	53

Sources: SEP; GSOEP; BHPS.

In Figure 5.2 we depicted the trend in real median income in the Netherlands, Germany and Great Britain. Real income grew in all three countries during the observation period, with the largest growth in Great Britain and the smallest in Germany. How did economic growth impact on inequality? Did inequalities diminish in the process of economic growth – as the trickle-down hypothesis would suggest – or did growth exacerbate them? The evolution of inequality through the years is depicted in Figures 5.7, 5.8 and 5.9 for the Netherlands, Germany and Great Britain, respectively. The conclusion is clear: in the period under study, economic growth did not result in a decrease of income inequality. Inequality remained more or less stable or, as in Germany, even increased.[6]

Table 5.3   Subgroup decomposition of Theil by household type and use of
work potential, the Netherlands (1994), Germany (1995) and
Great Britain (1995)

	Netherlands	Germany	Great Britain
Theil	0.147	0.140	0.179
Decomposition by household type			
Within-group	0.139	0.125	0.153
(in %)	(95)	(89)	(85)
Between-group	0.007	0.015	0.026
(in %)	(5)	(11)	(15)
Decomposition by use of work potential			
Within-group	0.114	0.125	0.139
(in %)	(78)	(89)	(78)
Between-group	0.032	0.015	0.040
(in %)	(22)	(11)	(22)

Sources: SEP; GSOEP; BHPS.

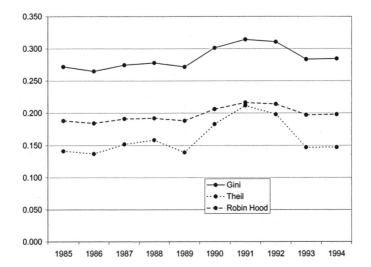

Source: SEP.

Figure 5.7   Trend in post-government inequality in the Netherlands,
1985–94

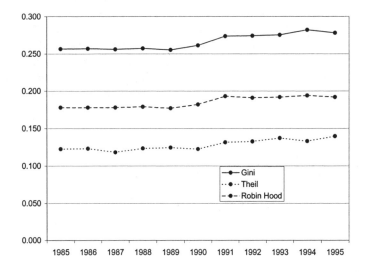

Source: GSOEP.

Figure 5.8 Trend in post-government inequality in Germany, 1985–95

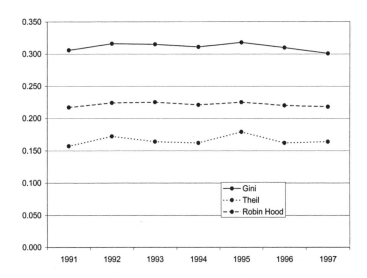

Source: BHPS.

Figure 5.9 Trend in post-government inequality in Great Britain, 1991–7

5.6   ISSUES IN THE MEASUREMENT OF POVERTY

Poverty covers many aspects of life that change from place to place and over time. In this study, poverty is defined in monetary terms, that is being at the lower end of the income distribution. In measuring poverty, three distinct steps have to be distinguished. The first one is conceptual and consists of defining the term poverty. The second step is empirical and consists of defining a poverty threshold which reflects the definition of poverty that was adopted. The third one, also empirical, is to measure the total amount of poverty. These steps have already been discussed at length in the literature, so instead of summarising here, we present a conceptual framework in which to view poverty and poverty dynamics (Section 5.6.1) and describe the poverty line adopted in this study (Section 5.6.2). Some cross-sectional results pertaining to the extent and determinants of poverty are presented in Section 5.7.

5.6.1   Conceptualisation of Poverty

Different types of poverty definitions are found in the literature. Definitions of poverty can analytically be distinguished along four lines (Muffels, 1993):

- The basic dimensions involved;
- Absolute–relative poverty line;
- Objective–subjective poverty line;
- The way the needs of households of various sizes are compared to one another (see Section 5.3.2).

Basic dimensions of poverty
In earlier work (Dirven et al., 1998) a classification of poverty definitions was used based on two dimensions: one relates to the difference between income and consumption; the other relates to the difference between static and longitudinal poverty. In his work, Amartya Sen (1979) had already made a distinction between the direct (deprivation-related method) and the income method of poverty measurement. Later, the sociologist Stein Ringen (1988) elaborated further on the distinction between direct (consumption-related) and indirect (income-related) definitions of poverty.[7]

With a consumption – or deprivation – definition, poverty is assessed in terms of a low level of living conditions. People are poor when they have a lower standard of living than what is judged decent in their community: that is when they are deprived of some resources. This standard of living is regularly measured multidimensionally, according to a broad set of achievements: food, health, education, housing, work, social contacts, and so on. The approach is termed direct since it focuses on the actual achievements and living conditions of households and/or individuals. With an indirect – or subsistence – definition poverty is defined in terms of income. Those who do not have at their disposal the minimum amount of resources deemed necessary to achieve a certain minimum living standard are labelled poor. This minimum amount of resources is referred to as the income poverty line. The income notion used is, in general, disposable household income. Here, only one aspect of the living situation – income – is considered. For the Netherlands, evidence has been produced indicating that income poverty is not the sole determinant of relative deprivation (Dirven and Berghman, 1991; Muffels, 1993). Other resources, including economic, social and cultural are also determinants of relative deprivation.

Very often, poverty is defined as a situation in which income is too low, according to a pre-defined standard. In fact, income is then taken as a measure of the actual economic outcome achieved by the individual or household. However, since the study of poverty is an attempt to measure people's welfare, income can be shown to be a rather poor determinant of welfare. In fact, it is not income itself that produces welfare (utility), but what people can actually afford with their income – the commodities and services they can buy – and what they can achieve with these commodities and services. Sen has thoroughly developed this line of reasoning in much of his work (see, for example, Sen, 1985, 1992).

In all these approaches, income – or resources – definitions are distinguished from definitions in terms of consumption patterns and standards of living. By making the distinction between direct and indirect poverty measurements, Ringen (1988) stressed the fact that, although poverty is often defined in terms of deprivation, it is frequently measured only in terms of income. However, the use of the words 'direct' and 'indirect' might be confusing because, in welfare economic theory, they refer to the way of measuring consumer preferences. The measurement of preferences might be pursued either by the method of 'revealed preferences' as in classical budget research (indirect) or by 'stated preferences' (direct), asking questions about the utility assigned to income levels in surveys (Kapteyn et al., 1985). Therefore, in welfare economic terms, income definitions are called 'direct' and consumption definitions 'indirect'. For this reason we prefer to make a distinction between income-related and consumption-related poverty definitions. Throughout this study we restrict our analyses to the income method, using it – instead of consumption or deprivation – as a yardstick for welfare.

In the second dimension of poverty definitions, it must be stressed that poverty is a gradual process. It can start short term and evolve towards a permanent situation through a process of marginalisation. Therefore, studying poverty in a static perspective is insufficient. Terms such as 'income poverty' or 'relative deprivation' are generally seen as instantaneous notions of poverty. In the conventional static approach, there is little consideration for the longitudinal aspect of poverty. In a dynamic approach, what matters is how poverty statuses evolve over time: whether people are able to escape transitory instances of poverty conditional on the length of stay in poverty, how stable or unstable income positions are over time and whether poverty is a recurrent phenomenon or not. In a dynamic approach, the interest goes, therefore, to longitudinal patterns of poverty and deprivation, as well as to the factors which determine impoverishment and exclusion from average living standards. This leads to a matrix for the classification of poverty definitions, as presented in Table 5.4.

The use of terms such as impoverishment (low income) and social exclusion (low consumption) reflect the longitudinal approach to poverty and the focus on poverty dynamics. In the dynamic approach, the attention is placed on changes, or the sequence of life events, leading people to enter into or to escape from poverty. The longitudinal concept of poverty adds the time dimension to the static poverty concept, making it fundamentally different. As Walker argued, it is not just another dimension: 'it is the medium within which poverty occurs and shapes the experience of being poor' (Walker, 1994: 11). Changes in employment status, household composition and position within the social protection system are all events that can generate these processes. Disincentives, stigmatisation and moral hazard may also contribute to these processes.

Table 5.4   Conceptualisation of poverty definitions

	Static (state at one point in time)	Dynamic (changes over time)
Income (cash income, command over resources)	Income poverty, income deprivation ⟶	Longitudinal poverty, impoverishment
Consumption (consumption budget, living standard)	Relative deprivation, consumption deprivation ⟶	Longitudinal deprivation, social exclusion

Source: adapted from Berghman (1995: 21).

Our use of the term 'social exclusion' in Table 5.4 must be distinguished from the way the term is generally used in the European context. In official discourse at the EU level, the term 'poverty' has gradually made place for the notion of 'social exclusion'.[8] The relative vagueness of the concept and its multidimensionality can account for its attractiveness in European debates (Matsaganis and Tsakloglou, 2001). It is broad enough to encompass whatever aspect the Member States wish to incorporate in the concept. However, it also enables them not to undertake new policies and use existing policies as illustrations of their actions. In any case, the use of the term social exclusion in European discourse does not necessarily refer to processes or dynamics. It is generally used to describe situations.

Throughout this book, we restrict our analyses to the income method, using it – instead of consumption or deprivation – as a yardstick for welfare. For evidence on consumption deprivation and its dynamics (social exclusion) in the EU countries, see Muffels and Fouarge (2002a, 2004) and Whelan et al. (2001a, 2001b, 2001c). Chapter 6 focuses on the dynamic aspects of poverty (impoverishment). In the remainder of this chapter we deal essentially with income poverty from a static perspective.

Absolute and relative poverty
With an *absolute* poverty line, a person can be said to be poor when he or she does not reach an absolute minimum level of resources, independent of the environment of that person (Townsend, 1979). It is clearly based on some notion of basic needs. Hence, the level of an absolute poverty line – though it can be indexed to account for inflation – does not change when the standard of living in society changes. A *relative* poverty line is linked to the standard of living in society. It recognises that 'the notion of poverty is strongly related to the average level of and the distribution of individual welfare in society' (Van Praag et al., 1982: 7) but has no explicit link with the notion of basic needs. It is sometimes argued that relative methods reduce poverty to a notion of inequality. For a discussion on relative versus absolute poverty lines and a critical view on poverty lines, the reader is referred to Sen (1983). Sen argues that, while poverty can be thought of absolute in the space of capabilities (see below), it translates into a relative approach in the space of income, commodities and resources. A similar point was illustrated by Adam Smith in *The Wealth of Nations* (Smith, 1976). He reckoned that, in eighteenth-century England, one would have been too ashamed to appear in public without leather shoes while this might not have been the case in earlier times. Customs of the country have made it a necessity to wear shoes (relativity) in order to avoid shame when appearing in public (absolute feeling).

Objective and subjective poverty
A further distinction is usually made between *objective* and *subjective* poverty lines. An objective poverty line is one set by experts. People are classified with respect to objective aspects of their situation that are measurable by an external observer. The level of a subjective poverty line is dictated by the view of people and their own feeling about their situation – their perceived level of utility or welfare. However, when they disagree, some aggregation procedure is required, which turns subjective approaches into inter-subjective approaches (see

Goedhart et al. 1977; Kapteyn et al. 1985; Van den Bosch, 2001).

Capabilities

Measuring poverty in terms of income is like viewing poverty in terms of command over resources or, rather, the lack thereof. Rather than measuring what people have – income, goods and other material resources – the capability approach concentrates on what people do and can do (Sen, 1983, 1985, 1992). In this approach, 'functionings' play an important role. They represent what 'the person succeeds in *doing* with the commodities and characteristics at his or her command' (Sen, 1985: 10). What is crucial here is that, while functionings are absolute, the means to achieve them are relative across individuals, time and space. It is the collection of such functionings that determines a person's capabilities: what he or she can do. What people actually do does not matter, as long as their capabilities set is broad enough. Within this framework, poverty can be defined as a state in which the level of capabilities is unacceptably low compared to the standards of the society one is living in. However, attempts to operationalise this concept of capabilities are scarce (see, for example, Desai, 1990) and so are empirical studies on the subject. These studies, moreover, tend to focus on functionings rather than capabilities (see Schokkaert and Van Ootegem, 1990).

Income

In advanced economies, income is an important determinant of people's possibility set and command over goods and services. Moreover, income is easily measurable and directly available from international comparable data sources. Income data are readily available for long periods of time, making the analysis of trends and dynamics possible. One should, however, keep in mind that a given net income level in one country does not open the same possibility set in another country. This will be the case, for example, when health care is publically financed in one country and privately in another.

Measuring the extent of poverty

Once the concept of poverty has been clarified and appropriately operationalised, the next step is to develop quantitative indicators of poverty. Having determined which households/people live in poverty, one has to compile this information into a single index. The most easily computable – and indeed the most popular – measure of poverty is the headcount ratio also called poverty rate. It is simply defined as the total number of poor relative to the total number of persons in the population. Despite the shortcomings of this index – it says nothing about the poverty gap (the question of how poor one is) or the variation in income among the poor (see Sen, 1976; Foster et al., 1984) – we use this index throughout this book.[9]

5.6.2   Making a Choice

The definition of poverty we adopt in this study is taken from the Third Poverty Programme of the EU:

> The poor shall be taken to mean persons, families and groups of persons whose resources (material, cultural and social) are so limited as to exclude them from the minimum acceptable way of life in the Member States in which they live (European Council Declaration of 19 December 1984).

The first important aspect of the definition is that it is relative, since the frame of reference for evaluating people's living standard is the 'way of life in the Member States' in which people live. Because of this relativity, it also fits the principle of subsidiarity included in the EU Treaty. Hence, poverty is not understood to be the inability to satisfy some physiological needs necessary for survival. The second aspect of this definition is that poverty encompasses both material and non-material aspects. We believe both aspects are significant. However, due to problems of data availability, international comparative studies focus mainly on income poverty.[10]

In this study, we chose to apply a statistical poverty line. More precisely, we set the poverty threshold at half-median national standardised income, where income is standardised using the modified OECD equivalence scale (see Section 5.3.2). Later in this book, we also define poverty line based on some proportion of EU median income (see Section 7.3). Although the method is unidimensional, arbitrary and subject to a number of other criticisms, it is becoming standard practice to use it in international comparative research. The standard practice at Eurostat, however, is to use 60 percent of standardised median income as the poverty threshold. To visualise the effect of the level of the poverty line on the poverty estimate, the poverty rates corresponding to various proportions of median income, ranging from 0 percent (no poverty) to 100 percent (half the population in poverty) of median income, are depicted in Figure 5.10. The figure shows that, for low values of the poverty line, poverty in Great Britain is less than in Germany and the Netherlands. This can be explained by the larger proportion of very low income in the latter two datasets. As the poverty line is set at higher levels of median income – above 40 percent – poverty in Great Britain is always greater than in the other two countries. The largest difference in poverty rate between the Netherlands and Great Britain and between the Netherlands and Germany is found for a poverty line equal to 64 and 60 percent of median income, respectively. The largest difference between the German and Great Britain poverty rates are found when the poverty line is set at 74 percent of median income. At the 50 percent of median income cut-off point, German and Dutch poverty rates are rather equally sensitive to small changes of the poverty line. However, the British poverty rate is more sensitive. This holds for all the values on the range of 35 to 65 percent of median income. The elasticities calculated for the half-median poverty line show that a 10 percent increase of the poverty line leads to a dramatic 32 percent increase in the poverty rate in Great Britain. This elasticity is much lower in Germany (19 percent) and lowest in the Netherlands (15 percent).

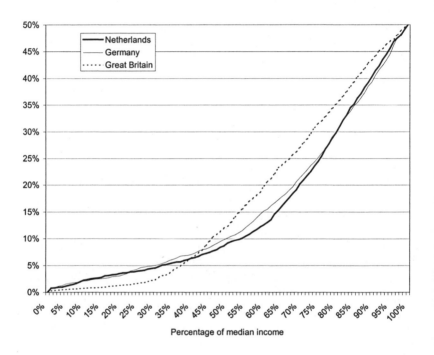

Sources: SEP; GSOEP; BHPS.

Figure 5.10 Sensitivity of the poverty rate to the poverty line, in the Netherlands (1994), Germany (1995) and Great Britain (1995)

5.7   THE INCIDENCE OF POVERTY

5.7.1   Trends in Poverty Rates

We first present general trends in pre- and post-government relative income poverty as measured by the headcount index (in Table 5.5). In the table, the degree of redistribution achieved though transfer income is also reported. Redistribution is measured as the proportional reduction in the poverty incidence. Considering the results across countries for 1994, Great Britain is found to have the largest post-government poverty rate. What is striking is that the pre-transfer poverty rate is more or less equal in all three countries, resulting in a lower redistributive efficiency of the British social protection systems. One could then conclude that the free play of the market results in similar (pre-transfer) poverty rates in all three welfare states but that – conform to the expectation – the continental and social-democratic welfare states do a better job at reducing poverty.

While pre-transfer poverty rates seem to have remained more or less constant over time in the Netherlands – though a slight increase is found by the 1990s – post-government poverty appears to have increased, reducing the redistributive efficiency of social transfers over the years. In Germany, noticeable changes took place at that time. Both pre- and post-government poverty have increased, leading to a general reduction of redistributive efficiency of the social protection system. While pre-transfer income poverty gradually increased during the first half of the 1990s in Great Britain, post-government poverty increased after the economic recession of the early 1990s to decrease again afterwards.

Table 5.5   *Percentage of poor according to 50 percent of median standardised income, pre- and post-government income, redistribution (%), 1985–95*

	1985	1986	1987	1988	1989	1990	1991	1992	1993	1994	1995
Netherlands											
Pre	32.2	31.3	31.2	31.2	32.3	34.4	33.7	32.9	34.3	34.4	–
Post	6.7	6.9	6.4	7.0	7.5	9.4	10.0	9.8	8.4	9.1	–
Redist.	79	78	79	78	77	73	70	70	76	74	–
Germany											
Pre	29.8	28.9	29.2	28.9	29.1	29.0	31.0	32.2	32.3	33.3	33.3
Post	7.1	6.7	7.0	7.3	6.2	7.1	8.1	9.2	9.2	9.2	10.2
Redist.	76	77	76	75	79	76	74	71	72	72	69
Great Britain											
Pre	–	–	–	–	–	–	31.9	33.5	35.2	35.6	35.0
Post	–	–	–	–	–	–	12.2	13.3	14.8	13.5	12.4
Redist.	–	–	–	–	–	–	62	60	58	62	65

Sources: SEP; GSOEP; BHPS.

5.7.2   The Distribution of Poverty

In this section, we take a closer look at the groups at high risk for poverty.

The results are summarised in contingency tables where the probability of being poor is related to a number of variables, that is demographics, income, labour market and human capital.

As to the demographic variables, we distinguish, as we did above, among seven family types. Alongside of the distinction between households with or without children, we also consider the impact of a larger number of children in the household (none, one, two, three or more) on the poverty status.

Table 5.6   Post-government poverty rate, by characteristics of the household, and redistribution (%) in the Netherlands (1994), Germany (1995) and Great Britain (1995)

	Netherlands		Germany		Great Britain	
	Poverty rate	Redist.	Poverty rate	Redist.	Poverty rate	Redist.
Total	9	68	10	69	12	65
Household type						
Single non-elderly	12	69	14	51	20	40
Single elderly	3	96	14	85	28	70
Couple without children	8	58	5	71	2	82
Couple with children	9	41	6	55	10	51
Elderly couple	10	84	6	93	6	92
Single parents	18	76	46	20	46	39
Other	15	67	17	61	10	65
Number of children						
0	9	75	9	80	10	75
1	10	47	14	40	12	51
2	9	45	9	43	13	51
3+	9	57	17	46	26	42
Age of head of the household						
25–	32	45	40	23	39	25
26–45	8	51	11	42	13	45
46–65	10	64	8	69	6	75
65+	7	89	10	89	16	79
Gender of head of the household						
Male	9	64	6	77	8	72
Female	13	79	17	61	20	58
Head's educational level						
Lower than high school	18	63	15	63	16	65
High school level	3	80	10	72	12	54
Higher than high school	3	72	4	77	5	69

Sources: SEP; GSOEP; BHPS.

The educational level of the head of the household is introduced as a measure of human capital. Because of problems of comparability of educational achievements involved in international comparative studies, we take a basic classification of educational level: low (less than high school); average (high school) and high (more than high school). In fact, this rough classification performs rather well in our analyses. Gender and age of the head of the household are included as general demographic characteristics of the household. In a sense, they can also be interpreted as measures of human capital of the household.

Three variables are used to represent the labour market status of the household. The first one indicates whether or not the head of the household has paid employment. Because we expect that there is less chance of being poor if more household members are engaged in gainful employment, our table also includes the total number of employed persons in the household. The last variable is a composite indicating the use of work potential by the household, as was defined earlier. Finally, the social security status is accounted for by the proportion of social security income in total disposable income.

Poverty in relation to demographic and human capital variables
From the point of view of the various household types, single parents display the highest poverty rate in all three countries (Table 5.6). In the Netherlands, however, the poverty rate among single parents is 'only' double the average – it is more than four times the average in Great Britain and Germany – and the redistributive effect is found to be large.[11]

Poverty incidence also tends to be larger than average among the non-elderly singles in all three countries and elderly singles in Germany and Great Britain. Large redistributive effects are found among elderly couples, single elderly – especially in the Netherlands – and, in Great Britain, among couples without children. In Great Britain, the poverty risk tends to increase as the number of children in the household increases. Something similar is found in Germany, but not the Netherlands. However, in all countries, the redistributive impact of social security transfers tends to decrease as the number of children increases.

Young household heads are generally at a higher risk of poverty. However, some are still studying and are thereby investing in human capital formation. Others are at the beginning of their working life and are gathering experience at a low wage. As human capital theories suggest, the earning potential of those youngsters is very likely to increase substantially over the years. These numbers, therefore, do not really reflect their true lifetime prospects.

Although the poverty rate in female-headed households is higher than average in all three welfare regimes, the redistributive effects of the welfare regimes are quite different. The Dutch regime is relatively more redistributive towards female-headed households, while the breadwinner (Germany) and liberal models (Great Britain) are relatively more redistributive towards male-headed households.

Table 5.7   Post-government poverty rate, by labour market and social security characteristics, and redistribution (%) in the Netherlands (1994), Germany (1995) and Great Britain (1995)

	Netherlands		Germany		Great Britain	
	Poverty rate	Redist.	Poverty rate	Redist.	Poverty rate	Redist.
Total	9	68	10	69	12	65
Head's employment status						
Not working	21	69	21	73	25	66
Working	3	63	4	55	4	58
Number of employed in the household						
0	18	75	25	74	32	64
1	11	52	9	62	8	67
2+	2	60	1	56	2	59
Use of employment potential						
0–10%	20	73	25	74	31	65
11–25%	38	44	25	68	23	67
26–50%	9	58	12	72	7	67
51–75%	2	70	3	77	5	60
75+%	2	39	2	33	2	59
Ratio of social security income in total household income						
0–10%	4	5	6	8	3	18
11–25%	9	28	6	59	10	52
25–50%	8	71	14	65	11	71
51–75%	13	85	15	80	12	84
75+%	26	74	20	80	38	62

Sources: SEP; GSOEP; BHPS.

Poverty by labour market and social security characteristics
As expected, the employment status of the household members greatly influences the probability of being poor (Table 5.7). The degree of association of the poverty status with the labour market variables is generally higher than with the demographic variables. The importance of the labour market is greatest for countries in the liberal tradition, such as Great Britain. For example, individuals in a household with a strong attachment to the labour market (making almost full use of their work potential) display comparable poverty rates. However, when little use is made of the work potential, the British are much more prone to poverty than the Dutch, and the Germans. Overall, the redistributive impact of transfers is larger for non-working households than for self-supporting, working ones. The larger the proportion of social transfers in total household income, the larger the chance

one is going to be poor. Twenty (Germany) to 40 percent (Great Britain) of those whose main income source is transfers are found to be poor.

5.7.3 Determinants of Poverty

In the previous section, we examined the independent effect of a number of socio-economic variables on poverty, without considering other factors. Using econometric models, we can measure the effect of these variables on the poverty status while, at the same time, controlling for the effect of other factors (Box 5.2).

BOX 5.2   Model for the determinants of poverty

The approach used here is to estimate logit models on the data so as to gain better insight into the determinants of poverty. When estimating a logit model for the poverty status, the probability of being poor is compared to the probability of not being poor, as in the following model:

$$P(y_i = 1) = \frac{\exp(x_i\beta)}{1 - \exp(x_i\beta)},$$

where y_i equals 1 if the individual is poor and 0 if not, x_i is a vector of covariates and β a vector of coefficients measuring the effect of the dependent variables on the poverty risk. The vector x_i includes a number of theoretically inferred variables, which are expected to impact one's economic position. These relate to relevant socio-economic characteristics of the person and the household: gender, human capital variables, employment status and employment profile of the household. Past poverty experience is included in the model to see whether having been poor in the recent past exacerbates the probability of being poor. The model was estimated for the last year available in the data. Only those living in a household where the head is of working age (16–65 years old) have been used for estimation. The Hubert–White estimator of variance was used. The fit of the model is measured according to MacFadden's R^2 = 1 – (log likelihood of the model/log likelihood of the model including only a constant). It expresses the reduction in log likelihood of the model including the explanatory variables compared to the model including only a constant term. The estimation results are reproduced in Table 5.8. The numbers in the table are the regression coefficients. A negative sign indicates that the variable under scrutiny reduces the poverty risk, compared to the reference category. A positive coefficient indicates that, compared to the reference category, the variable increases the risk of being poor.

The estimated model (Table 5.8) indicates, in the first place, the importance of educational attainment in reducing the poverty risk. Better-educated persons have a significantly lower probability of being poor. Similarly, the poverty risk is lower at higher ages. This could mean that older cohorts have maintained their human capital in terms of know-how, as well as earning potential.

Table 5.8   Parameters for the probability of being poor, the Netherlands (1994), Germany (1995) and Great Britain (1995)

Head of household aged 16–65	Netherlands (n = 10,464)	Germany (n = 14,114)	Great Britain (n = 8,339)
Number of children in household (ref: no child)			
One	0.479**	1.105**	0.036
Two	0.676**	0.308*	0.354*
Three or more	0.315*	1.219**	0.277
Age of head of the household (ref: 16–25)			
26–45	−2.023**	−0.796**	−1.506**
46–65	−2.302**	−1.435**	−2.387**
Female head (ref: male)	−0.109	0.697**	0.008
Educational level of head of the household (ref: less than high school)			
High school level	−1.131**	−0.479**	0.123
Higher than high school	−1.263**	−1.124**	−0.268*
Head is working (ref: not working)	−1.270**	−0.654**	−0.051
Use of work potential in household (ref: 0–10%)			
11–25%	1.272**	−0.408*	−0.279
26–50%	−0.068	−1.144**	−0.751**
51–75%	−1.090**	−2.639**	−1.289**
>75%	−0.850**	−3.112**	−2.332**
Proportion of social security income in total household income (ref: >75%)			
0–10%	−0.639**	−0.087	−1.666**
11–25%	0.097	−0.573**	−0.650**
26–50%	−0.502*	−0.068	−0.885**
51–75%	−0.651**	−0.679**	−1.123**
Number of times poor in previous four years	1.267**	1.145**	0.727**
Constant term	0.662**	-0.134	0.951**
R^2	0.46	0.43	0.45

Notes: * significant at 5%; ** significant at 1%.

Sources: SEP; GSOEP; BHPS.

A second aspect of the model indicates the importance of the labour market situation of the head of the household and household members in decreasing the probability of being poor. Those living in a household where the head is economically active have a lower probability of being poor. This does not, however, hold in the British case. When the activity status of the household was found to be significantly negative, including the indicator of the use of the work potential in the household suppressed that effect. In all countries, as expected, an increased use of the work potential of the household members results – through increased labour market income – in a lower poverty risk. This is, however, not true for marginal jobs (few hours) in the Netherlands (see also Figure 5.4). Similarly, a decreased share of social protection income results in a lower probability of being poor. This effect is especially strong in Great Britain, due to the generally low and means-tested social security transfer.

The household situation is also found to influence the poverty risk. Larger numbers of children in the household lead to an increased risk. With the exception of Germany, no significant gender effect on poverty has been found. The significant effect of gender in a bivariate setting is eliminated through the inclusion of labour market variables. The significant positive gender effect in Germany is interpreted as a typical feature of its corporatist breadwinner tradition. The significant and positive effect of past poverty experience suggests the possible existence of some state dependence in poverty.[12]

5.8 CONCLUSION

Whether or not income inequality and poverty are found to be high is, to a great extent, a matter of personal judgement. However, it is also a measurement issue. Using a variety of inequality measures we have shown here that, although income levels have been rising during the past decades in the Netherlands, Germany and Great Britain as a result of increased economic activity, the distribution of income has become more unequal. Using a relative measure of income poverty, we have also shown that the incidence of poverty increased during the past decades. Individuals in Germany are found to have the highest net income, followed by Great Britain and the Netherlands. The differences among the countries, though, are not very large. However, the three countries differ in the way income is distributed among individuals. Great Britain displays a higher level of inequality and poverty than Germany and the Netherlands. The Dutch and German welfare states both do a better job at redistributing income and, therefore, at reducing market-induced inequalities.

The computations carried out show that human capital variables and labour market participation are strong determinants of the poverty risk. The stronger the attachment to the labour market, the lower the probability that one will be poor. This holds for all three countries, but especially for Great Britain with its more liberal welfare system.

However, as discussed later, the true incidence of poverty in a society is determined by the level of transitions into and out of poverty and the extent of long-term poverty. In brief, if the turnover rate is high, the incidence is likely to be high and the length of poverty spells short. If turnover is low, the same people will be found to be poor year after year and poverty spells will be long. In the next chapter we investigate this at length using the possibilities offered by the panel datasets at our disposal.

NOTES

1. These include Mitchell (1991), Deleeck et al. (1992), Gustafsson and Lindblom (1993), Smeeding et. al. (1993), Van den Bosch et al. (1993), Atkinson et al. (1995), Jäntti and Danziger (2000). See Smeeding et al. (1990) for description of the LIS database.
2. The eastern sample is included from the 1992 wave onwards.
3. The data used in this book were made available through the UK Data Archive. The data were originally collected by the ESRC Research Centre on Micro-social Change at the University of Essex, now incorporated within the Institute for Social and Economic Research. Neither the original collectors of the data nor the Archive bear any responsibility for the analyses or interpretations presented here.
4. Social security transfers include pensions, maternity, unemployment, invalidity, widow(er), orphan and housing benefits, child allowances, study grants and cash social assistance. In this study, income data are expressed in terms of Euro Purchasing Power Standards (PPS). Strictly speaking, PPS adjustment is not designed for comparison of net household income, but for the comparison of real national income. PPS only account for average international prices while relative prices for goods and services within the country matter more to households. See Dowrick and Quinggin (1994) for a discussion. At present, however, there is no other alternative to PPS.
5. See, for example, Kapteyn and Van Praag (1976), Pollak and Wales (1979), Buhmann et al. (1988), Blundel and Lewbel (1991), Coulter et al. (1992).
6. Supposedly, this is one of the consequences of German reunification. Looking at the Western sample alone, we found that inequality had increased. Schwarze (1996) shows that post-transfer inequality decreased following German reunification. However, the income concept he uses differs from ours on some crucial points.
7. For an extensive treatment of the issue, see also Callan et al. (1996).
8. See Vleminckx and Berghman (2001) for a historical account of the concept of social exclusion.
9. In Chapter 7, use is also be made of the poverty gap index.
10. Note, however, that due to increased availability of comparable datasets such as the ECHP, comparative studies of non-monetary indicators of poverty are becoming more common. For comparative evidence on relative deprivation, see Dirven and Fouarge (1996, 1998), Halleröd (1998), Layte et al. (2001), Whelan et al. (2001a, 2001b, 2001c), Muffels and Fouarge (2002a, 2004), Tsakloglou and Papadopoulos (2002).
11. Note that in the Netherlands, the poverty rate among single parents is highly sensitive to the level of the poverty line. Setting the poverty line equal to 60 percent of median income, for example, results in poverty incidence among single parents that is substantially larger than average. An explanation for this high sensitivity is that many single parents live on social assistance, while the 50 percent threshold comes just short of the general assistance level. Hence, raising the poverty threshold results in a large increase in the poverty incidence in this group.
12. See Cappellari and Jenkins (2000) for an extensive treatment of the issue of state dependency.

6. The Dynamics of Poverty

6.1 INTRODUCTION

This chapter focuses on long-term income poverty and poverty dynamics using, as in the previous chapter, income as the yardstick for welfare comparisons across population groups. We have already indicated that previous international comparisons of poverty and inequality have generally been based on annual cross-sectional data, of which the most well known and comprehensive is the Luxembourg Income Study (LIS). Comparative studies of income and poverty dynamics are now becoming more common (see Duncan et al., 1993; Headey et al., 1997, 2000; Goodin et al., 1999; and more recently, OECD, 2001; Bradbury et al., 2001). Still, not many countries have long-running panels that allow for longitudinal analyses. It was a great opportunity to be able to use three unique long-running panel datasets for three rather distinct countries in terms of their poverty distributions and welfare state features. We have used panel data for 10 consecutive years for Germany and the Netherlands, and five consecutive years for Great Britain. A 10-year period seems sufficiently long to reflect the long term. The five-year period we use for comparing Great Britain with the other countries is meant to reflect the medium term. Hence, in this chapter, a comparison is made among the short- (annual as in the previous chapter) and medium-term (five years) results for three countries and the long-term (ten years) results for two. Within welfare regimes, we are, therefore, able to compare the social and economic efficiency of redistributive policy over time. We can also compare the long-term social and economic efficiency of the various welfare regimes. From the point of view of subsidiarity, we can show whether the market is capable of alleviating poverty in the longer run. If so, state intervention might not be necessary. Otherwise, if one wants to eliminate poverty, some degree of State redistribution might be required.

Section 6.2 of this chapter pertains to the definitions used in the literature for monitoring long-term poverty. Subsequently, we develop the notion of 'poverty profile', according to which a distinction is made among transient, permanent and recurrent poverty. In Sections 6.3 and 6.4, comparative evidence is presented on longitudinal poverty, using the previously explained measures. In Section 6.5, our focus shifts to the events that trigger entries into and exits from poverty, after which we turn – in Section 6.6 – to the investigation of the socio-economic determinants of poverty profiles over time. Finally, in Section 6.7, we briefly present some results from model-based estimates of permanent poverty. The findings are summarised in Section 6.8. These analyses are of interest because they will help gain insight into the economic efficiency of the various welfare regimes in the longer run.

6.2   APPROACHES TO PERSISTENT POVERTY

6.2.1   The Time Nature of Poverty

In Chapter 5, we introduced a theoretical scheme by which to view concepts of poverty and social exclusion (see Table 5.4). One of the dimensions of that classification points out the distinction between static and dynamic definitions of poverty. Such terms as 'income poverty' or 'relative deprivation' are generally conceived in their static meaning: instantaneous notions of low income or relative deprivation in which the person or household lives at a certain time. In the conventional approach, there is little consideration for the longitudinal aspect of poverty. However, for policy purposes, it is certainly significant whether those recorded as poor at different times are always the same or whether some have left poverty while others have become poor. For example, using data for the Netherlands, de Beer (2001) has shown that high levels of economic growth and a large increase in labour market participation in the 1980s and 1990s did not reduce poverty. Although the poverty rate remained more or less constant, there was much dynamics into and out of poverty.

In a dynamic approach, what matters is how poverty statuses evolve over time: whether people are able to escape transitory instances of poverty (conditional on the length of stay in poverty); whether or not income positions are stable over time and whether or not poverty is a recurrent phenomenon. In a dynamic approach, such as the one followed in this chapter, one is interested in the longitudinal patterns of poverty and deprivation and the factors which determine the process of impoverishment and exclusion from average living standards. In the dynamic approaches the attention goes to processes – or the sequence of life events – leading people into or out of poverty (see Sections 6.5 and 6.6).

The time nature, itself, should be part of the definition of poverty. The experience of short- and long-term poverty, the welfare assigned to the poor's standard of living and the strategies they adopt to cope with poverty and exclusion at the micro-level are quite distinct. In the short run, people may be able to make ends meet by drawing on their savings and reducing their expenditure. For the longer run, however, these strategies are often insufficient to cope with the income shortfall. Apart from the magnitude of that shortfall (poverty gap) and the duration of it (spell duration), attention should be paid to the distribution of poverty across the population over time. In particular, its recurrent nature – and, therefore, the prevalence of poverty in society over time – should be the concern of academic researchers.

The distribution of poverty over time depends not only on the number of people in poverty, but also on income mobility, the duration of poverty spells and the extent of recurrent poverty (Walker, 1994). The higher income mobility or income volatility is during a certain period and the shorter the spell duration, the higher the prevalence of poverty in society; that is the higher the proportion of people experiencing poverty at least once during the period. Similarly, the lower the share of recurrent poverty, the higher the prevalence. This means that, in the absence of income mobility over a given period, it is always the same individuals who are poor and the prevalence over time equals the cross-sectional poverty rate. This situation indicates the existence of an underclass: once poor, always poor. If, on the other hand, poverty is a once in a lifetime event, then economic positions are open to all and the probability of being poor is equally shared by all. This situation is to be preferred to the former one on the grounds of Rawls's principle of distributional justice (Rawls, 1971; see Chapter 3). However, the prevalence of poverty is directly affected by the length of the observation period. Lengthening of the observation period results in the observation of more short-term poverty spells and, hence, in a higher prevalence of poverty.

In summary, the time-dependent nature of poverty is characterised by four dimensions: 1) the length of the observation period; 2) the extent of recurrent poverty; 3) the length of the poverty spell; and 4) the volatility and stability of poverty statuses over time. For each of these dimensions, different measures are applied. Together, these four dimensions determine the pattern – or profile – of poverty for each individual over time. In this chapter, four types of poverty profiles are distinguished: persistent non-poverty, transient, recurrent and persistent poverty.

6.2.2   Length of Observation Period

With regard to the length of the observation period, the panels at our disposal give us the opportunity to make a distinction among short- (one year), medium- (five years) and long-term (ten years) poverty. Short-term indicators of inequality and poverty were presented in the previous chapter. What we do here is to compare the short-, medium- and long-term results within, as well as across, welfare regimes. Extending the observation period makes it possible to observe income patterns over time and gain insight on the total 'movie' – not just the 'snapshot' – of people's socio-economic status. Short- and medium-term comparisons can be made across the three countries. However, for the long term we only have data for Germany and the Netherlands.

What is attractive about looking at medium- and long-term poverty is that it clarifies how income-smoothing over the years can lead to a reduction of poverty. It is a fact that, by looking at cross-sections, one is comparing people in different phases of their working and non-working lives. These phases are associated with different income levels. Hence, one is comparing the income level of, for example, a student in economics to that of a successful manager with the same educational background. Extending the observation period allows us to alleviate such problems.

Pooling income data over the years and assessing the extent of poverty on these pooled incomes generates a measurement that has been referred to as the *n-years income-to-needs ratio* (Section 6.3.1).[1] This is one of the indicators of persistent poverty in the literature (Duncan and Rodgers, 1991; Rodgers and Rodgers, 1993), which will be used in this chapter. Concerning this measurement, it should be noted that, given the extent of poverty in society, a longer accounting period causes long-term poverty rates to fall since short-term changes in income positions are evened out in the longer run.

6.2.3   Extent of Recurrent Poverty

The extent of recurrent poverty is measured in Section 6.3.2 by the so-called *poverty hit rate* over time: the frequency of poverty experiences during the period in question. However, this indicator is problematic in various respects. There is still no answer to the question of how many years of poverty are enough to speak of persistent poverty. This method is also criticised by Bane and Ellwood (1986) because it is subject to a censoring problem. Let us take the example suggested by the authors:

> Suppose all poverty occurs in spells lasting exactly ten years. If we were to ask how many persons who were poor over a ten-year survey period remained poor the entire time, only those people who happened to begin their ten-year spell in the first year of the survey would be counted (Bane and Ellwood, 1986: 4).

Other spells beginning prior to the start of the survey and finishing before the end of the survey would be observed as shorter than 10 years. The same holds for spells beginning after the start of the survey. Nevertheless, despite these criticisms, we will use this measure as one of the indicators of persistent poverty.

6.2.4 Duration of Poverty Spells

Whether or not periods of poverty are consecutive matters to people. This aspect is not covered by the two indicators of long-term poverty suggested above. Since only annual information on the poverty statuses is available, the *duration of the poverty spell* is defined as the number of years people live in poor households from time t onwards, given that these people had lived in non-poor households at time $t - 1$. Here, it is the longitudinal sequence of experience of poverty that matters. The notion of spells and the implications for measurement are detailed below.

Whether or not long spells of poverty are to be judged to be worse than short spells depends, to a large extent, on the degree of one's aversion towards uncertainty. It stands to reason that, if one is to become poor, one would prefer to be poor for a short – rather than a long – time. However, long periods of poverty are not always worse than repeated short periods. Indeed, risk-averse individuals may prefer low but stable incomes to higher but unstable ones. For a complete picture, information on the volatility of income positions must complement the data on the duration of low-income spells.

6.2.5 Volatility and Stability of Poverty

Because incomes are mobile, snapshots tend to exaggerate the extent of poverty. From a labour market perspective, labour income mobility is desirable as an instrument to improve the overall efficiency of the labour market. However, as Atkinson et al. (1992) state, it is also desirable intrinsically, because mobility promotes equality of opportunities, and instrumentally, because mobility reduces lifetime inequalities.

Here, we will supply two methods to measure the volatility and stability of income positions over time. The first method is the *spell approach* (Section 6.4), derived from survival analyses in biological research (life table analysis). It is an approach that was used by Bane and Ellwood (1986) and Stevens (1994, 1999), among others. It gives information about the exit or escape rates out of poverty, conditional on being in poverty for a certain number of years. Whereas these exit rates give information on income mobility, the staying probabilities – the reverse of the exit rates – provide an insight into the stability of low-income positions over time.

The stability of income positions are also measured by a *model-based approach* (Section 6.7) to poverty persistence, derived from Duncan and Rodgers (1991). Here, persistent poverty is defined as a situation in which permanent income is below the poverty line. This is based on the fact that people have a rather permanent latent income-to-needs level from which occasional departures are possible because of temporary income shocks due to unemployment, disability, illness, overtime work, incidental income flows, and so on. The model is not able to identify individuals living in persistent poverty, since it can only provide a population-wide estimate of the existence of persistent poverty in society.

6.2.6   Poverty Profiles

The poverty hit rate and the spell approach can be used to define the notion of *poverty profiles* (Walker, 1994). We can distinguish among four types of poverty profiles (see Muffels et al., 1998, 1999):

- the persistent non-poor: never poor during the accounting period;
- the transient poor: poor only once during the accounting period;
- the recurrent poor: poor more than once, but never longer than two consecutive years;
- the persistent poor: poor for a consecutive period of at least three consecutive years.

The measure of poverty persistency seems rather arbitrary. However, the likelihood of escaping poverty diminishes rapidly after having been poor for two or more years (see Section 6.4). Given the longer-running panel data, distinct poverty profiles can be observed across the population.

6.3   WELFARE STATE TRANSFERS IN THE SHORT, MEDIUM AND LONG TERM

6.3.1   The Reduction of Poverty

In Table 6.1, the short-, medium- and long-term poverty figures are given for the Netherlands, Germany and Great Britain. They are computed using the *n*-years income-to-needs ratio. In all of those countries, income-smoothing over the years leads to a reduction in poverty. Provided the labour market offers opportunities for all to improve their income positions in the long run, one would expect the rate of reduction in pre-transfer poverty – when extending the observation period – to be larger than that of post-transfer poverty. That, however, is not the case: the rate of reduction in post-transfer poverty is larger than that of pre-transfers poverty. This means that the redistributive effect of transfers, in the long run, is larger than in the short run, even in a liberal regime such as Britain. Pre-transfer poverty remains high, presumably because of a high level of income volatility or economic mobility. This means that, due to the operation of the market, situations of income shortfall are followed by instances of income surplus. This suggests that it is certainly not the market that evens out poverty over time; it is the operation of the welfare state through income transfer policies. Welfare state policies are generally more egalitarian in the longer term. The downsizing of poverty in the longer run appears to be due to the success of the market–government nexus.

Table 6.1   Percentage of pre- and post-government poverty and welfare state redistribution: short, medium and long term

	Netherlands			Germany			Great Britain		
	Pre	Post	Redist.	Pre	Post	Redist.	Pre	Post	Redist.
Short term									
1987	26.4	6.4	78	29.2	7.0	76	–	–	–
1993	27.9	9.8	65	32.3	9.2	72	35.2	14.8	58
Medium term									
1985–9	25.0	3.7	85	26.6	4.0	85	–	–	–
1991–5ᵃ	26.9	4.8	82	28.7	4.8	83	33.2	8.9	73
Long term									
1985–94	25.6	2.4	91	23.9	2.6	89	–	–	–

Note: a) Data for 1990–94 for the Netherlands and 1991–5 for Great Britain and Germany.

Sources: SEP; GSOEP; BHPS.

The extent of post-transfer poverty is similar in the Netherlands and Germany. The Dutch welfare state, though, slightly outperforms the German one in terms of its long-term redistributive effect. Notwithstanding the success of the British government to reduce medium-term poverty, both pre- and post-transfer poverty rates are found to be highest there. This might reflect the lower level of the safety net in Great Britain for people dependent on a minimum labour income or social assistance benefits. The high level of pre-government poverty indicates that, in Great Britain, people at the lower end of the income distribution ladder are very dependent on the income transfer policies of the government to make a decent living. Obviously, the market is unable to provide for decent labour incomes for low-income earners.

6.3.2   Poverty Hit Rates

As stated above, longitudinal poverty accounts for the prevalence of poverty in society. In this section, results are given on recurrent poverty, based on the poverty hit rate: that is the frequency of poverty hits in the accounting period. The post-government poverty figures for the five-year period 1991–5 reveal that, in the Netherlands and Germany, about one in five people are prone to fall into poverty at least once (Table 6.2). Hence, more than 80 percent of all the people in these countries are never poor. In Great Britain, more than a quarter of the individuals experienced poverty at least once in the early 1990s.

Table 6.2   *Percentage of recurrence of poverty (poverty hit rates) in the Netherlands, Germany and Great Britain*

	Netherlands		Germany		Great Britain	
	Pre	Post	Pre	Post	Pre	Post
1985–9						
Never	58	84	60	86	–	–
Once	11	10	8	7	–	–
2 times	5	2	5	3	–	–
3 times	5	2	3	2	–	–
4 times	7	1	4	2	–	–
5 times	14	1	20	1	–	–
1991–5[a]						
Never	61	82	56	82	51	73
Once	8	10	9	8	9	10
2 times	4	3	6	4	6	6
3 times	4	2	5	3	5	5
4 times	5	1	5	1	5	3
5 times	19	2	20	1	24	3
1985–94						
Never	50	75	51	79	–	–
Once	9	13	10	10	–	–
2 times	5	5	6	3	–	–
3 times	4	3	4	2	–	–
4 times	3	1	3	2	–	–
5 times	4	1	3	1	–	–
6 times	4	1	3	1	–	–
7 times	2	0	2	1	–	–
8 times	3	0	3	1	–	–
9 times	5	1	3	0	–	–
10 times	12	1	14	1	–	–

Note: a) Data for 1990–94 for the Netherlands and 1991–5 for Great Britain and Germany.

Sources: SEP; GSOEP; BHPS.

If the accounting period is twice as long (10 years) one in four people in the Netherlands experience at least one single poverty spell. The prevalence of poverty is, therefore, much higher than suggested by annual 'snapshots'. The risk of becoming poor seems widespread. In the medium term, more people in Great Britain are frequently hit by poverty than in Germany and the Netherlands. The pre-government figures show the market to be more inegalitarian in Great Britain, for the medium term, compared to the other two countries. The German and Dutch figures for the shorter – as well as for the longer – accounting period look similar. Comparison of the pre- and post-government figures show that, particularly for the Netherlands and Germany, the system of public transfers leads to a large – but not complete – reduction of poverty.

It looks like the Dutch and British social security systems make more people poor for a single year than would have been the case if there were no government transfers and people had to live from their pre-government or market income. However, as was concluded elsewhere, this is actually good, rather than bad, news since these people would have been poor for at least two years if there had been no government transfers (Headey et al., 1997).

In Great Britain, the number of pre-government persistently poor (poor for the entire five-year period) is extremely high (24 percent). Some interesting results are found as to the effects of transfer systems. For Great Britain, the downsizing effect of public transfers on longitudinal poverty is particularly significant for the persistent poor and less so for the transient poor. This reveals the role of targeted public income transfers to the 'deserving' – persistent – poor, which is a typical feature of liberal social security systems. More evidence concerning this point is presented in Section 6.5.

In all three countries, the evidence suggests that the recurrence of poverty is less of a problem than persistent poverty. Most of the people are never poor and a significant proportion are poor once. However, except in Great Britain, the number of people who are frequently poor during a given period is rather limited.

6.4   ANALYSIS OF POVERTY SPELLS

From the findings presented so far, it might be concluded that the longitudinal poverty concept is multifaceted and complex. In order to understand this, it is essential to distinguish among the various forms of longitudinal poverty as they become manifest over time. The poverty hit rates simply count the number of times people are poor within the accounting period and, therefore, say little about the duration of poverty. In the next analysis, we turn to the study of the duration of poverty spells, that is the consecutive years spent in poverty (see Box 6.1).

Contrary to what might be expected, the distribution of pre-government spells is very similar in the three countries (see Figure 6.1). The pre-government spells show that, in the situation of no government intervention, the market would produce similar levels of poverty persistency across countries. Nevertheless, pre-government poverty spells tend to last longer in all countries, indicating, again, that the market does a poor job in terms of preventing persistent poverty. Government interventions are needed to shorten spells of poverty. Post-government poverty spells, therefore, appear to be much shorter. About 20 percent of the people who started a spell three years earlier are still poor and were not capable of escaping from poverty. The post-government survival rates for Great Britain are slightly higher than for the Netherlands and Germany. These outcomes suggest that more egalitarian welfare regimes do not generate strong disincentives on the labour market. More redistributive welfare regimes, such as the Dutch and the German, do not perform worse in terms of preventing pre-government poverty than liberal welfare regimes, such as the British.

BOX 6.1   The calculation of spells

For the calculation of the poverty spells, left-censored spells, for which the starting date is unknown, were excluded from the analysis but right-censored spells were included. Within this framework, the survival function $S(t)$ is equal to $1 - F(t)$, with $F(t) = Pr(T \leq t)$ being the distribution of time t that indicates the probability that the random variable T is smaller than or equal to some value t. In other words, it indicates that some event – an exit from poverty – has occurred by duration t. Hence, $S(t)$ indicates the probability that the event has not yet occurred by duration t. The survival rates were computed with the life table method (non-parametric approach). This involves counting the number of failures and censored observations that fall in each of the time intervals $[t_j, t_{j+1}], j = 1, \ldots, J$, with $t_{J+1} = \infty$.

Define n_j the number entering the interval $[t_j, t_{j+1}]$, d_j the number of failures occurring during that interval and m_j the number of censored observations during the interval. Then, $n^*_j = n_j - m_j/2$ is the adjusted number at risk during the interval $[t_j, t_{j+1}]$. In the absence of censoring $n^*_j = n_j$. The estimator of survival function is given by:

$$S(t_j) = \prod_{i=1}^{j} \frac{n^*_i - d_i}{n^*_i}.$$

The numbers in Table 6.3 are the cumulative staying probabilities, that is the probability to remain in poverty conditional on the number of years already spent in poverty.

Most spells end within the first or second year after they began. After the second year, the likelihood of escaping poverty diminishes rapidly. In principle, the results for the five-year period should be viewed with caution because of the limited time span, although a 10-year observation period does not seem to change the results. We found that in the longer run (10 years), most poverty spells in the Netherlands and Germany also tend to end within the first years after a spell has begun (for details, see Fouarge, 2002: 126). If spells last longer than three years, the likelihood of escaping from poverty is extremely low. Pre- and post-government spells in Germany were found to last longer than in the Netherlands.

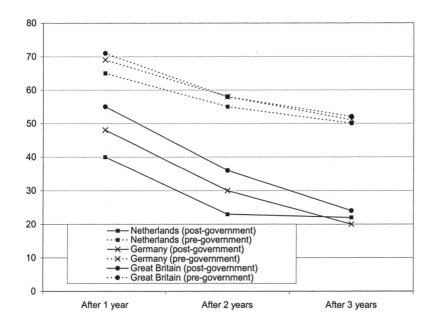

Note: Data for 1990–94 for the Netherlands and 1991–5 for Great Britain and Germany.

Sources: SEP; GSOEP; BHPS.

Figure 6.1 Cumulative staying probability after a set number of years in poverty (in percentages) for pre- and post-transfer income for the Netherlands, Germany and Great Britain, 1991–5

6.5 MOBILITY INTO AND OUT OF POVERTY

6.5.1 Transition Tables

Table 6.3 presents data for the dynamics of income poverty between 1985–9 and 1991–5 for the Netherlands, Germany and Great Britain. In both Germany and the Netherlands, inflow into poverty averaged 4 percent per year during both periods. Inflow into poverty in Great Britain, however, equalled 7 percent on average from 1991 to 1995. Moreover, outflow from poverty is somewhat less in Great Britain compared to Germany and the Netherlands. Although outflow from poverty was greater in the Netherlands than in Germany during the first five-year period, this ordering changed during the second five-year period. The odds of remaining non-poor rather than becoming poor for the non-poor equals 24 to 1 in the Netherlands and Germany in the 1991–5 period. The odds of being non-poor rather than poor for the poor were 0.8 to 1 in the Netherlands and 0.9 to 1 Germany. In Great Britain, the corresponding odds were 13 to 1 for the non-poor and 0.7 to 1 for the poor. The odds ratio is 30 in the Netherlands, 27 in Germany and 19 in Great Britain, suggesting more unequal mobility chances in the Netherlands and Germany compared to Great Britain. In other words, in liberal welfare states income positions are more open, at least at the lower end. A closer look should be taken at the processes underlying these transitions.

Table 6.3   *Transition table for poverty status in the Netherlands, Germany and Great Britain (row percentages), 1985–9 and 1991–5*

	Netherlands		Germany		Great Britain	
	Non-poor in $t+1$	Poor in $t+1$	Non-poor in $t+1$	Poor in $t+1$	Non-poor in $t+1$	Poor in $t+1$
1985–9						
Non-poor in t	96	4	97	3	–	–
Poor in t	49	51	43	57	–	–
1991–5[a]						
Non-poor in t	96	4	96	4	93	7
Poor in t	43	57	46	54	41	59

Note: a) Data for 1990–94 for the Netherlands and 1991–5 for Great Britain and Germany.

Sources: SEP, GSOEP, BHPS.

6.5.2   Explaining Poverty Transitions

The transition probabilities presented in Table 6.3 can be explained by a number of factors: socio-cultural attitudes and norms, demographic characteristics and socio-economic characteristics – that is the labour market status and the impact of economic shocks in the household budget. Such variables are also likely to explain differences in transition probabilities among countries. Here, we develop an empirical explanatory model where we look at the effect of these micro-level variables on the transition probabilities into and out of poverty in the Netherlands, Germany and Great Britain. We focus on year-to-year transitions taking place in the first half of the 1990s.[2] The variables to be included in the models are inferred from the economic and sociological literature on income and social mobility. We distinguish among: 1) individual or household characteristics; 2) indicators of labour market activity; and 3) social security status. Since we are interested in explaining transitions, we also included variables measuring the changes in those characteristics at the time of the transition. From the point of view of subsidiarity, individual or household characteristics are included in an attempt to measure the effect of self-help or traditional family help. The labour market status – and change thereof – is included to keep track of the relative importance of market mechanisms in explaining transitions into and out of poverty. The social security status – and change thereof – is included in the models to account for the effect of State intervention in promoting welfare through the mechanisms of the welfare state.

A number of labour market activity indicators are included in the models. As in Chapter 5, the labour market attachment is defined as the ratio of the number of hours worked by all household members of working age to the total number of hours of full-time work available. A change in this indicator of household labour attachment is defined as a 25 percent or more increase or decrease in the use of work potential. The reliance of the household on public transfers is defined as the proportion of social security transfers in the total household income. A change of 25 percent or more in this public transfer ratio between two years is defined as an increase or decrease of that ratio. The econometric model used is similar to the one discussed in Box 5.1, but what we scrutinise is the probability of entering or exiting poverty.[3] The estimations were limited to persons living in a household, the head of which was aged 16–65.

At first glance (Table 6.4), the demographic variables tell us that young households run a considerably higher risk of slipping into poverty. People living in a household where the head is of prime working age run a lower risk of becoming poor. In Germany and Great Britain – but not in the Netherlands – people in female-headed households are more likely to become poor. Dependent children or adults in the household contribute to a high risk of becoming poor, except in the Netherlands. The effect of a mutation in the number of children, however, is ambiguous. In Germany and Great Britain, both an increase and a decrease in the number of dependent children leads to an increased risk of becoming poor. A tentative explanation is that the effect is dependent on the age of the children. Young children coming into the household induce an additional financial burden that is generally less than compensated by child benefits. Children leaving the household are generally older and have their own income, which may have negative consequences for the financial situation of the household. Additional adults coming into the household are likely to bring their own income. This leads to a reduction of the poverty risk. However, adults leaving the household induce a negative shock on the household's income, which increases the risk of poverty.

Table 6.4   Parameters for the probability of entering poverty between
1991–5, in the Netherlands, Germany and Great Britain

	Netherlands[a] (n = 32,624)	Germany (n = 50,434)	Great Britain (n = 25,575)
Age of household head (ref: 16–25)			
26–45	–0.913**	–0.384*	–0.595**
46–65	–1.395**	–0.884**	–1.729**
Female head of the household (ref: male)	0.178	0.293**	0.241**
Educational level of household head (ref: less than high school)			
High school level	–0.504**	–0.252*	–0.275*
Higher than high school	–0.410**	–0.879**	–0.323**
Number of children	0.241**	0.349**	0.246**
Number of adults	0.513**	–0.133	0.233**
Number of employed persons	–0.416**	–0.306**	–0.803**
Use of work potential in household (ref: 0–10%)			
11–25%	0.802**	–0.289	0.596**
26–50%	0.514*	–0.036	–0.573**
51–75%	0.179	–0.697*	–1.216**
>75%	–0.333	–1.208**	–1.644**
Proportion of social security income in total household income (ref: >75%)			
0–10%	–2.255**	–1.048**	–0.961**
11–25%	–1.534**	–0.574	–0.856**
26–50%	–0.997**	–0.398	–0.343
51–75%	–0.506**	–0.093	–0.553**
Change in number of children (ref: no change)			
Increase	–0.401	0.763**	0.315*
Decrease	–0.004	0.603**	0.892**
Change in number of adults (ref: no change)			
Increase	–0.086	–1.850**	–0.753**
Decrease	0.619**	1.214**	1.203**
Change in use of work potential (ref: no change)			
Increase	0.158	–0.619**	–0.550**
Decrease	1.878**	2.017**	0.871**
Change in social security income receipt (ref: no change)			
Increase	1.777**	1.064**	0.779**
Decrease	0.502**	0.815**	–1.352**
Constant	–3.705**	–2.638**	–0.599*
R^2	0.23	0.24	0.35

Notes:
a) Data for 1990–94 for the Netherlands and 1991–5 for Great Britain and Germany.
* significant at 5%; ** significant at 1%.

Sources: SEP; GSOEP; BHPS.

As would be expected, a higher level of human capital leads to a reduced
risk of becoming poor. As far as indicators of labour market activity are
concerned, in all three countries – but more so in Great Britain – the poverty
risk decreases as more household members are employed. This could be the
result of Britain's liberal model of economic welfare. A similar conclusion
can be drawn from studying the use of work potential. In Great Britain,

increased use of the work potential substantially reduces the risk of slipping into poverty. This is less so in Germany and the effects are insignificant in the Netherlands. In both Great Britain and the Netherlands, however, a marginal use of the work potential (10–25 percent) of the household is likely to lead to a poverty entry. Hence, from the point of view of preventing poverty, marginal employment – associated with low labour market income – is not likely to be an adequate policy option.

Increasing the use of work potential in the household induces a reduction – except in the Netherlands – of the poverty risk. However, a decrease of the use of work potential in the household increases the risk of becoming poor. In all countries, even in the most de-commodified country such as the Netherlands, the labour market incentives to escape poverty are found to be strong.

When household income consists primarily of market income – with very little social security income – the risk of entry into poverty is significantly reduced. The less one is dependent on social transfers for his or her welfare, the lower the chance that one will become poor. This effect, however, is not found in Germany. In all countries, an increase in the proportion of social security income to total household income is likely to lead to an increased risk of slipping into poverty. This indicates the potential risk of welfare dependence. A decrease in social transfers also implies a higher chance of becoming poor in the Netherlands and Germany. In Great Britain, however, reducing welfare transfers appears to have a strong incentive effect in the sense that it leads to a reduced probability of becoming poor. However, one should keep in mind that the counterpart of this is a large percentage of persistent poverty.

Once poor, one is more likely to exit poverty in a household where the head is older than 25 years old (see Table 6.5). The returns on education – in terms of increasing the probability of exiting poverty – are high in the Netherlands, lower in Germany and insignificant in Great Britain. Dependent children or adults reduce the probability of escaping poverty, except in Germany.

Participation in the labour market is an escape route from poverty. With the exception of the Netherlands, an increase in the number of employed people in the household leads to an increased probability of leaving poverty. An increase in the use of work potential in the household also leads to an increased probability of exiting poverty, except in Germany.

In the Netherlands, some evidence of welfare dependence is found for particular ranges of social security income. Compared to those fully dependent on social transfers, people whose income depends on social transfers for 50–75 percent are less likely to exit poverty. The same holds for those receiving between 10 and 25 percent of social security transfers. In the other countries, especially Great Britain, lower levels of social transfers stimulate exit from poverty.

Table 6.5   Parameters for the probability of exiting poverty between 1991–5, in the Netherlands, Germany and Great Britain

	Netherlands (n = 3,068)	Germany (n = 3,911)	Great Britain (n = 3,503)
Age of household head (ref: 16–25)			
26–45	0.460*	0.220	0.389*
46–65	0.825**	0.482*	0.128
Female head of the household (ref: male)	0.228	–0.131	–0.124
Educational level of household head (ref: less than high school)			
High school level	0.516**	0.394**	–0.205
Higher than high school	0.787**	0.370	–0.057
Number of children	–0.207**	–0.044	–0.331**
Number of adults	–0.791**	0.087	–0.186**
Number of employed persons	0.000	0.503**	0.371**
Use of work potential in household (ref: 1–10%)			
11–25%	0.859**	0.004	–0.088
26–50%	1.472**	0.860**	0.940**
51–75%	1.784**	0.315	1.272**
>75%	0.529	–0.280	0.843*
Proportion of social security income in total household income (ref: >75%)			
0–10%	–0.117	–0.179	0.747**
11–25%	–0.649**	0.578*	1.077**
26–50%	–0.055	0.137	0.817**
51–75%	–0.444*	0.397*	1.189**
Change in number of children (ref: no change)			
Increase	–0.079	–0.560*	–0.358*
Decrease	0.259	–0.926**	–0.750**
Change in number of adults (ref: no change)			
Increase	0.082	1.466**	1.217**
Decrease	0.641**	1.057**	0.226
Change in use of work potential (ref: no change)			
Increase	1.619**	0.674**	0.239
Decrease	–0.987**	–0.867**	–0.279**
Change in social security income receipt (ref: no change)			
Increase	–0.134	–0.033	–0.869**
Decrease	–0.318**	0.517**	0.998**
Constant	–0.370	–1.564**	–0.628*
R^2	0.21	0.16	0.19

Notes:
a) Data for 1990–94 for the Netherlands and 1991–5 for Great Britain and Germany.
* significant at 5%; ** significant at 1%.

Sources: SEP; GSOEP; BHPS.

Just as a change – in whatever direction – of the number of dependent children leads to an increased probability of becoming poor, it also leads to a decreased probability of leaving poverty for the same reasons as mentioned above. With respect to the use of the work potential, it can be noted that a change thereof works in the expected direction: an increase in the use of work potential is likely to lead to an exit from poverty, while a decrease will have the opposite effect. A substantial decrease in social security benefits is found to have a strong incentive effect in Germany and Great Britain. However, the opposite effect is found in the Netherlands. In Great Britain, the increase of social transfers in total household income is also found to have a strong disincentive effect.

6.6 POVERTY PROFILES

Thus far, the analyses have provided a brief description of the current achievements of various welfare states in the three countries with respect to the reduction of short- and long-term poverty. The picture changes when we move from the conventional static to a dynamic approach. The conclusion was that over time, twice as many people are prone to fall into poverty at regular intervals compared to the conventional annual snapshots. The economic mobility in the three countries – particularly in Germany and the Netherlands – is higher than expected. According to neoclassical theory, these mature and fairly generous welfare states might cause disincentive effects that negatively affect mobility rates. However, most people, when they fall into poverty, seem capable of moving out rather quickly through labour market changes, changes in household formation or budget strategies.

Our analyses have shown that many people never experience poverty whereas others experience extended bouts of it. Some have a single experience of poverty during their lifetimes and others move into poverty at regular intervals but only for very short periods. A better understanding of the distribution of poverty over time can be obtained from poverty profiles, which include information on the prevalence, periodicity and duration (see Section 6.2). A poverty profile permits us to make a distinction among the never poor, the single year or transient poor, the multiple year or recurrent poor (poor more than once but never longer than two years in succession) and the persistent poor (at least three consecutive years in poverty).[4]

These profiles are different for various population groups, depending on their income and money flows over time. Poverty profiles combine the information on prevalence and duration of poverty. Table 6.6 shows how poverty is distributed across the various profiles. The results tell a similar story as above. Whereas the incidence of poverty on an annual basis was found to be highest in Great Britain, there is also a higher prevalence of transient, recurrent and persistent poverty there compared to the other countries. There are twice as many persistent and recurrent poor in Great Britain as in the Netherlands or

Germany. The number of transient poor is also higher in Great Britain and the number of recurrent poor is more than twice as high in Great Britain as in the Netherlands.

Table 6.6   Post-government poverty profiles (in percentages) for the Netherlands, Germany and Great Britain

	Netherlands			Germany			Great Britain
	1985–9	1991–5ᵃ	1985–94	1985–9	19991–5	1985–94	1991–5
Never poor	83.9	81.9	74.7	85.8	82.4	79.4	72.6
Transient poor	10.2	9.7	13.4	7.0	8.4	9.5	10.1
Recurrent poor	2.9	4.4	6.7	3.5	5.4	6.5	9.5
Persistent poor	3.0	4.0	5.2	3.7	3.8	4.6	7.8

Note: a) Data for 1990–94 for the Netherlands and 1991–5 for Great Britain and Germany.

Sources: SEP, GSOEP, BHPS.

Though the extent of transient poverty is lower in Germany than in the Netherlands, the percentage of recurrent poor is higher. No significant difference is found in terms of persistent poverty between the two countries. Hence, the evidence presented here supports the hypothesis that Great Britain, with its more liberal welfare state orientations, does a poorer job of preventing recurrent and persistent poverty. The differences among the three welfare regimes with respect to transient poverty are less well defined.

6.6.1   Who Are the Poor?

After our description of the distribution of poverty profiles, we now turn to examine the characteristics of the poor within the various profiles. According to the analyses in Chapter 5, it seems to matter whether someone lives in a household headed by a female, presumably because of the more precarious position of women in the labour market. From the point of view of subsidiarity, it is also interesting to relate the poverty profiles to indicators of the three levels at which income protection can be provided: the household level, the market and the State. Hence, we relate the poverty profiles to the household type, the labour market status of the household head and to whether the social transfers is the main income source in the household. The distribution – for the Netherlands – of persons across poverty profiles according to these characteristics is presented in Table 6.7.[5]

About 10 percent more people in female-headed households than in male-headed households run the risk of living in poverty. Although people in a female-headed household had a greater probability of living in poverty during the 1990–94 period, the gender differential is largest for transient poverty. The difference becomes smaller when related to recurrent and persistent poverty. With respect to the family type, single elderly and couples (with or without children) clearly run the lowest risk of being poor. A quarter of the single non-elderly are at risk for one type of poverty or another, mostly transient poverty. Nevertheless, the percentage of persistent poverty among couples with children is larger than average (5 percent). Single parents are rather likely to be poor at least once over the five-year period, and their poverty rate is highest for all profiles. This data partly support the idea that pooling resources through the formation of a household is an effective way to preserve oneself from poverty. This, however, does not hold for elderly couples, for they tend to pool relatively low – mostly pension – income.

Table 6.7   *Socio-economic characteristics of the poor by poverty profile (percentages), the Netherlands, 1990–1994*

	Never poor	Transient poor	Recurrent poor	Persistent poor	Total
Total	81.9	9.7	4.4	4.0	100
Gender of household head					
Male	83.3	8.6	4.2	3.9	100
Female	73.7	16.1	5.8	4.4	100
Household type					
Single non-elderly	75.3	15.0	7.4	2.3	100
Single elderly	87.7	11.8	0.5	0.0	100
Couple, no child	83.9	7.6	4.8	3.7	100
Couple with children	83.8	8.0	3.3	4.9	100
Elderly couple	77.6	16.0	3.8	2.6	100
Single parent	57.7	23.7	12.2	6.4	100
Employment status of household head					
Employed	89.6	7.6	2.1	0.7	100
Unemployment	65.6	14.2	9.2	11.0	100
Proportion of social security income in total household income					
Less than 50%	88.6	6.9	2.2	2.3	100
50% or more	66.0	16.4	9.7	7.9	100

Source: SEP.

Employment, as expected, is also an effective way to prevent poverty. While only 10 percent of those in a household where the head is working live in poverty – most of them are transient poor – two-thirds of those in a household where the head is out of employment live in poverty. Fourteen percent are transient poor, but 20 percent are either recurrent or persistent poor. Approximately the same picture holds with respect to the proportion of social transfers in total household income. A third of those whose main income source is social transfers live in poverty. Although most of them live in transient poverty, almost 10 and 8 percent, respectively, live in recurrent and persistent poverty. This is twice the average. In a well-developed welfare state, such as the Netherlands, there is still an effort to be made in order to alleviate long-term poverty.

In some respects, the situation in Germany (Table 6.8) is similar to that in the Netherlands. Approximately the same groups have a high probability of being in poverty. However, the distribution over the poverty profiles is quite different from that in the Netherlands. For example, while the poverty risk among persons living in a female-headed household is nearly equal in Germany and the Netherlands, Germans in such households have a higher probability of being either recurrent or persistent poor than the Dutch. Similarly, not only are single parents in Germany more likely to be poor than in the Netherlands, but almost a quarter of them are recurrent poor and 15 percent are persistent poor. This is twice the Dutch percentage. Another remarkable difference is that, in Germany, single elderly are more – and elderly couples less – likely to be poor. In the Netherlands, the opposite is true.

Table 6.8   Socio-economic characteristics of the poor by poverty profile (percentages), Germany, 1991–5

	Never poor	Transient poor	Recurrent poor	Persistent poor	Total
Total	82.4	8.4	5.4	3.8	100
Gender of household head					
Male	86.0	7.7	3.9	2.4	100
Female	74.5	10.0	8.8	6.7	100
Household type					
Single non-elderly	76.3	11.7	6.2	5.8	100
Single elderly	75.5	12.1	6.6	5.8	100
Couple, no child	87.0	6.6	3.7	2.8	100
Couple with children	85.6	7.1	4.9	2.4	100
Elderly couple	87.1	8.6	2.2	2.1	100
Single parent	43.4	17.8	23.9	15.0	100
Employment status of household head					
Employed	86.4	7.4	4.3	1.9	100
Unemployment	73.6	11.0	8.2	7.2	100
Proportion of social security income in total household income					
Less than 50%	85.3	7.7	4.2	2.8	100
50% or more	71.9	11.2	9.8	7.2	100

Source: GSOEP.

Living in a household where the head is out of employment or dependent on social transfers seems to have fewer consequences for the risk of poverty in Germany than it does in the Netherlands. The poverty rates in all profiles are lower in Germany than they are in the Netherlands.

The groups at risk in the Netherlands and Germany are even more at risk in Great Britain (Table 6.9). More than two-thirds of those in a female-headed household run the risk of being in one of the poverty profiles. Moreover, if they are poor, they are more likely to be persistent or recurrent poor than transient. This is even more blatant in the case of single parents, most of whom are female: 70 percent run the risk of being in one of the poverty profiles. Two-thirds of those in a single-parent household are persistently poor and a quarter are recurrent poor. The income position of the single elderly is also precarious. More than half of them are poor and, when they are, they are also more likely to be recurrent or persistently poor (20 percent in both cases). A particularity of the British situation is the poverty risk of couples with children: more than a quarter of the persons in this household type live in poverty, compared to 13 percent among couples without children. In Britain, children, therefore, seem to increase the risk of poverty.

Table 6.9   Socio-economic characteristics of the poor by poverty profile (percentages), Great Britain, 1991–5

	Never poor	Transient poor	Recurrent poor	Persistent poor	Total
Total	72.6	10.1	9.5	7.8	100
Gender of household head					
Male	77.9	9.5	7.6	5.0	100
Female	61.9	11.5	13.2	13.4	100
Household type					
Single non-elderly	73.2	10.9	8.1	7.8	100
Single elderly	45.5	14.6	20.1	19.8	100
Couple, no child	87.3	6.5	3.4	2.9	100
Couple with children	73.7	10.8	10.1	5.4	100
Elderly couple	82.1	8.4	6.4	3.1	100
Single parent	30.3	14.0	23.9	31.8	100
Employment status of household head					
Employed	83.5	8.4	5.3	2.8	100
Unemployment	54.4	13.1	16.5	16.0	100
Proportion of social security income in total household income					
Less than 50%	82.7	8.7	5.9	2.6	100
50% or more	46.8	13.8	18.6	20.9	100

Source: BHPS.

The consequences of unemployment in Britain are also much more dramatic than in the two other countries, which confirms our earlier findings. Almost half of those living in a household where the head is unemployed live in poverty. And if they are poor, they are likely to be recurrent (16.5 percent) or persistent poor (16 percent). Due to the generally low level of social transfers in Britain, having social transfers as the main income source results in an increased risk of poverty, especially persistent poverty.

6.6.2 Mobility In and Out of Poverty Profiles

In the previous tables, we examined the socio-economic characteristics of the individuals in the poverty profiles. We now turn to the investigation of the life events that might trigger the entry into or the exit from a poverty profile. Again, in accordance with subsidiarity, we distinguish among three types of life events: household formation events, changes in labour participation and changes in the share of social security income. Two types of household formation events are considered: a change in the number of household members (increase or decrease) or a change in the marital status of the household head – separation, divorce or death of partner, on the one hand, or a union through a marriage or cohabitation, on the other hand. Labour market changes are measured as a change in the number of working persons in the household and a change – five hours or more – in the total number of hours worked by household members. Changes of social security status are defined as a substantial increase or decrease (of 25 percent or more) of social security income in the household. We only coded such changes in social security income for the households where the number of workers remained unchanged at the time of entry into or exit from the poverty profile. The other enumerated events are not mutually exclusive. It is possible that a divorce, for example, is accompanied by a change in the number of employed persons in the household.

In Table 6.10, we show whether transitions into a poverty profile between year t and $t + 1$ are associated with life events occurring between the two years in the 1991–5 period. Poverty profiles that were in progress or starting up in the first year of the observation period – left-censored spells – are left out of the analyses because, for those spells, we are unable to measure changes in demographic, labour market and social security variables at the time of entry into the poverty profile. In general, it appears that adverse labour market events are more often associated with entries into poverty than adverse demographic events. This is particularly true for the Netherlands (especially for the persistent poor), but it also holds – to a lesser extent – for the other two countries. This shows that labour market dynamics tend to play a significant role in explaining entries into poverty.

In the Netherlands, around 7 percent of those entering persistent poverty during the early 1990s experienced the loss of a partner or a decrease of the household size. The corresponding figures for Great Britain are 18 and 19 percent, respectively. The figures for Germany are even larger: 26 and 44 percent, respectively. We attribute this to the breadwinner model of the German welfare state, according to which the income consequences of break-ups are expected to be large.

Table 6.10   Change in characteristics at the time of inflow into transient (T), recurrent (R) and persistent (P) poverty, the Netherlands, Germany and Great Britain (percentages), 1991–5

	Netherlands[a]			Germany			Great Britain		
	T	R	P	T	R	P	T	R	P
Household formation events									
Loss of partner[b]	14.8	9.4	7.7	19.7	16.9	25.9	19.4	12.1	18.4
Gain of partner[c]	0.8	0.5	4.8	1.1	0.6	0.0	1.0	1.1	2.5
Increase of household size	3.3	8.5	7.5	5.1	4.6	4.3	6.6	8.2	7.1
Decrease of household size	21.4	15.1	6.5	25.7	21.2	43.9	20.0	13.0	19.3
Labour market event									
Increase number of employed	8.0	8.5	2.3	4.0	5.6	0.0	11.7	9.7	1.2
Decrease number of employed	30.4	26.5	35.0	41.2	27.2	44.3	22.9	17.3	25.7
Increase number of hours (+5)	10.9	13.3	0.0	8.4	10.6	3.7	13.8	9.8	5.0
Decrease number of hours (−5)	32.1	27.5	43.3	52.3	42.6	67.1	29.9	17.8	24.4
Changes in social security income									
25% increase social security income	3.7	1.6	4.3	7.9	6.9	11.6	14.4	9.6	4.5
25% decrease social security income	39.4	36.1	20.3	26.4	37.0	15.3	27.6	30.1	26.7

Notes:
a) Data for 1990–94 for the Netherlands and 1991–5 for Great Britain and Germany.
b) Separation, divorce or widowhood.
c) Marriage or cohabitation.

Sources: SEP; GSOEP; BHPS.

In all countries, adverse labour market shocks, either through a reduction of the number of employed people in the household or decrease in the number of hours worked, tend to be most associated with transitions into persistent poverty and least with transitions into recurrent poverty. The only exception to this is the effect of decreased number of hours in Great Britain. From the data in Table 6.10, it appears that transitions into poverty – transient, recurrent or persistent – are less strongly associated with labour market shocks in Great Britain than in the Netherlands and Germany. This could be explained by the generally better quality of the jobs in the latter two countries, so that losing a job implies larger financial consequences. It can, however, also be explained by the difference in labour participation in the three countries. In the period under investigation, the labour market participation was higher in Great Britain (67 percent) than in Germany and the Netherlands (around 60 and 55 percent, respectively). Moreover, the proportion of single earners was larger in Germany and the Netherlands than in Great Britain. Hence, job losses would have a larger effect on the household's economic status in those countries. Aside from labour market shocks, a substantial loss of social security income will also potentially lead to inflow into transient or recurrent poverty.

The same exercise is repeated in Table 6.11 for transitions out of poverty. The table shows the bivariate association between exit from one of the poverty profiles and the aforementioned life events. Poverty profiles that were not completed in the last year of the observation period (right-censored spells) were left out of the analysis.

Demographic changes do not account for a large part of the poverty exits. In the Netherlands, however, 15 percent of the persistent poor experience a poverty exit together with the loss of a partner through separation, divorce or widowhood, and 24 percent through a decrease of the household size. These numbers cannot be explained by the presence of elderly in the data.

From the evidence in the table, it is clear that exits from poverty are associated with favourable labour market shocks. In all countries, the effect of a substantial increase in the number of hours seems to be stronger than the effect associated with an additional earner. This can be understood from the fact that those already in the labour market tend to earn more than those entering. The measured effects tend to be larger in Germany than in the other two countries. Whereas in Germany and the Netherlands the percentages of poor exiting poverty through a favourable labour market event are similar across profiles, in Great Britain, the percentages tend to decline with the length of the period in poverty. This seems to indicate that, in a liberal welfare state such as Great Britain, the effectivity of the labour market to lift people out of poverty diminishes with the length of the poverty spell. Therefore, as it increases, the poor seem to lose their labour market value. More than the other poor – and also in the two other countries – the persistent poor in Great Britain have to rely on social transfers in order to exit from poverty.

Table 6.11   Change in characteristics at the time of outflow from transient (T), recurrent (R) and persistent (P) poverty, the Netherlands, Germany and Great Britain (percentages), 1991–5

	Netherlands[a]			Germany			Great Britain		
	T	R	P	T	R	P	T	R	P
Household formation events									
Loss of partner[b]	3.9	1.9	14.5	8.1	6.3	5.7	3.6	3.2	1.1
Gain of partner[c]	1.9	2.1	3.1	2.5	2.8	3.5	6.0	7.1	4.7
Increase of household size	5.0	5.2	9.3	13.6	15.8	19.3	14.9	10.2	7.2
Decrease of household size	8.6	4.9	23.7	4.0	5.8	3.7	4.9	2.0	1.4
Labour market events									
Increase number of employed	18.0	17.1	19.8	28.6	23.2	31.2	22.5	16.1	9.6
Decrease number of employed	8.2	7.1	1.9	8.3	6.2	5.9	7.5	6.0	9.8
Increase number of hours (+5)	23.3	21.5	24.5	42.3	37.5	40.8	28.6	19.4	18.7
Decrease number of hours (−5)	7.3	9.2	7.7	13.8	11.1	8.2	11.1	9.0	11.6
Changes in social security income									
25% increase social security income	51.6	51.2	46.8	41.4	37.3	33.3	39.4	46.2	52.9
25% decrease social security income	3.2	5.9	14.0	6.1	7.9	3.0	6.8	6.9	3.1

Notes:
a) Data for 1990–94 for the Netherlands and 1991–5 for Great Britain and Germany.
b) Separation, divorce or widowhood.
c) Marriage or cohabitation.

Sources: SEP; GSOEP; BHPS.

6.6.3   The Determinants of Poverty Profiles

Recurrent poverty appears to be less of a problem for the three welfare states than persistent poverty, although the number of people in recurrent poverty, particularly in Great Britain, is quite high. This reasoning holds only when recurrent poverty is not a preliminary state or entrance gate to persistent poverty. This issue will be examined in more detail in this section. To what extent are the persistent poor different from the transient and recurrent poor? Persistent poverty appears rather modest in the long term, but substantial in the medium term. Even if persistent poverty is, on average, low it should be of concern for policy-makers. This is because the likelihood of extended stays in poor living conditions rapidly rises with increasing spell duration and might create social and psychological problems. Persistent poverty is also of concern since it is very unevenly spread across the population and hits particularly vulnerable groups in society. In this section, the events that trigger membership in the various poverty profiles – poverty 'careers' as we called it in Muffels et al. (1998) – are examined.

Econometric models (see Appendix 4) were applied to estimate the likelihood of belonging to each of the longitudinal poverty profiles. In the model, four types of variables are included which are likely to be important factors characterising these different profiles: 1) personal and household characteristics (age, sex, marital status, household composition, number of children and marital status); 2) socio-economic characteristics (education level, labour market status of the head of the household, number of employed persons in the household and total number of hours worked); 3) household formation events (divorce or separation); and 4) labour market events (increase or decrease in the number of employed adults in the household or in the number of hours worked).

Let us first examine the results for the persistent poor compared to the never poor (Appendix 4, Tables A.4.1, A.4.2 and A.4.3). In the Netherlands, we find that male heads of households are less likely to belong to the persistent poor than female heads. Note also the very strong impact of the number of children on the likelihood of persistent poverty. Considering the impact of household formation events, it is clear that separation during the observation period strongly increases the likelihood of persistent poverty. Though separated (widowed or divorced) heads at the beginning of the spell have higher chances to become persistently poor, single parents are less likely to be persistently poor than unmarried singles. Widowhood and divorce appear to raise the likelihood of poverty persistence. This also holds for the number of children; caring for children necessitates earning additional income to cover the additional costs. Married heads running into poverty have fewer chances to escape from it than single persons, probably because of lack of labour market opportunities.

Labour market-related variables appear to exert an even stronger impact on persistent poverty. The more people in the household who work, the less likely the household falls into poverty. For the same reason, households in which the head is unemployed at the beginning of the poverty spell are more likely to be persistently poor. If the head or a household member loses his or her job, the likelihood of persistent poverty increases sharply. The reverse holds if they get into work. Given the impact of labour market events on the likelihood of becoming persistently poor, it is interesting to look at the impact of human capital variables. A low educational level has a positive impact on poverty persistence. Therefore, education has a pay-off in terms of preventing persistent poverty.

The results for the other countries are similar. In Great Britain and

Germany, it is found that households with a separated head are more likely to be persistently poor. The larger the number of children, the more likely the household will become persistently poor. In Great Britain, younger heads are more likely to become persistently poor, although the likelihood falls with increasing age. In all three welfare states, separation during the time of the spell has, again, a strong impact on the likelihood of becoming persistently poor.

The effects for the labour market variables and labour market events are similar to the effects found for the Netherlands. The more workers there are in the household the less likely that the household members are persistently poor. Job loss by either the head or another household member during the observation period raises the probability of becoming persistently poor. A high educational level decreases the likelihood of being persistently poor in Germany but not in Great Britain. However, as in the Netherlands – and unlike Germany – a lower educational level raises the probability of being persistently poor in Great Britain.

To what extent are the persistent poor different from the recurrent and transient poor? The models suggest that the variables explaining the membership to the transient, recurrent or persistent poor are the same for the various categories. The magnitude of the effects, however, is larger for the persistent than for the recurrent poor, and larger for the recurrent than the transient poor. Membership into any of the groups seems particularly affected by human capital characteristics. The weaker the association with the labour market – because of obsolete skills, low qualifications, or a low human capital due to age or caring obligations – the higher the likelihood of being persistently poor. In the Netherlands and in Great Britain, about 80 percent of the persistent poor are unemployed. More than 60 percent of the recurrent poor and less than 50 percent of the transient poor are unemployed. In Germany, these figures are 53, 50 and 34 percent for the persistent, the recurrent and the transient poor, respectively.

6.7 PERSISTENT POVERTY, INCOME SHOCKS AND WELFARE REGIMES

From an economic point of view, it is important to make a distinction between temporary and persistent income inequalities. The more persistent income inequality is, the lower the income mobility. This could indicate the existence of institutional rigidities that strongly affects one's life-cycle income, implying that the burden of inequality over time is passed on to the same individuals. However, if cross-sectional inequalities were due to short-term income disparities, a high degree of income mobility would imply a more equal distribution of income. The same reasoning applies to poverty. Since both persistent and transient poverty require distinctive policy responses, it is essential to develop tools for measuring the extent of each types.

With an explicit reference to Friedman's notion of permanent income and elaborating on the existing literature on modelling income dynamics, a panel regression model has been estimated in order to disentangle the permanent and transitory components of income in a sophisticated way.[6] The methodology is similar to the one developed by Lillard and Willis (1978) and applied by Duncan and Rodgers (1991) and Stevens (1999) on US data. With the model applied, people's income level at one point is equal to their level of permanent income over their whole life plus temporary income changes. These can be positive (for example, winning a lottery) or negative (for example, a drop in income when one loses his or her job).

The basic idea behind this approach is that people are most concerned with maintaining their welfare level in the long run – their permanent income – and not with short-term changes. Within this model, poverty can be seen as a state in which permanent income falls below a pre-defined threshold. Hence, the model can be used to estimate the size of the population in persistent poverty and to compare it across welfare regimes. The analyses do confirm our earlier results. They reveal that the largest proportion of persistent poverty is found in Great Britain (around 5.5 percent), followed by the Netherlands and Germany, which have similar proportions (around 2 percent). Permanent income turns out to be both lower and less equally distributed in Great Britain than in the Netherlands and Germany. It is shown that a larger percentage of overall British and German income inequality (56–58 percent) is due to permanent income differences than in the Netherlands (47 percent). This indicates a relatively more 'open' institutional structure in the Netherlands that permits people to change income positions more easily than in the two other countries. This is in contradiction with the finding in Section 6.5.1. However, there the focus was on the lower end of the income distribution only, while here we look at the whole income distribution.

The model was also used to monitor the effect of socio-economic variables on persistent poverty. In particular, we looked at the long-term income effects of shocks on the labour market and at the household level. The motivation is that the increasing degree of interrelation among European economies might affect the ability of the welfare states to react adequately to asymmetric labour market shocks and to accommodate them by varying their level of spending. The findings confirm that living in a household with an unemployed head makes persistent poverty much more likely. That holds *a fortiori* for households with a non-working female head, because their labour market position is not as good as males. In Table 6.5, gaining employment was shown to be an adequate way of escaping poverty. However, employment policy is only likely to be effective for the cyclical or short-term poor. Often, the long-term poor are permanently excluded from the labour market. Hence, they lack the experience and capacity to compete in the modern labour market and information society. If this is true, employment policy must be flanked by an adequate income policy.

Table 6.12   Estimation results of panel model for persistent income poverty, seven years

	Netherlands	Germany	Great Britain
Proportion of permanent inequality	47	56	58
Estimated persistent poverty rate			
Total	2.0	1.6	5.5
Single parents	22.2	29.5	38.6
Male unemployed	4.8	3.0	9.8
Female unemployed	10.1	9.1	18.2

Sources: SEP (1988–95); GSOEP (1989–95); BHPS (1991–7); adapted from Fouarge (2002: 159–62).

As to household shocks, one must realise that increased individualisation impedes traditional networks of solidarities, such as the family, to function as welfare providers. Our analyses have shown that persistent poverty among single parents appears to be high in all three countries, corroborating the results of many poverty studies. In Great Britain single elderly are also more likely to be persistently poor than average. To the extent that the family is a basic provider of welfare at the base of the subsidiarity chain, the dismantling of families and increased individualisation – processes that tend to trigger long-term poverty – can be seen as a potential threat to economic welfare. In that context, the reliance on self-help and traditional family structure for the provision of welfare is bound to increase inequities in an individualising community.

6.8   CONCLUSION

The first aim of this chapter was to develop longitudinal measurements of poverty and to apply them to some of the long-running panel studies for Germany, the Netherlands and Great Britain. This allowed us to gain insight into the extent of long-term poverty. Modelling this micro-data also allowed us to gain additional insight into the processes leading to poverty entries and exits, as well as into the processes conducive to long-term poverty. The results are reported from two perspectives. The first one, *across welfare states,* raises the question of how welfare states perform in terms of preventing poverty and in particular, poverty persistence. The second one, *across time,* focuses on a comparison of the short-, medium- and long-term results in terms of preventing poverty. The results largely follow the expectations derived from Esping-Andersen's typology of welfare regimes. We found some clear and – from a theoretical viewpoint – coherent differences across the three welfare regimes. From the point of view of the European Union (EU), the analyses presented here make it clear that persistent poverty should be on the social agenda. The extent of, and the processes leading to, persistent poverty should be monitored carefully.

Across welfare states, it is clear that the Dutch and German welfare states do a good job in preventing poverty and inequality – not only in the short term, but also in the medium and long term – without greatly distorting efficiency. The British system produces higher levels of poverty, whether transient, recurrent or persistent. Great Britain had 50 percent more recurrent and persistent poverty during the first half of the 1990s than Germany or the Netherlands. Comparing the Dutch and German welfare systems, it appears that they perform equally well in preventing welfare state dependency in the medium and longer term. Great Britain, however, does a poorer job, especially in the short term. In the longer term, the redistribution results become much better and similar to the ones for Germany and the Netherlands. Comparison of pre- and post-government poverty rates makes it clear that the market does a much poorer job than the welfare state in preventing poverty in the short, medium and long term. The overall performance of these systems to reduce recurrent and persistent poverty appears very successful in Germany and the Netherlands, as well as in Great Britain with its different and more liberal welfare system. Nevertheless, Great Britain has to accept fairly high levels of recurrent and persistent poverty among particular groups, that is single-parent families and the unemployed.

Across time, it was shown that these governments perform better in the medium and long term than in the short term. The Dutch and German welfare systems are very successful in reducing poverty, particularly in the longer term. The British welfare system is also successful, albeit more in the long run than in the short run. For all the countries – including the liberal Great Britain – it is not the market that prevents long-term poverty. It is through government intervention that poverty is successfully tackled. Nonetheless, in all three countries, there are strong labour market incentives to both prevent entry into and to stimulate exit from poverty. The labour market incentives, however, seem to work more effectively for the short-term than for the long-term poor. Whether the State should be subsidiary to the market depends on one's perspective. From the point of view of incentives, the market should be given priority since it does a rather good job – at the micro-level – of preventing poverty and promoting poverty exits. The labour market, however, is not very likely to help the long-term poor. From the point of view of social efficiency, social transfers seem to do a good job in reducing long-term poverty, with limited disincentive effects.

Longitudinal poverty measurements provide a better view and tell a different story than the usual snapshots. On the one hand, they show that poverty is not simply a problem for a small group of low-income people in society. It appears to be a widespread social phenomenon because, in the longer run, many more people are prone to poverty than in the short run. On the other hand, it makes it clear that, in the long term, a great deal of the poverty is transient. Many people experience poverty only once and do not need much help to escape from it permanently. In general, there is much more economic mobility than the annual snapshots suggest, even at these low levels of income. There is another story told by these figures which is that, apart from the high levels of economic mobility among the poor, within particular categories – long-term unemployed, disabled and separated households – there is a great deal of persistent poverty. Although instant poverty can be unpleasant, it does not threaten subsistence and, in some circumstances, hardly matters at all. Running down savings, borrowing and belt-tightening can be adequate strategies when such short-term income shortfalls occur. However, these are not likely to help in the long run.

Income mobility and poverty persistence go hand in hand, even in growing economies and matured and developed welfare states. The explanatory models estimated in this chapter suggest that human capital, household formation and labour market events are responsible for people falling into as well as escaping from poverty. Where the transient and recurrent poor share many characteristics of the persistent poor, the likelihood of being part of a separated household and having a low education level is, in all instances, larger for the persistent poor. They share the experience of divorce and family break-ups and the occurrence of significant changes in the labour market status of household members due to work loss or work gain. They have a lower human capital value on the labour market and they lack the resources in terms of skills, education and work experience that can be exchanged on the market for jobs.

NOTES

1. For each person, the income-to-needs ratio equals the standardised income divided by the poverty line. Remember, however, that the relative poverty line used here does not really refer to the notion of 'needs'.
2. For this purpose, the data have been pooled over the years, to obtain a person–year dataset.
3. We used a pooled logit model to analyse all individual entries into and exits from poverty.

4. The definition is based on the length of the last poverty spell. Note that the poverty profile depends on the time window in which measurement is made. Extending the observation period changes the distribution of the poverty profiles. No attempt has been made here to account for left- and right-censoring when constructing the poverty profiles.
5. The characteristics are measured at the start of the observation period.
6. The method is based on the estimation of panel models for income dynamics. The models have been estimated on a seven waves panel (see Appendix 2). For details see Fouarge (2002: 153–6). See Jenkins (2000) for a critical comment on such methods.

7. Social Europe: Fiscal Competition or Co-ordination?

7.1 INTRODUCTION

The inclusion of the social chapter in the Treaty of Amsterdam has given a new impetus to the debate on social issues at the European Union (EU) level. At the Lisbon summit, the Council managed – for the first time – to draw attention to the balance among economic, employment and social policy (Vandenbroucke, 2001). The Lisbon conclusions (March 2000) formulated a new strategic objective for the EU in the next decade: 'to become the most competitive and dynamic knowledge-based economy in the world, capable of sustainable economic growth with more and better jobs and greater social cohesion' (European Council, 2000a: 2). This goal is to be achieved by, among other things, modernising the European social model, investing in human resources and combating social exclusion. In order to implement this strategy, the open method of co-ordination was preferred, the method that is currently used in the field of employment policy and the intention is to apply it in other policy fields, as well. The need to take steps in order to eradicate poverty – as mentioned at the Lisbon European Council (European Council, 2000a: 11) – has now steadily put the issues of poverty and social exclusion on the political agenda. However, the measures suggested by the Council – promoting more and better jobs for vulnerable groups, reviewing the functioning of the European Social Fund, increasing the involvement of social partners and reaching agreement on aims, targets and statistics – appear very tame in view of the more general aim of combating social exclusion (Begg and Berghman, 2001). The principle of subsidiarity, which constrains the action scope of the EU might be held responsible for that. Nevertheless, the Nice Council (December 2000) requested that Member States have a national action plan (NAP) to fight social exclusion (NAP/inclusion) prepared by June 2001. As with the NAPs in the area of employment, these plans for inclusion are meant to monitor progress in the area of poverty and social exclusion.

As requested at the Lisbon and Feira Council (European Council, 2000a, 2000b), the Commission has now released a Communication on 'Structural

Indicators' (European Commission, 2000c) which proposes a set of indicators to be used for the synthesis report at the Stockholm Council (March 2001). Six of these are concerned with social cohesion: 1) distribution of income; 2) poverty rate before and after transfers; 3) persistence of poverty; 4) jobless households; 5) regional cohesion; and 6) early school-leavers, not in further education or training. In the preceding chapters, we presented evidence with respect to the first three indicators for the Netherlands, Germany and Great Britain, while the fourth indicator has been the object of separate studies (Muffels and Fouarge, 2002b, 2002c).[1] The fifth and sixth indicators fall beyond the scope of our research.

In this chapter, we consider various hypothetical poverty targets for EU Member Sates and estimate what it would take – in terms of additional transfers – for the Member States to achieve them. Moreover, as we explained in Chapter 4, we elaborate further on the effect on poverty of fiscal competition among Member States in the field of minimum protection. By making various assumptions as to the outcome of the process of fiscal competition among Member States, we simulate the effect of these processes on poverty and inequality. The assumptions made are described in Section 7.2 and the methods followed are highlighted in Section 7.3. The results are presented in Sections 7.4, 7.5 and 7.6. Section 7.7 concludes the chapter.

7.2   FISCAL COMPETITION: RACE TO THE BOTTOM OR CALIFORNIA EFFECT?

The recent move towards the monitoring of social exclusion and the explicit formulation of national action plans for inclusion – as agreed at the Nice summit – demonstrate the desire, at the European level, to add a social dimension to the European Monetary Union (EMU). For a number of reasons, a consolidated EMU and a single market generate the need for some integration of social policies. The free market and the single currency constrain the budgetary and monetary autonomy of the Member States so that they cannot use these instruments to correct regional economic imbalances. Other possible ways of correcting the imbalances include the flexibilisation of the labour market, a reduction in taxes and social security contributions and the international mobility of labour. However, these are not without consequences for the social security systems. Another potential risk results from the enlargement of the EU, with the possibility of migration flows of workers (mostly low-qualified) from these countries.

Focusing on minimum protection, one can argue that the possibilities of social dumping and social tourism might threaten the sustainability of minimum protection systems because they are likely to lead to a race to the bottom. However, a careful analysis of theoretical insights concerning the possible involvement of the EU in issues of redistribution (see Chapter 3) shows that there is no clear-cut answer concerning whether or not the EU should intervene in the field of income redistribution. Depending on the assumptions made in the models of fiscal federalism, the question of whether or not there is a role for higher entities in income redistribution can be answered positively or negatively. It is also uncertain if the process of fiscal competition will indeed lead to a race to the bottom. In this chapter, we formulate hypotheses concerning the possible outcomes of the fiscal competition process among Member States, on the one hand, and concerning the direction the EU will take in shaping 'Social Europe', on the other hand. Using the micro-data at our disposal, we then undertake to test the effect of these scenarios in terms of their impact on poverty and the distribution of income.

Three alternative outcomes of the process of fiscal competition are considered here. First, one could assume that a *race to the bottom* will indeed take place among Member States, leading to a dismantlement of the welfare state to the lowest common denominator. Secondly, one can imagine that co-ordination among Member States will lead to a *convergence* of systems towards some average level in the EU, with some countries upgrading their systems and others downgrading them (let us call this EU convergence). In the third and final hypothetical case, we make use of the principle of subsidiarity in the positive sense (see Chapter 2). Here, the principle has a strong moral content and can be taken to mean that authorities of higher rank have an obligation to support and assist entities of lower rank. This leads us to consider the possibility of a general upgrading of minimum protection arrangements under the leadership of countries with elaborate social protection systems or – with respect to positive subsidiarity – under the guidance of the Commission. This upgrading will be referred to as the *California effect* (see Chapter 4).

By the same token, it is worth considering what the scope of the future social Europe will be. At present, integration is primarily concerned with workers and those seeking employment. We are still far from the notion of European citizenship, involving free movement of citizens and equal social security rights for all European citizens. One can then either suppose that the situation will remain as it is or, alternatively, that Europe will evolve towards the recognition of full citizenship. The matching of these expectations with the possible outcomes of the process of fiscal competition has determined the research questions that will be scrutinised in this chapter (see Table 7.1). More precisely, we simulate these options and measure their effect on poverty and inequality in European welfare states.

If the Commission is to promote European citizenship alongside of the broader economic goals that are already recognised and encouraged, by virtue of positive subsidiarity it must encourage Member States to co-operate in that direction. This is the ideal of a truly economically and socially integrated Europe. From an empirical point of view, we are primarily interested in measuring the effects that the three scenarios (a race to the bottom, the EU convergence and the California effect) would have on poverty in the Member States, in which EU-based – as opposed to country-based – poverty lines are implemented to account for them (Section 7.4).

As far as the possibility of social dumping is concerned, we measure the effect that changes in the level of replacement incomes (unemployment, sickness and social assistance) have on income distribution and poverty. In the case of a race to the bottom, we simulate a reduction of replacement income to the lowest common denominator. An overall equalisation to the mean is simulated in the EU convergence scenario, while an upgrading towards the highest level in Europe is simulated in the emergence of the California effect (see Section 7.5).

Table 7.1   Matrix of the scenarios under investigation

	EU of citizens	EU of workers
	Poverty target	Replacement income	Labour income
Race to the bottom	Use poverty line of poorest	Equalisation of replacement income to lowest level	Equalisation of labour income to lowest level
EU convergence	• Use EU poverty line • Let poverty rate converge to average	Let replacement income converge to average	Equalisation of labour income to average
California effect	• Use poverty line of richest country • Let poverty rates converge to lowest level	Equalisation of replacement income to highest level	Equalisation of labour income to highest level
	↓	↓	↓
	Costs?	Effect on poverty rate and inequality?	

If, however, attention remains focused on workers, then fiscal competition is likely to take place through reductions in wage costs. The first scenario relates to the effect on poverty and inequality of a reduction in wages towards the lowest level in Europe as in the event of a race to the bottom. The second scenario reflects the idea of convergence of wage levels to the EU median and aims at estimating the effect this would have on poverty and income distribution. Finally, in the event of the emergence of the California effect scenario, we simulate the rise in wages towards the highest level in Europe and see how this affects poverty and the distribution of income (Section 7.6).

Limitations: abstracting from behavioural effects

Although we believe that studying these scenarios is useful since they suggest a number of boundaries for the development of poverty in Europe, the exercise carried out in this chapter should be viewed as merely illustrative. To begin with, we focus exclusively on financial poverty while it is widely agreed that poverty is more than that (see Sen, 1992). We also do not take into account the rich history in the design of social security systems as they developed in the course of the past century. Nor do we take the question of social and political acceptability of the simulations into account. Moreover, because we simulate changes in replacement incomes and wages without considering the effect on labour market behaviour, we do not provide a complete picture of the true effects these changes imply for the distribution of income and poverty. A careful modelling of the tax-benefit system of the Member States as well as of behavioural effects should complement the preliminary results presented here. However, to our knowledge no such EU-wide model is currently available.[2] For now, we will stick to some qualitative comments.

As far as the behavioural effects of social security income are concerned, Jehoel-Gijsbers et al. (1995), in their review of the Dutch literature, have shown that no conclusive evidence can be found with respect to the effect of the level of unemployment benefits on the duration of unemployment. The effects found are often insignificant. When significant effects are reported, they are generally small. Moffit (1992), when reviewing the US literature, concludes that welfare programmes (Food Stamps, AFDC) affect people's behaviour: higher benefits lead to more participation in these programmes. He does, however, point out that the effects on the labour supply are not very large. Layte and Callan (2001) have found significant, but small, negative effects of unemployment benefits on unemployment duration for Ireland. Moreover, no significant effect was found for unemployment assistance recipients. The above findings suggest that the labour supply effects of our simulations in Section 7.5 will be small.

Whether or not the simulated changes in the wage level (as in Section 7.6) will affect labour supply depends on the elasticity of that supply. For men, estimated labour supply elasticity is small and ranges between 0 and 0.45 (MaCurdy, 1981; Altonji, 1986). The corresponding elasticity for female workers ranges between 0.45 and 1.35 (Filer et al., 1996: 59). In the Netherlands, elasticities around 0 and 1 for men and women, respectively, have been reported (Theeuwes and Woittiez, 1992). Hence, although our calculations on wages (Section 7.6) are likely to affect the female labour supply, the effects on the male labour supply are expected to be small.

7.3   DATA AND METHODS

Whereas the preceding chapters only used data for three EU countries, the analyses in this chapter incorporate a larger number of countries. The data used in this chapter are from the European Community Household Panel (ECHP), a survey providing comparable micro-level data on the socio-economic conditions of individuals and households in the EU Member States. At the time of research, the first three waves of the data were readily available to us through the so-called users' database.[3] They cover the years from 1994 to 1996 and 14 EU Member States.[4] The data include income variables for the year preceding the interviews. In 1996, 61,000 households were surveyed, representing approximately 170,000 individuals. For reasons of consistency with the previous chapters, we substituted the Dutch, German and British data in the ECHP for the national panels used above – the Dutch Socio-Economic Panel (SEP), the German Socio-Economic Panel (GSOEP) and the British Household Panel Survey (BHPS) – for the corresponding years. As argued in Chapter 4, the countries are grouped according to the welfare state regimes they belong to: liberal (Great Britain and Ireland), southern (Italy, Greece, Portugal and Spain), corporatist (Belgium, Germany, Austria, Luxembourg and France) and social democratic (Denmark, Finland and the Netherlands).

As in the preceding chapters, the income concept used here is net total household income (expressed per equivalent adult). However, we also present some data on gross household earnings and gross household replacement income. In that respect, gross replacement income equals the sum of gross unemployment benefits, unemployment assistance, social assistance and disability payments to individuals in the same household. Earnings include the sum total of wages and income from self-employment, for persons in the same household.

The analyses here, as in the previous chapters, are based on a poverty line that equals half of the median standardised income in the country. However, comparing relative poverty rates across countries does not account for the fact that the real standard of living varies among countries. Because of the higher median income in richer countries, the poor there might have higher incomes than the rich in poorer countries. When considering the use of a common poverty line, this has to be taken into account (see Box 7.1). Moreover, once common objectives in terms of growth and welfare have been recognised, the relevance of considering a single poverty line for the whole of the EU is considerably increased. Moreover, distributional issues at the EU level cannot be tackled without bearing in mind that the purchasing power among Member States varies enormously; in Portugal, it is about one-third of the purchasing power in Luxembourg. When using an EU-wide poverty line, we allow for the effect of economic growth on poverty in the EU to be affected by the relative growth rates of the Member States (Atkinson, 1995). Applying such an overall threshold could prove to be a useful instrument for the study of poverty in Europe as it would complement the statistics provided by a poverty line set at the national level.

In Sections 7.5 and 7.6, we make selections of observations used for the analyses to include only the working-age population and people in employment. The selections are then made explicit, but it must be remembered that, in all cases, the poverty line used was computed on the whole sample.

BOX 7.1   Country-specific and common poverty line

Analytically, the two options – country-specific poverty line or one that is common to all countries – can be linked according to the following formula:

$$PL_c = \frac{1}{2}\left(y_{med,c}^{\alpha}\ y_{med,r}^{1-\alpha}\right),$$

where PL_c is the poverty line for country c, $y_{med,c}$ the median income in country c, $y_{med,r}$ the median income in a reference state – for example, the EU – and α a weighting factor. The value of α lies between 0 and 1 and determines whether the poverty line is computed on the national median income ($\alpha = 1$), the overall EU median income ($\alpha = 0$) or a weighted average of EU median income and national median income ($0 < \alpha < 1$). In the following section, we present poverty statistics for the Member States based on a poverty line set at the national level, on the one hand, and at the EU level, on the other hand. Setting the poverty line at the level of the EU median income endorses the idea of EU convergence and poverty achievements that are measured with respect to one common criterion. One could also evaluate the relative achievement of EU welfare states by referring to the standard of the richest or the poorest Member State. This would mean replacing $y_{med,r}$ in the above formula by the median income of the richest or poorest country and setting α to 0.

7.4   EUROPE OF CITIZENS?

Although it is likely that in the longer run an attempt will be made to bring social security systems in Europe closer together, this is not likely in the short run. Just as we hypothesised in Section 4.2, the future could provide an opportunity for an EU convergence of systems, a race to the bottom or even, in the case of a truly social Europe, an upgrading. In a first attempt to outline the general picture, we start by presenting poverty and inequality statistics for EU Members States where the poverty line is allowed to take these possibilities into account. Then, we investigate in greater detail the possible implications of social tourism and fiscal competition[5] on replacement incomes, poverty and inequality.

Table 7.2   Theil inequality, within- and between-country inequality, 1993–5

	1993	1994	1995	Rank 1995
Liberal				
Great Britain	0.164	0.162	0.179	9
Ireland	0.212	0.198	0.200	12
Southern				
Greece	0.224	0.190	0.198	11
Spain	0.198	0.183	0.189	10
Italy	0.176	0.163	0.235	13
Portugal	0.277	0.254	0.239	14
Corporatist				
Belgium	0.159	0.140	0.138	4
Germany	0.137	0.133	0.140	6
France	0.217	0.146	0.147	8
Luxembourg	0.160	0.141	0.138	5
Austria	–	0.135	0.123	3
Social democratic				
Denmark	0.138	0.111	0.096	1
Netherlands	0.147	0.147	0.145	7
Finland	–	–	0.101	2
EU12[a]	0.188	0.175	0.182	–
Within-country	0.174	0.160	0.168	–
Between-country	0.014	0.015	0.014	–

Note: a) Excluding Austria and Finland.

Sources: ECHP; SEP; GSOEP; BHPS.

7.4.1   Country and EU-specific Poverty Lines

Table 7.2 reports the cross-national differences in terms of inequality of income distribution in Europe. The index used is the Theil coefficient, which allows for decomposition by population sub groups (see Appendix 3). This property is applied here to compute inequality between and within countries of the EU. The data in the table show that inequality is higher than average in southern Europe. Denmark and Finland, two typical social-democratic welfare regimes, display the lowest degree of inequality.[5] Although overall inequality in Europe appears to have decreased between 1993 and 1994 –

only to increase again the year after – the changes were not found to be significant. In the course of these three years, between-country inequality has remained constant so that one can conclude that, during the first years following the Treaty of Maastricht, the efforts made to meet the Maastricht criteria have left the income disparities among Member States unchanged.

Table 7.3 *Poverty incidence in Europe: percentage of individuals with standardised household income below half of national median, 1993–5, income gap ratio and rank in 1995*

	1993 % poor	1994 % poor	1995 % poor	1995 Rank	1995 Income gap	1995 Rank
Liberal						
Great Britain	14.8	13.5	12.4	11	28.8	4
Ireland	8.1	8.7	8.3	5	27.1	2
Southern						
Greece	16.3	14.1	14.3	13	28.8	5
Spain	12.5	12.0	11.6	10	27.9	3
Italy	13.1	11.3	12.8	12	32.0	8
Portugal	17.7	16.8	14.6	14	36.9	11
Corporatist						
Belgium	10.1	10.9	10.7	9	45.0	13
Germany	9.2	9.2	10.2	8	48.0	14
France	10.0	9.2	9.2	6	26.7	1
Luxembourg	7.0	8.7	6.1	2	38.4	12
Austria	–	8.9	6.6	3	35.5	9
Social democratic						
Denmark	4.6	5.4	6.1	1	28.9	6
Netherlands	8.4	9.2	9.4	7	36.7	10
Finland	–	–	6.8	3	31.5	7
EU12[a]	11.5	10.9	11.1	–	–	–
EU14	–	–	10.9	–	35.4	–

Note: a) Excluding Austria and Finland.

Sources: ECHP; SEP; GSOEP; BHPS.

In Table 7.3, we present the poverty rates for all European countries in the mid-1990s. As can be seen from the table, approximately 11 percent of all EU citizens were living in poverty in 1995, representing around 39 million people. Over the three-year period, that percentage showed little variation: poverty decreased by less than half a percentage point between 1993 and 1995. The poverty rate, however, varies greatly among countries. In 1995, it ranged from more than 14 percent in Greece and Portugal to about 6 percent in Luxembourg and Denmark. Large absolute changes in the poverty rate between 1993 and 1995 were found in Portugal, Great Britain and Greece (decreases of 3, 2.5 and 2 percentage points, respectively). Over the same period, poverty increased by one percentage point or more in Germany, the Netherlands and Denmark.

According to the income gap ratio (the ratio of the average income shortfall of the poor to the poverty line), it appears that the income shortfall of the poor amounts to 35 percent. That a low poverty rate is no guarantee for a small income gap is well illustrated by the data in the table. Germany, which has an average poverty rate, has by far the largest income gap. The lowest income gaps are found in France, Ireland and Spain. The ranking generated by the income gaps looks rather different from the ranking found on the basis of the poverty rates.

Shifting the threshold

Of course, the half-median method is just one of the possible methods for determining the poverty threshold. Standard practice at Eurostat is to set the poverty threshold at 60 percent of median standardised income. One possible way of monitoring poverty in the future in the EU could be to use various thresholds. In Figure 7.1, we depict poverty levels in 1995 generated by using three different poverty thresholds: 40, 50 and 60 percent of national median income. For most countries, using the various thresholds does affect the relative ranking, though only for one or two positions. However, Germany and Great Britain are two important exceptions. The relative position of Germany in terms of the poverty rate is greatly improved when the poverty line is set higher (60 instead of 40 percent). The relative position of Great Britain is greatly worsened when the poverty line is shifted from 40 to 60 percent of median income (see also Section 5.6). This indicates that one must be cautious in deciding upon one particular threshold in cross-country poverty research. It is clear, however, that whatever the definition, the four best performing countries are Denmark, Finland, Austria and Luxembourg. Using the 40 percent poverty threshold, the four worst performing countries are within the southern European welfare cluster. When using the 60 percent poverty line, Great Britain takes the place of Spain in the top four of the worst performing countries.

Suppose that in the process of open co-ordination, as initiated at the Lisbon summit, European countries were to agree on a poverty target according to which EU Member States would reduce their poverty figure to the EU average. This would imply that some countries would need to make additional efforts to reduce their poverty rate. Using the 50 or 60 percent income threshold, it would mean that countries in the southern regime cluster, as well as Great Britain, would need to adjust their poverty rate downwards. With the 40 percent of median income poverty line, that would hold true for the southern welfare states, together with Germany. This illustrates the fact that, depending on the threshold, the 'laggards' in league tables might not always be the same.

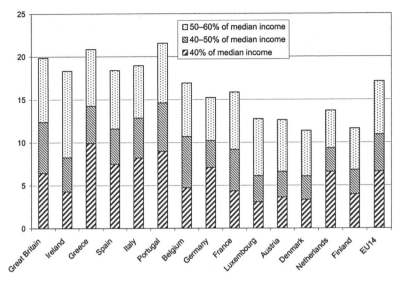

Sources: ECHP; SEP; GSOEP; BHPS.

Figure 7.1   Percentage in poverty for the 40, 50 and 60 percent of national
median standardised income threshold, 1995

7.4.2   Union-specific Poverty Lines

If the EU were to emphasise the idea of European citizenship and work towards the creation of a truly social Europe, an approach with a EU-specific poverty line – as opposed to a country-specific one – would become relevant. To give one an idea of what this would mean for poverty statistics, we have chosen to apply three EU-specific poverty lines to our data.[6] From the point of view of the race to the bottom hypothesis, we monitor poverty in the EU according to the poverty line of the country with the highest poverty rate: Portugal. In this case, the poverty rate in Portugal remains unchanged. Next, we take half of the EU median equivalised income. Finally, we set the poverty line in all countries equal to the poverty line of Luxembourg – the richest country with the highest poverty line – in which case the poverty rate in Luxembourg will remain unchanged. We take this as a relevant benchmark for the situation in which one is interested in comparing welfare levels across Europe using a high absolute standard.[7] Table 7.4 reports on the incidence of poverty in 1995 using these three scenarios. Obviously, taking the two extreme cases (the poverty lines of the richest and the poorest countries) provides us with an indication of the range of the poverty rates that ensue from EU-based poverty lines.

Table 7.4   *Poverty incidence: percentage of population with standardised household income below half of Portuguese, EU and Luxembourg median (rank order), 1995*

	Portuguese poverty line		EU poverty line		Luxembourg poverty line	
Liberal						
Great Britain	2.1	(5)	11.2	(9)	39.8	(7)
Ireland	3.1	(8)	17.8	(10)	53.4	(10)
Southern						
Greece	11.3	(13)	30.8	(13)	68.5	(13)
Spain	8.1	(12)	25.1	(12)	64.8	(12)
Italy	7.1	(11)	19.8	(11)	55.9	(11)
Portugal	14.6	(14)	40.1	(14)	75.1	(14)
Corporatist						
Belgium	2.5	(7)	5.5	(4)	29.3	(5)
Germany	4.6	(9)	7.9	(6)	27.2	(4)
France	1.5	(3)	6.1	(5)	33.2	(6)
Luxembourg	0.8	(1)	1.5	(1)	6.1	(1)
Austria	1.6	(4)	3.8	(3)	24.5	(3)
Social democratic						
Denmark	1.2	(2)	3.4	(2)	19.6	(2)
Netherlands	4.7	(10)	9.2	(7)	39.8	(8)
Finland	2.4	(6)	9.5	(8)	48.8	(9)
EU	4.8	–	13.4	–	42.3	–

Sources: ECHP; SEP; GSOEP; BHPS.

Setting the poverty line at the lowest EU level – using the Portuguese poverty line for all countries – will result in a lower poverty rate in all countries except, of course, in Portugal. The way this affects the poverty rate in other countries depends on the level of the national poverty line compared to the Portuguese poverty line. The smaller the difference, the smaller the discrepancy will be when using the national poverty line. It also depends on the shape of income distribution at the lower end. The higher the concentration of individuals around the national poverty line, the larger the effect will be. The overall EU poverty rate is then reduced to 4.8 percent. However, poverty in all southern European countries will remain high. Note that, although the poverty rate is then reduced due to the use of the Portuguese poverty line, the feeling and perception of poverty in the various countries will not change since, as we argued earlier, poverty is a relative concept.

Setting the poverty line to half-median household income in the EU is an alternative that is probably more realistic than the previous one. The consequence is that poverty is increased in countries with median income below the EU median while it is decreased in countries where median income is higher than the EU median. Using this poverty line, the EU rate equals 13.4 percent. This is approximately 2.4 percentage points more than when using the national poverty lines. The poverty rate ranges from 1.5 in Luxembourg to 40 percent in Portugal. In countries where median income is close to EU median (the Netherlands and Great Britain), this scenario does not substantially affect the poverty rate.

The highest poverty rates by far are found for a poverty line that equals that of Luxembourg. Although, by definition, this scenario leaves the poverty rate in Luxembourg unchanged, it increases poverty substantially in all other countries. The average poverty rate in the EU is almost four times the average when using poverty lines set at the national level. More than half of the population in Ireland, Italy, Greece and Spain, and three-quarters of the Portuguese would be defined as poor according to this scenario.

The three scenarios tested above not only produce poverty rates that are different than those found when using the national poverty lines, they also result in changing the rank order of the countries. Although, in general, the lowest poverty rates are found in Luxembourg, Denmark and Austria (in that order), and the highest ones in Portugal, Greece, Spain and Italy (in that order), the ranking of the other countries is affected by the poverty line used. For example, Belgium ranks ninth when using a country-specific poverty line (5 countries out of 14 have a poverty rate that is higher), it ranks fourth when the poverty line is set to half of EU median income. Obviously, the computations based on these two extreme scenarios – using the Portuguese and the Luxembourg poverty line for all EU countries – must be taken with a grain of salt. We interpret these alternatives as providing the range within which the poverty rates will be found when one considers using common lines for all EU countries. In this respect, we consider the use of the overall EU median to be the most useful alternative.

7.4.3 What Does it Take to Satisfy a Poverty Target?

Computing the costs of reducing poverty
It goes without saying that the attainment of a particular target (that is the reduction of poverty to some agreed maximum) will be costly. Additional efforts have to be made in terms of, for instance, investments in human capital, job creation or subsidising low-skilled employment. Here, however,

we only estimate what it would take in terms of additional money transfers to achieve the poverty target. We do not believe that making unconditional transfers to the poor is an efficient way to combat poverty (see below). Yet, the computations presented can give us some insights into the depth of poverty and the level of incentives that have to be generated to induce the poor to exit it.

Suppose that the countries were to agree on a poverty line equal to half-median standardised income. They could then agree on a poverty target: that is a maximum poverty rate that no country should exceed (see for such suggestions Atkinson et al., 2003). In its NAP/inclusion, for example, Portugal sets the reduction of its relative poverty rate to the current EU average or the reduction of absolute poverty by half as policy targets (European Commission, 2002a). This 'ideal' poverty rate translates into a target number of poor, denoted Np^*, for the country in question. To illustrate this, we distinguish three alternative poverty targets and compute the costs implied by achieving these.

In Figure 7.2, we depict the cumulative distribution of income $F(y)$. Point z denotes the poverty line and Np the actual number of poor (Np/N is then the poverty rate).[8] Suppose that the abolition of poverty is the objective the Member States have set ($Np^* = 0$). The total cost of this first target (denote it C_1) will be given by the 0 *a z* area, or:

$$C_1 = \int_0^z F(y)dy .$$

C_1 then denotes the aggregate poverty gap. The income of the poor could be supplemented through, say, a tax credit to those who live below the poverty threshold. How large the income gap is will depend on the level of the poverty line and the shape of the income distribution below the poverty line. The income distribution resulting from this policy option will run from z to a and then follows $F(y)$ (see Figure 7.2). Of course, it does not seem very likely that Member States will agree to set themselves such a stringent target, yet it remains interesting to estimate what it would take to abolish poverty.

It is presumably more realistic to assume that Member States agree to set a poverty target that is larger than 0. We illustrate this by computing how large the financial effort should be in order to reduce their poverty rate 1) by half, 2) to the EU average and 3) to the average of the four countries with the lowest poverty rate. Obviously, reducing the poverty rate by half will induce costs for all countries, while reducing the poverty rate to some average level will only mean additional costs for the countries with above-average poverty. In any case, the cheapest option to reduce the number of poor towards the target (Np^*) is to lift those closest to the poverty line out of poverty – give them just enough additional income such that their total income equates the poverty line – and thereby avoid any spillover effects (Beckerman, 1979). Total cost (C_2) of the operation is the area $a\ b\ c$, or:

$$C_2 = \int_d^z F(y)dy - [Np^*(z-d)].$$

The new income distribution will be given by $0\ c - b\ a$ and $F(y)$ beyond that point. Hence, this option generates discontinuity in the income distribution (between c and b). Moreover, this policy line is unfair towards the very poor.

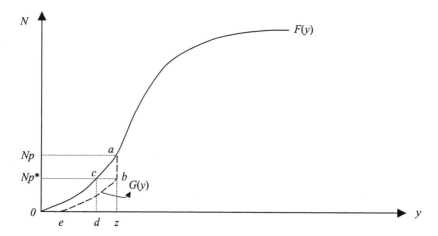

Figure 7.2   The cost of satisfying a poverty target

It would presumably be a more acceptable policy option to give an equal part of the transfer to all the poor while, at the same time, preventing inefficiencies by not giving more than necessary to reach the poverty line. This means that the amount $(z - d)$ is to be transferred to those with income below d. It corresponds to shifting the original income distribution to the right from that amount so that up to z, $G(y) = F(y) + (z-d) = F(y) + e$. For those with income between d and z, the size of the transfer is the same as in the previous case. The total cost (C_3) is then given by the area $0\ a\ b\ e$, or:

$$C_3 = \int_0^z F(y)dy - \int_e^z G(y)dy.$$

As far as the costs of these three policy options are concerned, the most expensive policy measure is obviously to lift everyone to the level of the poverty line, while the cheapest is to pull the least poor out of poverty. Hence we have $C_1 > C_3 > C_2$. We estimate the costs C_2 and C_3 that have to be incurred in order to reduce the poverty rate 1) by half, 2) to the EU average and 3) to the average of the four countries with the lowest poverty rate (see Table 7.3). Obviously, alleviating poverty completely or reducing it by half will be costly to all countries. However, for a particular country, the costs of achieving one of the other two targets will be zero if it already meets the target.

The costs are expressed in proportion of the total income of the non-poor. In this way, one can interpret the numbers as indicating the proportion of income of the non-poor that should be taxed away in order to fill the poverty gap associated with the poverty target. The total costs can also be related to a measure of the governments' budget, to indicate the magnitude of budget shifts that would be needed in order to alleviate poverty.

The costs for the EU Member States
In the first column of Table 7.5 we depict the cost associated with a complete reduction of poverty according to the 50 percent of the country's median household income (option C_1 as previously explained). In columns two and three, we report the costs associated with halving the poverty rate. The costs are computed under two alternative assumptions as already explained: lifting only the least poor out of poverty (C_2) and making an equal payment to all the poor (C_3). The fourth and fifth columns indicate the cost to be incurred in order to reduce poverty to the EU average, either by only lifting those closest to the poverty line (C_2) or by transferring income to all the poor as set out under option C_3. The last two columns report corresponding costs associated with a reduction of poverty so that the poverty rate in each country does not exceed the average poverty rate in the countries where poverty is lowest.

In 1995, removing all poverty in Europe would have cost approximately 112 billion euros. This is equivalent to, on average, 2,800 euros per poor household. In some countries, however, the costs are higher, due to a large poverty gap (Germany), or a large poverty incidence (Greece). The amount required to fill the poverty gap in Europe represents approximately 1.7 percent of the total income of the non-poor Europeans. This would mean that, by taxing away 1.7 percent of the income of the non-poor and redistributing it towards the poor, poverty could be alleviated. Such a measure might, however, not be very popular and could induce large disincentives, both among the non-poor and the poor. Whether or not economic growth would succeed in eliminating poverty can be questioned. As demonstrated in previous chapters, long spells of economic growth have not been able to reduce the incidence of poverty and they have exacerbated income inequalities (de Beer, 2001). Filling the gap with the fruits of economic growth would mean that, given an average growth rate of 2 percent, an estimated 0.3 percent would be left after redistribution to the poor.

Bearing in mind the limitations of this exercise (see Section 7.2), Table 7.5 shows that it would take 1 percent of the income of the non-poor to make additional transfers to all the poor and, therefore, reduce the total poverty rate in Europe by half. This represents a total of 67 billion euros, a little more than twice the amount spent within the framework of the structural and cohesion funds in 2000.[9] Should the transfers only be made to the 'richest' of the poor, the costs would only be 0.3 percent of the income of the non-poor. This represents a total of 21 billion euros, approximately half the total budget of the Common Agricultural Policy of the EU. Using the fruits of economic growth to fill this gap would supposedly be less of a problem than in the case of the total reduction of poverty. Given a growth rate of 2 percent, 1.7 percent would remain after transfers towards the least poor. The budgets involved are smaller and so are potential disincentive effects. Here again, it would be relatively more costly for southern European countries, Germany and the Netherlands to reduce their poverty rate by half than it would be for other countries. In particular, Denmark, Luxembourg, Finland, Ireland, Austria, France and Belgium are able to reduce poverty at the relatively lowest cost.

Given that only the southern European countries and Great Britain have poverty rates that exceed the EU average, they will be the only five countries to incur costs in order to reduce their poverty rate to the EU average. If only the least poor receive additional payments, the total costs would be almost insignificant (0.01 percent of the total income of the non-poor), especially in comparison with the other options. The relative costs of transferring income to all the poor will, however, be somewhat higher: 0.7–0.8 percent of the income of the non-poor in Greece and Portugal.

When the poverty target is set equal to the average of the four countries with the lowest poverty rate, only Denmark and Luxembourg appear to satisfy the criterion.[10] All other countries have a poverty rate that exceeds the target. In total, in Europe, an amount equivalent to 0.2 percent of the income of the non-poor (or 14 billion euros) would have to be transferred to the least poor in order to reach the target. Should a transfer be paid to all the poor, an additional gap equivalent to 0.8 percent of the income of the non-poor would need to be filled. The costs would then be approximately 55 billion euros.

The dynamics of poverty discussed in Chapter 6 show that labour market status and labour market transitions appear to account for a great deal of the mobility into and out of poverty. The reason is that there are strong financial incentives for having, or gaining, employment (see also Muffels and Fouarge, 2002b). Unconditionally lifting the poor out of poverty might, therefore, induce disincentives and create inefficiencies in the labour market. One should keep this in mind when viewing these results.

Table 7.5   *The cost of reducing poverty, in percentage of the total income of the non-poor, 1995*

	Remove poverty	Halving the poverty rate		Reduction to the EU average (11%)		Reduction to average of four best countries (6.5%)[a]	
	transfer to all the poor (C_1)	transfer to the least poor (C_2)	transfer to all the poor (C_3)	transfer to the least poor (C_2)	transfer to all the poor (C_3)	transfer to the least poor (C_2)	transfer to all the poor (C_3)
Liberal							
Great Britain	1.51	0.29	0.86	0.02	0.29	0.26	0.84
Ireland	1.11	0.16	0.54	–	–	0.03	0.24
Southern							
Greece	2.34	0.52	1.61	0.09	0.80	0.62	1.74
Spain	1.77	0.35	1.10	0.00	0.14	0.27	1.00
Italy	2.19	0.39	1.28	0.02	0.34	0.38	1.26
Portugal	2.28	0.41	1.37	0.09	0.68	0.52	1.47
Corporatist							
Belgium	1.46	0.18	0.59	–	–	0.12	0.48
Germany	2.15	0.41	1.33	–	–	0.20	1.01
France	1.12	0.17	0.56	–	–	0.05	0.32
Luxembourg	0.75	0.12	0.39	–	–	–	–
Austria	0.95	0.15	0.49	–	–	0.00	0.01
Social democratic							
Denmark	0.84	0.15	0.47	–	–	–	–
Netherlands	2.02	0.38	1.23	–	–	0.12	0.73
Finland	0.92	0.16	0.57	–	–	0.00	0.03
EU	1.73	0.32	1.01	0.01	0.13	0.21	0.82

Note: a) Denmark, Luxembourg, Austria and Finland have the lowest poverty rate.

Sources: ECHP, SEP, GSOEP, BHPS.

7.5   FISCAL COMPETITION AND REPLACEMENT INCOME

7.5.1   Operationalisation

In models of fiscal federalism, factor mobility plays an important role in determining the effect of fiscal competition. In Section 7.6, we address the issue of labour migration. In this section, migration of the unemployed and the poor is discussed. According to theories of fiscal federalism (Musgrave, 1959; Oates, 1972), if federal entities conduct different redistributive policies – with some states redistributing more than others – there are incentives for the poor and unemployed to migrate towards regions where they can get higher replacement incomes and incentives for the rich to migrate towards regions where taxation is lower. While migration as a result of relative price or wage differences is an economically efficient process, migration resulting from differences in levels of social protection is inefficient since it results in the aforementioned selection effect between rich and poor and undesired changes in the fiscal base. One possible solution is to centralise, or at least co-ordinate, redistributive policies (Lejour, 1995).

The fear is that fiscal competition might lead to social dumping (see Chapter 3). However, presently within the EU, migration flows are low and consist largely of high-qualified workers. The unemployed are only mobile under restrictive conditions. Moreover, as OECD (2000) data show, the spread in unemployment rates within regions of the EU is much larger than in the USA, Canada or Japan while, at the same time, internal mobility is lower (see Figure 7.3). It can be concluded that mobility flows within Europe are not responsive to differentials in unemployment rates (see also van Riel, 2001).[11] Therefore, the fear of a large flow of welfare migrants seems to be unwarranted.

However, migration within and from outside of the EU is expected to continue to play a role in the growth of European economies in the future (Smit, 2001). The wage differentials within Europe (with the exception of the southern countries) are apparently not large enough to induce migration flows within the EU or to compensate for potentially large migration costs. However, the difference in unemployment rates and income levels between EU countries and the acceding and candidate countries from central and eastern Europe are larger. As a consequence, migration flows are expected to be larger than they are now (van Riel, 2001; SER, 2001). Given the large number of vacancies in most of the EU countries, new workers from the applicant countries could easily be inserted into the labour market. However, as the educational level of those workers is generally lower, this is likely to affect the income distribution in the EU, especially at the lower end (de Mooij, 2000). Lejour et al. (2001) show that migration indeed negatively affects the low-wage/high-wage differential and, at least in some countries, the level of GDP per capita. Migrants from the applicant countries are also expected to be more responsive to welfare differentials than the EU citizens. As Borjas (1998) demonstrated using data for the USA, the income-maximising behaviour of individuals implies that a clustering of immigrants in high benefit states is likely to take place. He shows that the welfare participation of immigrants is more sensitive to changes in welfare benefits

Poverty and Subsidiarity in Europe

than that of natives: less skilled immigrants will be more concentrated in high benefit states. This sorting effect, he argues, will take place irrespective of migration costs.[12]

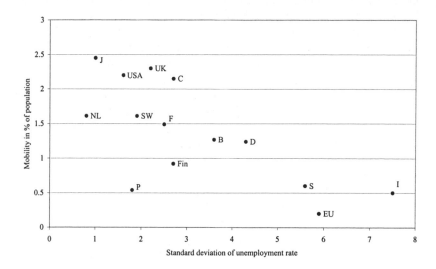

Note: EU: Europe; UK: United Kingdom; NL: Netherlands; S: Spain; F: France; SW: Sweden; Fin: Finland; P: Portugal; B: Belgium; D: Germany; I: Italy; J: Japan; C: Canada; USA: United States of America.

Sources: Dispersion of unemployment between regions are from OECD (2000: 39); all countries 1997. Mobility data are from OECD (2000: 53); Portugal 1990, UK 1998, all other countries 1995. Mobility between European countries: Krueger (2000: 122).

Figure 7.3   Internal migration in percentage of total population and disparities in unemployment rates around 1995

The hypothesis of welfare migration also becomes more relevant when the idea of EU citizenship is introduced. Creating an EU of citizens implies that all barriers to migration are removed and that the poor are free to cross borders where conditions for receiving benefits are more favourable. In this section, we assume that the creation of an EU of citizens is indeed the direction in which Europe is heading. Assuming this, we simulate various policy reactions of the Member States in the field of minimum protection. First, if Member States indeed engage in a process of social dumping, we assume that replacement incomes will converge towards the lowest level in the EU (race to the bottom), until they reach the point where there is no incentive left to reduce replacement incomes.[13] Secondly, we assume that

Member States engage in a process of co-ordination that leads them to equalise the level of replacement incomes to some average level so that, again, incentives for welfare migration are removed. Finally, we assume that Europe is evolving towards the creation of a strong social model. In that process, the countries strive for high levels of social benefits and the nation with the highest benefits, in fact, exports its benefits conditions (California effect). Once again, the race to the bottom scenario and the California effect scenario set the lower and higher boundaries, respectively, for the convergence process of replacement income.

As we stated earlier, replacement income is computed at the household level. It equals the sum of unemployment benefits, unemployment assistance, disability payments and social assistance received by all individuals in the household. The analyses in this and the following sections are limited to people living in households where both the head and his or her partner (if there is one) are of prime working age (aged 25–55). We will refer to them as people in a working-age household. In the race to the bottom scenario, we simulate a situation in which replacement income is adjusted downwards in all countries so that, on average, it equals the lowest level in the EU.[14] In the EU convergence scenario, we simulate that household replacement income is adjusted in such a way that it equals the EU average in all countries. In the California effect we simulate an increase of replacement incomes in all countries such that it equals the highest level in the EU. For each scenario, we estimate how it affects the distribution of income in the EU and the level of poverty. Every time, the poverty line equals half of the national median standardised household income.

We have argued in favour of a relative view on poverty by saying that people compare their income positions to those of others in the same community. Thus, the unemployed compare their incomes to those of the workers. For this reason, we simulated changes in household replacement incomes relative to household labour earnings. In terms of the scenarios just described, we assume that replacement income, relative to earnings, converges to the lowest, the average and the highest ratio in the EU for the race to the bottom, EU-convergence and the California effect scenario, respectively. However, absolute welfare gains are probably more important in triggering welfare migration than relative welfare gains. Hence, the scenarios are also implemented by simulating changes in absolute replacement income to equal the lowest, the average and the highest level in the EU for the three respective scenarios. Before proceeding, however, we present some data on replacement income dependency and replacement rates in EU Member States.

7.5.2   Replacement Income and Replacement Rates

Assuming that the poor and the unemployed are indeed mobile, the extent of potential welfare migration will depend on the numbers receiving replacement income and the income gain from migration: that is the level of replacement income relative to wages and the difference in absolute level of replacement income (see Table 7.6 and Figure 7.5). The first column in Table 7.6 shows that, in the EU, a fifth of those in working-age households receive at least some replacement income. As the scenarios implemented here will only affect the income positions of those receiving replacement income, the simulations performed will affect a fifth of all income recipients. However, those for whom replacement income is the main source of income will be more affected.

Table 7.6   Replacement income of people in a working-age household, 1995 (percentages)

	In receipt of replacement income	Replacement income as main source of income	Empirical replacement rate[a]
Liberal			
Great Britain	26.1	9.1	80.6
Ireland	39.3	13.1	67.7
Southern			
Greece	10.4	0.7	55.3
Spain	26.0	5.9	68.2
Italy	8.5	1.3	55.7
Portugal	16.1	1.8	64.1
Corporatist			
Belgium	36.4	8.9	76.8
Germany	12.3	1.8	71.2
France	25.4	2.6	75.4
Luxembourg	11.3	1.7	79.8
Austria	18.4	1.2	–
Social democratic			
Denmark	34.6	7.4	80.4
Netherlands	20.9	7.4	73.7
Finland	43.4	6.3	–
EU	20.0	4.0	70.6

Note: a) The empirical replacement rate is the average ratio of gross household replacement income in $t + 1$ to gross household earnings in t for people making a transition from employment to unemployment between t and $t + 1$ in the 1993–5 period.

Sources: ECHP; SEP; GSOEP; BHPS.

The second column in Table 7.6 shows that the percentage of people whose main income source is replacement income varies largely among EU Member States. On average, 4 percent of those in working-age households have replacement income as their main source of income, but this percentage is significantly higher in Ireland (13 percent), Great Britain and Belgium (9 percent). The third column in Table 7.6 displays the empirical replacement rates for those who made a transition from employment to unemployment during the 1993–5 period. The data are interesting because they provide insights into the labour market incentives of the social security system. However, the numbers are merely indicative of the true effects since the computations are made on annual income and no attempt was made to control for the number of months that replacement income was received. Moreover, we did not examine whether or not conditions for full entitlement were met. Nevertheless, the data do not differ significantly from other published data (see, for example, OECD, 1998). From the point of view of replacement rates, the numbers do show that these are substantially lower in Greece and Italy, but that the magnitude of the differences among the other EU countries is much smaller. These differences are indeed not very likely to induce large flows of welfare migration.

7.5.3 Simulating Changes in Replacement Income

Relative approach
Median gross replacement income, related to gross median earnings, can be seen as an indication of labour market incentives. Figure 7.4 shows the ratios for the various EU countries.

Adopting a relative view on poverty, one can assume that there are incentives for the poor to migrate when replacement income relative to earnings is higher in the destination country. By moving, the poor can improve their income position relative to those in employment. Overall in the EU, median replacement income represents some 15 percent of median wages. Therefore, other things being equal, there are large incentives to work rather than to be unemployed. However, the ratios differ greatly among countries. This ratio is relatively low in Greece (4.4 percent) but relatively high in the Netherlands (almost 26 percent).

The idea of the race to the bottom scenario is that replacement income will have to be adjusted downwards such that the ratio of replacement income to earnings is everywhere equal to the lowest level in the EU (Greece). In practice, for each country, we multiply replacement incomes by a factor such that the ratio of replacement income to earnings equals that of Greece (see Box 7.2). Only then are there no more relative gains to migration.[15] To simulate the EU convergence hypothesis, a similar procedure is adopted such that the ratio of replacement income to earnings is made equal to the EU average, assuming this is the convergence point. To simulate the California effect scenario, replacement incomes are corrected so that the ratio to earnings is equal to that in the Netherlands.

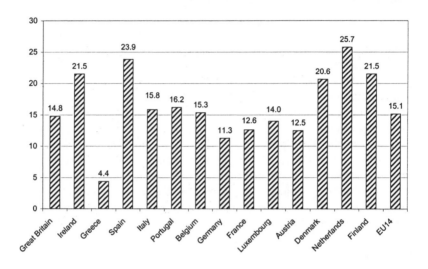

Note: People in a working-age household.

Sources: ECHP; SEP; GSOEP; BHPS.

Figure 7.4   Percentage of gross replacement income relative to gross household earnings, 1995

BOX 7.2   Simulated incomes

Relative approach
For each household i in country c, the procedure followed in the relative approach simulates a new income vector $\tilde{y}_{ic}$ for each of the scenarios according to the following formula:

$$\tilde{y}_{ic} = y_{ic} \text{ if } RI_{ic} = 0, \text{ and } \tilde{y}_{ic} = y_{ic}^* + \left(1 - tx_c\right)RI_{ic} \, {}^{q_r}\!\!\Big/\!_{q_c} \text{ if } RI_{ic} \neq 0,$$

where y_{ic} is the net standardised household income of individual i in country c, y_{ic}^* is the net standardised household income excluding replacement income, RI_{ic} is the gross standardised household replacement income, tx_c is the average tax rate and q_c and q_r are the ratio of gross median replacement income to gross median earnings in country c and the country of reference, respectively. q_r is the ratio of replacement income to earnings in Greece, the EU and the Netherlands in the case of the race to the bottom scenario, the EU convergence scenario and the California effect scenario, respectively.

Absolute approach
In the case of convergence of absolute replacement income, the simulated incomes ($\tilde{y}'_{ic}$) were computed as follows:

$$\tilde{y}'_{ic} = y_{ic} \text{ if } RI_{ic} = 0, \text{ and } \tilde{y}'_{ic} = y^*_{ic} + (1 - tx_c)(RI_{ic} + (RI_r - RI_c)) \text{ if } RI_{ic} \neq 0,$$

where y_{ic} is the net standardised household income of individual i in country c, y^*_{ic} the net standardised household income excluding replacement income, RI_{ic} the gross standardised household replacement income, tx_c is the average tax rate, RI_c and RI_r are the median gross standardised household replacement income in, respectively, country c and the country of reference. RI_r is taken to be the median household replacement income in Greece, the EU and the Netherlands in the case of the race to the bottom, the EU convergence and the California effect scenario, respectively. These simulations change the distribution of income and have consequences for the poverty rates in the various countries.

The simulated incomes are compared to the national poverty line in order to evaluate the impact of the scenarios on poverty. The results of this exercise are displayed in Table 7.7. The numbers in the first column of the table depict the actual situations in the 14 countries.[16] The numbers in the other three columns depict the outcome from the simulated incomes. They are to be compared to those in the first column.

Let us first consider the situation in which countries engage in social dumping in order to avoid welfare migration and diminish their replacement income, in percentage of earnings, to the lowest level in the EU. The countries with large numbers of replacement income recipients (Finland, Ireland, Belgium and Denmark) are the most affected by this scenario. Poverty would more than double in Finland, Ireland and Denmark. In Belgium, it would increase by some 6.5 percentage points. Poverty would increase in other countries as well (except, of course, in Greece), but these changes would be less spectacular. Overall, poverty among people in working-age households would increase from 10.2 to almost 13 percent. Due to an increase in inequality within countries, this scenario is expected to increase overall inequality within the EU.

By definition, the EU convergence scenario leaves the overall EU poverty rate unchanged, but it does affect the poverty rate within the countries. It leads to a poverty reduction of about one percentage point in France, Germany and Greece and a large absolute increase in the poverty rates in Ireland (from 9.2 to 17.1 percent), Spain (from 12.5 to 14.4 percent) and the Netherlands (from 8.5 to 12.9 percent). Simulating an increase in replacement income in all EU countries – making the ratio of replacement income to earnings equal to that in the Netherlands – results in an overall EU decrease in poverty of two percentage points, from 10.2 to 8.3 percent. With some exceptions (Great Britain, France and Belgium), the magnitude of the effect of this scenario on the poverty rate is smaller than that resulting from the race to the bottom scenario. The simulated California effect does result in an overall decrease in inequality. More precisely, within-country inequality is decreased in this simulation while between-country inequality is unchanged.

Table 7.7   Simulations on replacement income (relative). Percentage of individuals with actual and simulated household income below the poverty line, within- and between-country inequality, 1995

	Actual poverty rate	Simulations		
		Race to the bottom	EU convergence	California effect
Liberal				
Great Britain	10.9	15.5	10.7	5.2
Ireland	9.2	23.2	17.1	7.5
Southern				
Greece	10.1	10.1	9.4	9.1
Spain	12.5	17.4	14.4	12.3
Italy	13.3	14.0	13.3	12.5
Portugal	12.5	13.6	12.7	11.9
Corporatist				
Belgium	9.5	15.9	9.5	6.2
Germany	9.6	10.5	8.7	8.2
France	7.9	10.1	6.9	5.2
Luxembourg	5.5	7.1	5.3	4.9
Austria	6.6	7.9	6.3	5.5
Social democratic				
Denmark	3.6	10.1	4.0	3.2
Netherlands	8.5	15.0	12.9	8.5
Finland	5.3	11.5	6.9	4.7
EU	10.2	12.9	10.2	8.3
Theil coefficient:	0.179	0.196	0.180	0.172
Within-country	0.165	0.180	0.165	0.157
Between-country	0.014	0.014	0.015	0.015

Note: People in a working-age household.

Sources: ECHP; SEP; GSOEP; BHPS.

The outcomes of the three scenarios depict the expected poverty outcome of fiscal competition in the field of replacement income: 8 percent poor at best, 13 percent in the event of a race to the bottom. This relatively small range results from the fact that we considered relative adjustments to replacement incomes. In the next section, we consider absolute adjustments and show that the expected effects on poverty are much greater.

Absolute approach
It is probably more realistic to suppose that potential 'welfare migrants' seek to improve their absolute income position instead of their relative one. Hence, one could assume that the poor compare the absolute level of replacement income in the various countries and base their decision to migrate on that. In this case, there is an incentive to migrate to a particular country when it offers more generous benefits than the country of origin. With the introduction of the euro, such comparisons have indeed become easier.

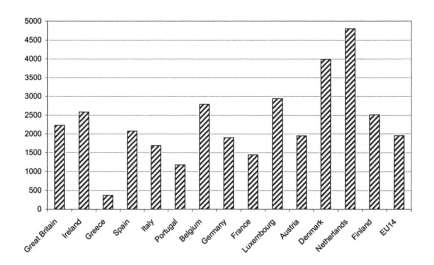

Note: People in a working-age household.

Sources: ECHP; SEP; GSOEP; BHPS.

Figure 7.5   Gross median standardised household replacement income, in Euro PPS, 1995

By analogy with the previous analyses, what we do here is to simulate new incomes for the recipients of replacement incomes, where their income is corrected to make them equal, in absolute terms, in all EU countries. In the race to the bottom scenario, countries engage in social dumping until replacement income in all countries is equal, on average, to the level in the country where this income is lowest. Following the EU convergence scenario, countries are expected to co-ordinate the level of their replacement incomes so that it is equal to the EU median. Eventually, assuming the Member States are working towards the creation of a strong social Europe, they are expected to upgrade their minimum to the level of the country paying the largest amounts. Figure 7.5 displays median standardised household replacement income in 14 EU Member States in Euro purchasing power standard (PPS). Median standardised household replacement income in the EU amounts to about 2,000 Euros PPS per year. In Greece, however, it is less than 400 Euros PPS per year and in the Netherlands as much as 4,800 Euros PPS.

Table 7.8 shows the poverty rates and inequality indices resulting from these simulations. Broadly speaking, the results are comparable to the previous ones; only the magnitude of the effects on the poverty rate and the inequality index is much larger. A consequence of subtracting sometimes large, absolute amounts of replacement incomes – in countries other than Greece – is that the relative poverty rates are substantially increased. They are, in fact, increased to such an extent that all poverty rates then exceed the Greek one. The overall EU poverty rate resulting from the simulated race to the bottom equals 17 percent, instead of the actual 10.2 percent. Poverty is increased to 28 percent in Ireland and 19 to 23 percent in Great Britain, the Netherlands and Spain. This scenario also leads to a substantial increase in within-country inequality.

Should median replacement income in all countries converge towards the EU median, poverty would be aggravated in countries where replacement incomes are larger than the EU median, while it will diminish in countries where these incomes are lower. This scenario results in poverty rates ranging from 5 percent in Greece to almost 17 percent in the Netherlands.

Improving the income position of benefit recipients such that, across Europe, median replacement income is equal to the Dutch level, obviously results in a sharp decrease in poverty and inequality. The EU poverty rate is reduced from 10.2 to 3.1 percent while overall inequality is reduced by some 30 percent. Within-country inequality, in particular, is reduced sharply, as is between-country inequality, albeit to a lesser extent. According to this scenario, poverty is reduced below 3 percent in Denmark, Greece, France, Austria, Portugal, Finland and Great Britain. However, whether this scenario is a realistic one can be questioned. It would indeed require massive money transfers towards replacement income recipients which implies that their incomes would be increased to such an extent that, in many instances, labour incentives would be removed.

Table 7.8 *Simulations on replacement income (absolute). Percentage of individuals with actual and simulated household income below the poverty line, within- and between-country inequality, 1995*

	Actual poverty rate	Simulations		
		Race to the bottom	EU convergence	California effect
Liberal				
Great Britain	10.9	19.2	12.4	1.5
Ireland	9.2	28.1	14.9	3.3
Southern				
Greece	10.1	10.1	5.0	0.7
Spain	12.5	23.1	13.3	3.8
Italy	13.3	19.9	12.1	5.0
Portugal	12.5	17.9	9.1	0.6
Corporatist				
Belgium	9.5	17.9	12.3	3.6
Germany	9.6	14.0	9.1	4.1
France	7.9	13.1	5.4	0.7
Luxembourg	5.5	11.2	7.1	3.6
Austria	6.6	10.4	6.6	2.7
Social democratic				
Denmark	3.6	10.6	6.9	2.4
Netherlands	8.5	22.3	16.8	8.5
Finland	5.3	12.0	6.6	1.7
EU	10.2	16.9	10.2	3.1
Theil coefficient:	0.179	0.206	0.176	0.125
Within-country	0.165	0.192	0.163	0.115
Between-country	0.014	0.014	0.013	0.011

Note: People in a working-age household.

Sources: ECHP; SEP; GSOEP; BHPS.

7.6 FISCAL COMPETITION AND LABOUR COSTS

Thus far, we have focused on the poverty incidence of various outcomes of fiscal competition in Europe, assuming the achievement of European citizenship. However, in the short run, it is more realistic to assume that competition among Member States will take place through the reduction of production costs. Here, we focus solely on labour costs. The sample considered for the analyses in this section consists of people in working-age households where an average of at least 15 hours a week is worked.[17] We refer to them as people in working households. Median gross standardised household earnings of people in working households with positive earnings are reproduced in Figure 7.6.

The figure shows that the differences among the countries are large. Gross wages are lowest in Portugal (about 55 percent of the EU average), Greece and Spain (about 65 percent of EU average). Other things being equal, these countries have a competitive advantage compared to other countries. Labour costs, including employer's contributions, as measured by gross median income, are highest in Luxembourg, followed by Denmark, the Netherlands and Belgium.

The final simulations in this chapter relate to the assumptions made with respect to the effect of fiscal competition on wages. The wage is but one aspect of the terms of employment. Employee benefits, working conditions and safety standards, labour market regulations and social protection are also part of the package. These are all aspects of the labour relations that determine a company's competitive advantage. Aspects of social protection were discussed in the previous section and in previous chapters. However, due to a lack of data on the other aspects of the terms of employment, we will focus on wages.

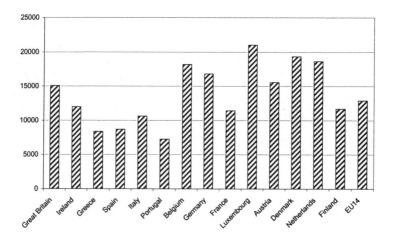

Note: People in a working-age household.

Sources: ECHP; SEP; GSOEP; BHPS.

Figure 7.6   Gross median standardised household earnings, in Euro PPS, 1995

As in the previous simulations, we first assume that fiscal competition – the race to the bottom – among Member States will drive them to adjust the level of their gross income to the lowest level in the EU: Portugal (see Box 7.3). Then, we assume that mean convergence will take place and that gross wages will converge towards the EU average. Eventually – through investing in a well-educated and skilled workforce – wages will converge towards the highest level in the EU. Although Luxembourg has the highest earnings – due to its special labour market situation highly specialised in commercial services and banking – we take Denmark (second highest earnings) as the reference country for the California effect scenario. As we did previously, the simulated incomes are compared to the national poverty line.

BOX 7.3   Simulated labour earnings

Following these hypothetical scenarios for wage competition, we simulate the household income ($\tilde{y}_{ic}^{"}$) for people in a working household (head and partner (if any) are aged 25–55 and average number of hours worked per adult is at least 15 hours a week):

$$\tilde{y}_{ic}^{"} = ynl_{ic} + (1 - tx_c)yl_{ic}\,{yl_r}\big/{yl_c}\,,$$

where ynl_{ic} is the net non-labour household income of person i in country c, yl_{ic} gross household labour earnings, tx_c the average tax rate, yl_c national median gross household labour earnings and yl_r median gross household labour earnings in the country of reference. The country of reference is Portugal in the race to the bottom scenario, as it has the lowest gross median earnings. In the EU convergence scenario, we take the EU median earnings as the reference point. In the California effect scenario, we take Denmark as the country of reference.

From the first column of Table 7.9, we see that 5 percent of the individuals can be said to live in working-poor households. This amounts to half that percentage in the Netherlands, but twice that in Portugal. Obviously, because labour income is the main income source for the great majority of EU citizens, implementing the above scenarios has a tremendous impact on poverty statistics. Assuming that Member States engage in wage competition, which induces them to reduce wages to the lowest EU level, implies that the poverty rate among workers will increase from 5 to almost 28 percent. This race to the bottom scenario particularly affects the income position of individuals in countries where earnings are high. Hence, substantially high poverty rates are found in Belgium (39 percent), Germany, the Netherlands, Denmark (47–48 percent) and Luxembourg (52 percent). According to this scenario, inequality within countries is increased but, due to the levelling-down effect of the simulation, inequality among countries is diminished.

By construction, simulating the EU convergence scenario increases poverty in countries with median earnings above the EU median (the poverty rate in Luxembourg is increased from 3.7 to 17.4 percent) while it reduces poverty in countries where median earnings are below the EU median (the Portuguese poverty rate is reduced from 10 to 5.4 percent). Overall, poverty and inequality are slightly increased. Once again, this scenario reduces inequality between countries but increases within-country inequality. The final scenario implemented here, the California effect scenario where earnings are assumed to converge towards the highest level in the EU, implies that poverty is halved to 2.7 percent but that inequality is increased by 8 percent. Compared to the actual situation, within-country inequality is substantially increased but between-country inequality is decreased. Under this scenario, the number of working-poor people ranges from 1.1 percent in Ireland to 4.8 percent in Belgium.

Table 7.9   *Simulations on gross wages. Percentage of individuals with actual and simulated household income below the poverty line, within- and between-country inequality, 1995*

	Actual poverty rate	Simulations		
		Race to the bottom	EU convergence	California effect
Liberal				
Great Britain	2.8	26.0	4.5	1.8
Ireland	2.8	10.3	2.5	1.1
Southern				
Greece	7.9	11.3	4.7	2.6
Spain	7.7	11.8	5.1	3.9
Italy	9.2	21.6	6.4	4.2
Portugal	10.0	10.0	5.4	4.2
Corporatist				
Belgium	5.8	39.0	9.9	4.8
Germany	3.4	47.0	6.7	2.5
France	4.1	15.4	2.7	1.3
Luxembourg	3.7	52.9	17.4	4.5
Austria	4.8	31.7	7.1	3.6
Social democratic				
Denmark	2.7	48.1	6.5	2.7
Netherlands	2.5	47.9	8.2	2.2
Finland	3.6	8.7	3.0	2.1
EU	5.0	27.7	5.4	2.7
Theil coefficient:	0.152	0.151	0.157	0.164
Within-country	0.138	0.143	0.148	0.154
Between-country	0.014	0.008	0.009	0.010

Note: Persons in a working-age household working at least 15 hours.

Sources: ECHP; SEP; GSOEP; BHPS.

7.7   CONCLUSIONS AND PROSPECTS

As we have shown, substantial amounts of money are needed to completely alleviate poverty in Europe. In financial terms, filling the poverty gap would absorb a large part of the fruits of economic growth. Both from an economic and political point of view, this is undesirable. A more modest objective in terms of poverty reduction, such as halving the poverty rate in all EU countries could, however, be achieved at substantially lower costs. A budget equivalent to half the Common Agricultural Policy budget would be enough to lift half the poor out of poverty. Of course, we do not suggest that poverty could be alleviated through money transfers. Not only would that be inefficient, but poverty is not solely a matter of insufficient income. It is a multifaceted concept associated with, for example, the lack of elementary goods, a low educational level, poor housing and few labour market opportunities. It can also be associated with psychological and social distress, which are not helped by money transfers. Keeping in mind their limitations, the calculations aim at presenting some relevant boundaries when it comes to discussing income poverty.

The basic simulations carried out in this chapter have shown that the cost of fiscal competition in terms of increased poverty and inequality – leading to social dumping – are high. Downward adjustments in the level of replacement income, whether relative to earnings or in absolute terms, lead to a rise in the poverty rate and in the inequality index. However, downward equalisation of the absolute level of replacement income has a larger effect than downward equalisation relative to earnings. The reverse holds true for the hypothesis that a social Europe with high standards of minimum protection is the ideal. This California effect scenario implies a reduction in poverty and inequality rates. This reduction is more substantial when absolute levels of minimum income are upgraded rather than when this upgrading is only relative to earnings. Upgrading of the absolute level of replacement income in Europe also leads to a reduction of income inequalities among EU Member States.

Whether or not substantial geographic mobility among EU regions is going to take place in the near future and generate a race to the bottom is questionable. As Krueger shows, migration within Europe is low and more or less constant over the years (around 0.2 percent; Krueger, 2000: 122). Only a very small increase was witnessed in the period following the Treaty of Maastricht. As to migration from non-EU countries, it has been falling since 1992. The pressure from migration is, therefore, not likely to provoke a race to the bottom in social transfers or wages. It is also not likely that social protection arrangements will be dismantled since, as we showed in Chapter 3, they contribute positively to the economy (Atkinson, 1999; Fouarge, 2003).

These results, however, also show that, at present, cross-border labour mobility is unlikely to be an effective instrument to correct for local economic shocks in the EU. Alternative answers to economic unbalances can be found, for example, in the flexibilisation of the labour market. In the prospect of the open method of co-ordination, it is possible that increased political integration will induce countries to raise their labour and living standards (see also Krueger, 2000). The 'laggards' might be induced to improve their standards while the 'leaders' are encouraged to keep their standards high. Such a process, along with of the setting of minimum standards, should be stimulated. From the point of view of positive subsidiarity, the EU could play a role here.

NOTES

1. See also Fouarge and Dirven (1995), Dirven and Fouarge (1998), Fouarge and Muffels (2000), Muffels and Fouarge (2002a) for comparative evidence on the first three indicators.
2. Gelauff and Graafland (1994) offer such simulations using an applied general equilibrium model for the Netherlands.
3. This chapter was written within the framework of the EXSPRO project 'Social exclusion and social protection; the future role for the EU'. The EXSPRO research project was funded by the European Commission under the *Targeted Socio-Economic Research* programme.
4. The ECHP users' database for the first three waves of the ECHP does not include data for Sweden. Austrian data for 1994 are missing. Finish data are only available for 1996. See Eurostat (1996) for additional information.
5. The Belgian data should be taken with caution. Large disparities between the ECHP income data and the original Belgian data have been indicated in Van Hoorebeeck et al. (2000).
6. A similar exercise was carried out by Hagenaars et al. (1994) on Household Budget Surveys held in EU Members States in the late 1980s.
7. In terms of the formula in Box 7.1 the three alternatives amount to taking either the Portuguese, overall EU or Luxembourg median income, with α set 0, to compute the poverty line.
8. See Creedy (1996: 104) for a detailed graphical presentation.
9. For details on the composition of the EU budget, see European Commission (2000d).
10. As Table 7.3 shows, the four countries with the lowest poverty rates are Luxembourg, Denmark, Finland and Austria. The weighted average of poverty rate in these four countries equals 6.5 percent.
11. In 1995, the coefficient of variation of unemployment rates in the various regions of the EU equals 5.7. In the USA, Canada and Japan it equals, respectively, 1.1, 2.3 and 0.7 (OECD, 2000: 39)
12. This is because immigrants are part of a selective group who have chosen to endorse the costs of migration, in any case (Borjas, 1998: 3).
13. Ultimately, social dumping will induce states to reduce benefits to zero.
14. A more sophisticated way to perform such simulations would be to use EUROMOD (see Immervoll et al., 1999). At present, EUROMOD does not contain behavioural equations.
15. For example, in the Netherlands, the simulated replacement income for each household equals the replacement income of that household times 4.4/25.7.
16. The data diverge for those in Tables 7.2 and 7.3 because they refer to people in households where the head or partner is of working age.
17. This was done in order to pin-point our analyses to households with a substantial attachment to the labour market.

8. Poverty in Europe: Which Way to Go Now?

8.1 INTRODUCTION

Large efficiency gains are expected from market integration in the European Union (EU). However, market integration also limits the way Member States can operate independently from one another. Monetary, budgetary and fiscal policies are constrained by the Stability and Growth Pact and the framework of the European Monetary Union (EMU). As a consequence, the possibility for the Member States to use such policies as corrective mechanisms for temporary shocks is limited. This has implications for the social protection systems. However, the European construction is primarily based on economic integration and social policy issues have generally remained in the background. The basis for this book is the following question: is there a role for the EU to play in social policy or should social policy remain an area of exclusive competence of the Member States? Within the limited scope of this study, only a partial answer could be given. First, we only examined the question from an economic point of view.[1] Secondly, we focused almost exclusively on redistribution and minimum income protection to the poor.

Several steps were taken to tackle this broad question, the findings of which could be useful for reshaping socio-economic policy in Europe and for defining the role of Europe in this policy field. First, it was noted that the improvement of the standard of living and quality of life of those living in the EU – as well as economic and social cohesion and solidarity among Member States – are among the objectives of the EU (article 2 of the EU Treaty). The fight against social exclusion is also recognised as one of its fundamental aims (articles 136 and 137 of the EU Treaty). The EU competencies in this policy field, however, are subject to the unanimity rule and the subsidiarity test. Hence, the first step towards answering the general question formulated above was to investigate the theoretical basis of the principle of subsidiarity and its implications for redistribution policy (Section 8.2). This is one of the novelties of this research.

The second step was to argue that future developments in the EU are likely to affect poverty and redistributive policies within the Member States. These developments relate to the consolidation of the EMU, the presence of economic shocks and the EU enlargement. From a theoretical perspective, fiscal federalism literature suggests the need for balancing mechanisms in such a context. From an empirical perspective, we investigated the effect on poverty and inequality of a number of scenarios pertaining to the future of social policy in Europe (Section 8.3). Such an investigation was, thus far, absent in the literature.

Finally, throughout this book we elaborated and quantified a number of poverty indicators, one of the dimensions of social exclusion. Using panel data for a number of EU countries, we evaluated their performances with respect to these indicators. We paid particular attention to the distinction between short- and long-term poverty and investigated the processes underlying poverty transitions. We used these empirical insights to emphasise that social protection, far from being just a financial burden to the economy, can be seen as a productive factor (Section 8.4). Hence, more equity is not necessarily conducive to less efficiency. This is one of the interesting findings of this study. The resulting effect of the interaction between equity and efficiency does in practice, however, depend on the welfare state design. With respect to poverty relief, the research findings endorse active policies to stimulate the processes leading to favourable socio-economic outcomes and preventing the deterioration of living conditions. Active labour market policies have an important role to play in this respect, since unemployment and employment loss were found to be strong determinants of poverty. Human capital formation is also significant because it contributes to the improvement of life chances. High-skilled people have better socio-economic prospects and less probability of moving into precarious economic positions.

We also support an increased involvement of the EU in social matters. Within the limits of subsidiarity, however, the open method of co-ordination seems to be the only workable option. It is also the most respectful of the great diversity in institutional settings in Europe. Within the framework of the open method of co-ordination, the role of the Commission should be to promote and stimulate the exchange of information on and improve economic and social policy. Encouraging the Member States to set up minimum guaranteed income schemes could also be part of this process. The policy implications of this research are discussed in Section 8.5.

8.2 SUBSIDIARITY, INCOME REDISTRIBUTION AND THE EU

The creation of a common market was the primary goal of the six original founding countries of the EU (the Benelux countries, France, Germany and Italy). At the time – despite the ongoing debate about social security – harmonisation of the social protection systems was not thought to be a prerequisite to the creation of a common market. Successive enlargements have strengthened the idea that harmonisation was impossible and unnecessary because of the great diversity of the various social protection frameworks (Chassard, 2001). However, the EU does have some competencies at its disposal for harmonisation of social security systems (Vansteenkiste, 1995; Jaspers et al., 2002). Free mobility, the working of the internal market and general as well as social objectives (Social Chapter) of the EU Treaty can be the basis for harmonisation of the social security laws of the Member States. Any action at the EU level, however, is subject to the subsidiarity test. In practice, efforts to co-ordinate or harmonise social policy schemes have been strongly opposed (Chassard, 2001). Nonetheless, softer forms of policy co-ordination might well be possible (Section 8.5).

8.2.1   The Dual Character of Subsidiarity

Subsidiarity applies both to the distribution of responsibilities between lower- and higher-tier levels of government (vertical subsidiarity) and the distribution of responsibilities among the individuals, the family, social partners and the State (horizontal subsidiarity). In general terms, the principle of subsidiarity states that it would be wrong for entities of higher rank to assume the tasks that could be performed at a lower plane. Subsidiarity involves an efficiency test favouring decentralisation – needs and preferences are better perceived at decentral levels – where the burden of the proof for shifting responsibilities to higher levels of government lies with the advocates of centralisation. This principle is central in policy practice at the European level. It is used by the Member States to limit the transfer of national competencies to the EU. However, subsidiarity has distant historical origins and implications that go beyond its actual usage in the EU. In Chapter 2, we indicated a second meaning of subsidiarity. There, it was argued that subsidiarity has a broader interpretation: higher entities have the duty to aid the fuller development of lower entities, in particular when human dignity and human rights are at stake. This aspect, which was termed positive subsidiarity, originates in Catholic social teaching. Positive subsidiarity has implications for defining the role of higher levels of governance when it comes to poverty relief. To the extent that poverty is a breach of human dignity, it is the role of the State to support and assist individuals. Moreover, higher levels of governance also have the duty to support and assist lower-plane entities. This does not necessarily contradict individual liberties: it is not that higher authorities are a substitute for the individuals or lower-tier entities, but rather that higher authorities are to help to protect and uphold these liberties. Such support should not be seen merely in terms of money transfers to secure people's standard of living. It can be seen more broadly in terms of developing people's ability to cope for themselves, for example, by providing jobs and education, and by developing social and economic skills. The duty of the central entities is to support the lower tiers of government in the design and development of the policies they wish to implement.

8.2.2   Economic Subsidiarity and Redistribution

Justification for support to the poor does not have to be based on normative precepts alone. Subsidiarity is also rooted in economics, so that there is a case for public interference in income distribution. In compound states, economic subsidiarity suggests that, when productive factors are immobile, social protection should be assumed by the lowest level of governance because preferences for redistribution are better perceived at that level. However, the literature also suggests that, when production factors are mobile, decentralisation of redistribution is not efficient. Hence, economic theory does not seem to provide a definite answer concerning the most efficient level of governance to carry out redistributive policy. Much depends on the assumed level of factor mobility and the degree of homogeneity in the preference for redistribution. Nevertheless, developments at the EU level, such as the consolidation of the EMU, the existence of asymmetric economic shocks and the EU enlargement, are expected to affect Member States in their redistributive policy. This is likely to lead to inefficient policy outcomes (see Section 8.3). As we argue below, an increased role for Europe would lead to a more efficient outcome in that the existing differences in the social protection settings impede factor mobility or are conducive to inefficient factor mobility. With respect to positive subsidiarity, the EU could stimulate co-operation among Member States in shaping a strong European social model and preventing the negative effects of fiscal competition.

On the individual–State nexus, economic subsidiarity suggests that the labour market and the family are the primary institutions for the support of one's standard of living. Minimum income protection by national governments compensates for the failure of the market to offer such schemes. We have shown that social protection, rather than simply a financial burden, could be seen as a productive factor and have argued that it can enhance both social and economic efficiency (Section 8.4).

8.3 MIGRATION, FISCAL COMPETITION IN THE EU

8.3.1 Theoretical Insights

In the wake of the Luxembourg Process, the European Employment Strategy was launched, primarily in order to render labour more flexible so that Member States could accommodate upcoming structural changes. The idea is to elaborate and monitor the employment policies of the Member States along four pillars: employability, entrepreneurship, adaptability and equal opportunity. These guidelines constitute the template for drawing up annual national action plans (NAPs). Within the European Employment Strategy, participation in the labour market is perceived as the key way to fight social exclusion. Although the fight against exclusion was introduced in the Treaty of Amsterdam – despite the Commission and Member States' recognition that social exclusion is 'one of the major challenges faced by our economies and societies' (European Commission, 2000b: 4) – social protection and social exclusion are primarily the responsibility of the Member States. Nevertheless, following the Nice summit and as part of the Social Policy Agenda, the European Council also requested that the Member States draft NAPs to fight poverty and social exclusion (NAPs/inclusion), much in the spirit of the NAPs/employment. As was the case with the European Employment Strategy, the open method of co-ordination was chosen.[2] This so-called soft law approach leaves the Member States free to decide on the details and implementation of policies, within a common framework and using common objectives set at the European level. Four aims of this process have been agreed upon: to facilitate participation in employment and public access to resources, rights, goods and services; to prevent the risks of exclusion; and to help the most vulnerable and to mobilise all relevant bodies. By now, the first NAPs/inclusion have been sent to and evaluated by the Commission (European Commission, 2002a). The Commission also wishes to set out a new social agenda in the near future (European Commission, 2003).

What can economic literature tell us about whether or not Europe should play a role in redistributive policy? Although the EU is not a federation, parallels can be drawn from the teachings of fiscal federalism literature. In Chapter 3, it is further argued that there are some risks involved with decentralised redistribution for countries operating in a federal setting or within the framework of an economic and monetary union. In the presence of factor mobility, social tourism and social dumping frustrate the possibility for decentral governments to conduct redistribution policies. The volatility of the tax base is conducive to this. To put it bluntly, the poor – or the unskilled workers – will tend to migrate to regions with attractive redistribution policies (social tourism) while the rich – or the skilled – will tend to migrate towards regions with low levels of redistribution and, correspondingly, low levels of taxation. Decentral levels of government, in turn, will compete for productive factors by sobering their fiscal policies (social dumping). These processes, at least in theory, lead to an inefficient allocation of production factors and the rolling-back of the welfare state. Decentral authorities are impeded in their ability to deliver the socially preferred level of income redistribution. Depending on the assumptions of the theoretical models in the presence of factor mobility, a centralised redistribution policy (when there is one single social welfare function to maximise at the level of the federation) or a co-ordinated solution involving compensation mechanisms (when decentral entities differ with respect to their preference for redistribution) would make it possible to internalise these externalities. When production factors are immobile, decentral redistribution is optimal since it most closely corresponds to the local preference for redistribution.

Apart from the fact that the EU lacks the legitimacy (and the necessary budget) to carry out interpersonal income redistribution, many would argue that the fears of social tourism and social dumping are unfounded. Primarily, this is because the mobility argument is not a strong one in the EU context. Although workers are freely mobile across Europe, there is, at present, no such thing as free mobility of citizens and free access to general assistance schemes. The social tourism argument is, therefore, largely unconvincing. Though capital is highly mobile, workers are not that willing to cross borders. Cross-border labour mobility is found to be significantly lower in the EU than in the USA. It is also far less responsive to unemployment differentials. This means that the pressure on social dumping in Europe is low.

However, labour mobility is expected to increase in the future, as a consequence of EU enlargement. This will make it difficult for the Member States to deliver their preferred level of redistribution. The prospective member countries from central and eastern Europe are characterised by a different socio-economic structure. The wage differentials between these countries and EU countries are large – indeed, larger than with the Iberian countries at the time of accession to the EU. Labour mobility from these countries – especially from low-skilled workers – is expected to be large and to affect the general level of welfare and its distribution in EU Member States (de Mooij, 2000; Lejour et al., 2001). It is no coincidence that Germany and Austria are willing to introduce a temporary migration stop when the applicant countries join the EU and other countries are considering the introduction of similar barriers.

In addition, by taking part in the EMU Member States have, de facto, constrained themselves in the use of budgetary and monetary policy as balancing mechanisms. It was argued in Chapter 3 that, while the local level responds best to the local demand for redistribution, a centralised system of redistribution is superior when economic shocks are asymmetric. This is even more the case when local jurisdictions are constrained in their possibilities to correct imbalances through monetary and fiscal policies. This leaves the Member States with a limited set of corrective instruments. Stimulating in- and out-migration of production factors is one of them, but we noted already that mobility, at present, is low and biased towards high-skilled workers. Above all, it is a variable that is difficult to steer. This implies that the possibility for labour migration to operate as a corrective mechanism for regional imbalances is limited. Increased labour market flexibility, or variations of the costs of production factors through taxation, are other ways to accommodate economic shocks. However, implementing either of these measures is not without consequences for the well-being.

8.3.2 Fiscal Competition and Co-ordination: Effects on Poverty

The inclusion of a social chapter in the Treaty of Amsterdam has given a new impulse to the debate on the social dimension of Europe. The subsequent European Councils at Lisbon, Feira, Nice and Laeken have put the issue of social exclusion on the policy agenda. The principle of subsidiarity, however, constrains the scope of action of the EU in this policy field. Still, the Council has urged the Member States to draw up national action plans against social exclusion. Although the debate at the EU level is formulated in terms of social exclusion, all the analyses in this book focus on income poverty and income distribution. The concept of social exclusion has a rich history (see Vleminckx and Berghman, 2001). It is a broad – but also vague – concept that encompasses many aspects of life: bad health; poor living conditions; low socio-economic status; absence of social contacts, and so on. Nevertheless, the concepts of income poverty and social exclusion are related, and – as we showed elsewhere (Muffels and Fouarge, 2004) – the relationship between both is stronger in the long run than the short run: the long-term income poor display higher levels of deprivation. Therefore, while financial hardship, in the short run, does not automatically lead to social exclusion, the longer one remains income-poor, the higher the probability that one will become socially excluded.

We used data from the European Community Household Panel (ECHP) in order to describe the poverty situation in the EU in Chapter 7. In 1995, 11 percent of the EU citizens were living in income poverty, but the disparity among countries was large. The number of poor ranged from 6 percent in Luxembourg and Denmark to almost 15 percent in Portugal. With a common poverty line for all EU countries – half of the EU median income rather than half of the national median – the differences among countries are even more pronounced. The poverty rates then range from 1.5 percent in Luxembourg to 40 percent in Portugal. The absolute differences in welfare are, we see, even larger than the relative ones.

In dealing with social policy in the EU, the open method of co-ordination was chosen because it is not binding for the Member States. But where will this method lead? Will the Member States agree to set common poverty targets and how much effort will it take them to achieve the set target? We carried out some simple computations to illustrate the magnitude of the effort needed to achieve alternative poverty targets. Suppose the Member States set themselves the target of the complete eradication of poverty. Bearing in mind the limits of our exercise, we computed that, in that case, 1.7 percent of the total income of the non-poor would need to be taxed away and redistributed towards the poor. This is not to say that transferring income is the ultimate solution to the poverty issue. Indeed, assuming a growth rate of 2 percent a year, that would mean that almost all the fruits of economic growth would be swallowed up by such transfers. This would have large disincentive effects. A more modest poverty target – the Member States reducing poverty to the EU average – would be far less costly, amounting to 0.01 and 0.13 percent of the income of the non-poor depending on whether transfers are made only to the least poor or to all of them (see Chapter 7 for details). The disincentive effects of such a scenario would be much smaller. However, the major drawback of this scenario is that it only has the poorest countries of the EU – or rather the countries with above-average poverty rates, that is the southern European countries and Great Britain – committed to reducing their poverty rate. An alternative target that would commit all Member States is one that opts for reducing poverty by 50 percent. Again, the costs incurred to meet this target will depend on to whom these transfers are made. If we mean all the poor, then 1 percent of the income of the non-poor would have to be transferred to the poor. If we mean only the least poor, then that implies a transfer of 0.32 percent of the income of the non-poor. This latter scenario, supposedly, would have lower disincentive effects.

Some of the theories scrutinised in Chapter 3 predict that, for countries operating in a federal setting, fiscal competition will lead to a race to the bottom on replacement income. One can also point to the possible deflationary effect on wages of low-skilled labour migration. Alternatively, one could hypothesise that, under the open method of co-ordination, some spontaneous convergence of replacement income and wages towards the EU average will take place.[3] Finally, it is possible that the open method of co-ordination will result in strengthening the European social model. In that respect, it can be assumed that countries with the best developed model manage – for example, through the peer review process embedded in the open method of co-ordination strategy – to export their social model. This could lead to an upgrading of the replacement income schemes. Alternatively, starting from a similar premise, one could assume that the European Employment Strategy will result in a general upgrading of the qualification level of the labour force, leading to the convergence of wages towards higher levels. The scenarios will affect economic well-being and its distribution. The substantive results presented in Chapter 7 show that there are clear risks of increased poverty and inequality, should the Member States fail to co-ordinate their policies and engage in policy competition. We showed that social tourism and social dumping – resulting in a race to the bottom – would significantly affect the income distribution and the level and distribution of poverty in Europe. Fiscal competition, leading to downward adjustments of replacement income to the lowest common denominator in Europe, would have a large effect on the poverty figure – poverty for those in working-age households could increase from 10 to 17 percent – and would exacerbate inequality. However, a general upgrading of the minimum protection level and wages would result in lower poverty rates. The numbers in Chapter 7 are, as stated above, merely illustrative for the true effect.

8.3.3 Conclusion

The conclusion is that increased co-operation and co-ordination of social protection policies among Member States is required in the future. This need emanates from the lack of instruments available for the Member States to correct for economic shocks as the EMU consolidates and from the probable increase in low-skilled labour mobility in the wake of the EU enlargement. The consolidation of the EMU constrains Members States in the use of budgetary and monetary policy to correct for economic shocks. Structural funds are also inadequate as corrective mechanisms. The risk is that Member States will engage in fiscal competition in order to correct imbalances and to gain competitive advantage. Because of the potential risk of social dumping, this will have a large effect on poverty and jeopardise the European social model.

The increased labour mobility following enlargement is also expected to have a major effect on welfare and hamper Member States in their redistributive policy. In accordance with positive subsidiarity, the role of the EU should be to stimulate co-operation among the Members States in this policy field, following a model that is respectful of the institutional diversity within the Member States. The open method of co-ordination fits well into this line of thought.

8.4 SOCIAL PROTECTION AND THE PROMOTION OF ECONOMIC AND SOCIAL EFFICIENCY

The discussion on the redistributive function of the welfare state is generally framed around equity and efficiency. From a theoretical point of view, as Okun (1975) pointed out, there appears to be a trade-off between the two. However, the relationship between equity and efficiency is a complex one. Considering economic and social efficiency solely in the light of this assumed trade-off would be a simplification of reality. Economic and social performance are interrelated in such a way that more of the one does not necessarily imply less of the other. Applauding fiscal competition as a way to tame Leviathan fails to appreciate the productive aspect of social protection. Aside from its obvious function in terms of redistribution, social protection also has an allocative and stabilisation function. More precisely, social protection is not only profitable from the point of view of equity or social efficiency, it can also be a productive factor since it promotes economic efficiency. Both aspects, as summarised in Figure 3.1 (Chapter 3), are conducive to improving well-being. The equity and productive contribution of social protection and minimum protection in particular have been investigated from a theoretical (Chapter 3) and empirical point of view (Chapter 5 and 6). The findings are summarised in the next paragraphs.

8.4.1 Subsidiarity and Welfare State Design

How social protection works in terms of social and economic efficiency depends on the way the welfare state is designed. A substantial part of the empirical chapters (Chapters 5 and 6) focused on monitoring poverty and the redistributive effects of public transfers in various welfare state settings. Emphasis was placed on the distinction between short- and long-term poverty and on identifying the events triggering poverty entries and exits. This approach makes it possible to compare the economic and social performance of the various welfare state settings. Moreover, within the welfare state, the approach also permits the evaluation of economic and social performance over the course of time. Social efficiency was measured in terms of income inequality, income poverty and the extent of income redistribution through public transfers. Economic efficiency was assessed in terms of income levels, growth and labour market incentives.

Esping-Andersen's typology of welfare regimes (Esping-Andersen, 1990) has been used to investigate the effect of welfare state design on economic and social efficiency. This typology distinguishes among the liberal, the corporatist and the social-democratic types of welfare regime. We added another type – the southern regime – to these types (see Chapter 4). These regime types represent a particular institutional framework, a particular type of policy intervention and set of policy tools. In terms of horizontal subsidiarity, these types vary as to who is primary responsible for the individual's welfare: the individual him or herself, through the workings of the market as in the liberal regime; the family, as in the southern regime type; social groups or the corporation, as in the corporatist regime; or the State, as in the social-democratic regime. In reality, no country fits perfectly into one of these types, nor are they stable features of a country's socio-economic policy over time. Nevertheless, such a typology is found to be a useful analytical tool.

In this study we present one of the first in-depth analyses – based on micro-data – of poverty dynamics in Europe within the framework of the above typology (see also Goodin et al., 1999). For three European countries – the Netherlands, Germany and Great Britain – we use longitudinal data to carry out the analyses. As argued in Chapter 4, data for the Netherlands (SEP) are used to describe the social-democratic model and Germany (GSOEP) is taken to illustrate the corporatist model. Great Britain (BHPS) exemplifies the liberal welfare model. The income data used cover the years 1985–94 for the Netherlands, 1985–95 for Germany and 1991–7 for Great Britain.

Welfare regimes and social efficiency
With respect to poverty levels and the income distribution, the British welfare state, which operates in the liberal tradition, tends to produce more inequality and poverty (Chapter 5). This finding confirms our expectation. Welfare states with a universal character (the Netherlands) produce lower levels of poverty and inequality. To some extent, this also holds for the German welfare state. Given the residual role of the state in liberal welfare regimes and the stress put on labour incentives, income redistribution through state transfers is found to be lowest in Great Britain. Again, this conforms to our expectations. The redistributive efficiency of social protection transfers in Germany and the Netherlands is more or less equal.

Across time, poverty turns out to be lower due to income-smoothing over the years and the resulting elimination of single-year poverty (Chapter 6). There are large turnover rates in and out of poverty. We have used several methods to demonstrate this. One of these was the notion of poverty profiles. Poverty profiles distinguish among the never poor, the transient poor, the recurrent poor and the persistent poor. When studied over a long period, more people experience poverty than over a short period. In the first half of the 1990s, some 18 percent of the Dutch and German population were hit at least once by poverty, compared to 9–10 percent on a cross-sectional basis. A quarter of the British experienced poverty at least once during that period, as opposed to a little more than 12 percent in 1995. Mobility is large: between 40 and 50 percent of the poor manage to escape poverty from one year to the next. Nevertheless, large numbers remain persistently poor. In the five-year period 1991–5, about 4 percent of the Dutch and German population and 8 percent of the British could be said to have been persistently poor. In Great Britain, another 9.5 percent were recurrently poor and 10 percent transient poor. The corresponding percentages for the Netherlands and Germany are 4.4 and 9.7, and 5.4 and 8.4, respectively. The long-term poor are primarily concentrated among single parents and unemployed and – especially in Great Britain – among women, single elderly and social transfer recipients. These findings illustrate the great added value of considering panel data (or the film of people's socio-economic condition) rather than only cross-sectional information (or snapshots of their socio-economic position).

8.4.2   Allocation and Stabilisation: Theoretical and Empirical Insights

Allocation and equity
In the first place, as was shown in Chapter 3, social protection, because it accommodates market failures and (some) informational problems, contributes to the improvement of allocative efficiency which, in turn, can lead to an improvement of well-being. A first theoretical argument is that public provision makes it possible to use plainly increasing returns to scale. As increasing returns to scale lead to an inefficient market outcome, enlarging the scope of the insurance programme is a method of dealing with this type of market failure. Income externalities can also justify the existence of public income transfers. Whenever the income of the poor matters to the rich, then income transfers from the former to the latter can be warranted. However, the free-rider problem makes a market solution difficult so that compulsory cash transfers might be preferable on efficiency grounds. Public provision is also better able to produce merit goods, such as education and training. Furthermore, evidence in the literature suggests that, to the extent that human capital is a determinant of growth, greater income equality will contribute to better economic performance (Chiu, 1998). The reason for this is that redistribution to the poor allows them to purchase education and build up human capital. This is an important argument within the framework of the knowledge-based economy. In our empirical analyses (in particular, Chapters 5 and 6), human capital was shown to be an important determinant of the poverty risk: the higher the educational level, the lower the probability of being or becoming poor.

Sinn (1996) also pointed out that income protection schemes stimulate risk-taking behaviour (see Chapter 3). When people know that they are protected by a benefit system, they are more likely to engage in risky and profitable economic activities that they would probably not undertake otherwise. In support of this, Bird (2001) indeed showed empirically that measures of risk are positively correlated to the share of GDP used for social spending.

Finally, it was argued in Chapter 3 that income protection schemes can improve job matching. Income protection for people out of employment allows them to look for a job that best matches their abilities and human capital endowment. Income protection schemes can, therefore, also contribute to increased labour market flexibility. The corollary, however, is that social protection schemes induce disincentive effects. Although there is some evidence suggesting that specific welfare programmes affect labour participation, taxes and transfers generally have a greater effect on female than on male participation (see also Chapter 7). According to our empirical analyses in Chapter 5, on a cross-sectional basis and with respect to economic efficiency, the British system generates stronger work incentives. Relative income differentials between the employed and unemployed are larger than in the Netherlands and Germany. The other side of the coin is that differences in poverty risk between those who are working and those who are not is smaller in the Netherlands and Germany than in Great Britain. From a dynamic point of view, however, the Netherlands – despite its high level of social spending – has managed to keep incomes relatively high and to maintain labour market dynamics as an effective mechanism in triggering poverty exits. At the same time it has kept poverty and inequality low compared to Great Britain (see Chapter 6). From this perspective, the redistributive Dutch welfare state does not seem to have resulted in economic inefficiencies.

From a theoretical perspective – with respect to informational problems and equity – the following points were made (see Chapter 3). Although the market performs well in terms of wealth creation, it does a poor job of bringing about the socially optimal income distribution (see Chapters 5 and 6). This equity argument can be introduced to justify the existence of redistributive mechanisms through the welfare state. The other side of this equity argument is one of efficiency and is based on incomplete information. When placed behind the veil of ignorance – without knowing what their factor endowments or market perspectives will be – risk-averse individuals are willing to insure themselves against possible income risks. However, there is no straightforward way to organise such an insurance market once the veil of ignorance has been lifted. Adverse selection will lead to the breakdown of the insurance market. The welfare state can solve this problem by making insurance compulsory.[4] Interdependence of the insured risk (when individual risks are positively correlated) can also make the market solution impossible. This will be the case for private income insurance with respect to unemployment because the unemployment risk cannot generally be spread over a large enough risk pool.

Stabilisation, growth and equity

Macroeconomic literature points out that social protection acts as a stabilisation instrument. Social protection has a counter-cyclical effect in that it works as a buffer during economic downturns, and thereby contributes to the diminishing volatility of aggregate demand. Our empirical findings show that welfare states with a social-democratic or corporatist tradition have large redistributive effects (Chapter 5). These effects are even larger in the long term than in the short term (Chapter 6). Although this increased redistributive efficiency in the longer term also holds for countries in the liberal tradition – and thus with small transfer programmes – the effects are smaller. In addition, in Chapter 6 we showed that permanent income displays larger fluctuations in liberal welfare states. Using advanced econometric techniques, we disentangled permanent and transitory components of household income. Although such models are commonly used to study the dynamics of wages, there are only very few applications in the context of household income dynamics. To our knowledge, ours is the first international comparative study using such techniques. The idea behind the model is that people are poor when their permanent income falls below the poverty threshold. Using seven years of panel data – ranging from the end of the 1980s to the early 1990s – the results presented show coherent differences among the regime types. As expected, permanent income inequalities and permanent poverty are largest in Great Britain. An estimated 5.5 percent of the British population is found to live in permanent poverty, as opposed to 2 percent in the Netherlands and 1.6 percent in Germany. Our computations confirm that adverse shocks in the labour market (unemployment) and at the household level (single parenthood) exacerbate the poverty risk.

In Chapter 3, reference was made to theoretical and empirical developments in relation to the notion of social capital. It was argued that social protection acts as a stabilisation instrument because it contributes to social capital and social peace and, therefore, to a stable investment climate. Dense social relationships enhance social trust and reciprocity and thereby increase the chance that people will engage in economic exchange. Hence, social integration and the development of social capital – which are enhanced by the social protection systems – are key elements of economic progress.

As shown in Chapter 6, government transfers are even more effective at reducing poverty and inequality in the medium or long term than in the short term. What our results show is that, in the counter-factual situation of no government intervention in the area of social security, the market does a poor job at reducing spells of poverty. Not only does the market fail to generate fair income distribution on a cross-sectional basis, it also fails over the course of time. Nevertheless, when modelling poverty entries and exits, labour market events prove to be highly influential. A low attachment to the labour market (working few hours), for example, tends to increase the poverty risk. The strong effect of labour market variables in the dynamic context found in all three countries leads us to conclude that the higher social efficiency of the social-democratic and corporatist models do not necessarily lead to lower economic efficiency.

A review of the literature discloses that the evidence of the alleged negative effect of social spending on economic growth is non-conclusive (Atkinson, 1999). There is also evidence that large amounts of public spending lead to better outcomes in terms of social indicators and have only minor effects on economic performance. There are, however, boundaries to this relationship. As Mayes and Virén (2002) demonstrate, the relationship between social spending and economic performance is asymmetric. While increasing social spending will initially stimulate economic performance, the relationship is reversed when some turnover point is passed. Moreover, it seems that spending on active policy is better for economic growth than spending on passive policy (Arjona et al., 2001). In the period under scrutiny (1985–95), the Dutch model has managed to keep poverty and inequality lower than the liberal British model while, at the same time, the economy generated above-EU average GDP and labour market participation growth rates. Nevertheless, although income and employment have been rising in all three countries over the past decade, poverty and inequality levels have certainly not decreased. In all three countries, both pre- and post-government inequality and poverty increased during this period. Hence, contrary to Kuznet's hypothesis, the fruits of economic growth do not seem to have trickled down to the poor in a way that reduces the incidence of poverty.

8.4.3 Conclusion

While it must be recognised that welfare states face some major challenges, social protection systems do have social and economic efficiency-enhancing effects. From the point of view of distributional justice, social protection compensates people for their economic weaknesses. Social protection is also a productive factor because it remedies market failures and informational problems: it makes up for failures of the insurance market. It is also a productive factor through its effect on factor endowments (human capital), on allocative efficiency and as an automatic stabiliser. The subsidiary role of social protection does not necessarily result in less economic efficiency. On the contrary, active social security spending seems to be profitable for growth. Reforming the welfare state to make it even more efficient would require governments to switch – rather than diminish – spending towards activation policies. To some extent, a switch towards more active policies is already taking place in Europe (Madsen et al., 2002).

Employment, both at the individual and the household level, was shown to be an efficient way to prevent poverty and promote poverty exits (Chapters 5 and 6). Nonetheless, periods of economic and employment growth have not led to decreasing poverty and inequality levels (see also de Beer, 2001; Muffels and Fouarge, 2001; Cantillon et al., 2002). In particular, poverty traps seem to be in effect so that the lower end of the distribution does not automatically take advantage of economic growth. Substantial parts of the population still live in persistent poverty, even in welfare states which had high levels of economic growth during the 1990s. Upon studying the effects of the welfare regime, however, we found that long-term poverty is lower in countries with social-democratic or corporatist characteristics (Chapter 6). Targeted policy seems necessary to ensure that those people at the lower end also take part in the economic process.

8.5   DISCUSSION

8.5.1   The Time Nature of Poverty

The economic reality is that short- and long-term poverty coexist. At any time, some of the poor will probably manage to exit poverty rapidly while others will remain poor for a longer period of time, or even permanently. To some, it may sound strange to speak of poverty in the relatively wealthy nations of Europe. In a way we can agree with this. Discussing poverty without distinguishing between short-term and persistent poverty masks the temporary aspect of some poverty spells. We believe that people's long-term economic prospects and positions – more than their cross-sectional economic status – matters more for policies. Hence, poverty research in developed countries should focus much more on the time nature of poverty and understand better the processes leading to it.

Aspects of mobility are important, as well. In this study, we showed that adverse household formation events (loss of partner through separation or divorce, a reduction in the household size) positively affect the probability of becoming poor. Chapter 6 supplied evidence that single parenthood increases the risk of persistent poverty. Hence, increased individualisation is likely to keep poverty on the policy agenda. Labour market events – at the individual but also at the household level – also significantly affect one's economic position (Chapter 6). Losing employment or working fewer hours decreases market income and increases the probability of being poor. The reverse holds for job gains and increases in the number of hours worked.

8.5.2 Flexible and Dynamic Labour Market

The coexistence of short- and long-term poverty has policy implications. In order to be effective, it is important that anti-poverty programmes differentiate between the two types. Given the positive contribution of labour market dynamics to the probability of escaping poverty, an employment policy and temporary income support will supposedly be sufficient for the short-term poor. For the long-term poor, however, an active labour market policy is not likely to be sufficient. Because the long-term poor lack the skills and work experience, they require an adequate level of income protection and more targeted measures, such as reintegration programmes and debt management. When paid employment is not a solution for avoiding poverty (for the elderly, the sick, and so on) an adequate level of income protection should be offered through social protection programmes in order to prevent these people from sliding into long-term poverty. More generally, investing in human capital – in the form of productive and social capabilities – is a prerequisite for both social and economic efficiency (see Section 8.5.3).

Although increased participation, at the macro-level, does not lead to a general decrease in poverty rates finding or losing employment, at the micro-level, it accounts for a substantial part of the transitions into and out of poverty. In particular, unemployment significantly affects the probability of long-term poverty. Because it is easier to get people out of short-term than long-term poverty, it is better, from the point of view of both economic and social efficiency, to keep people employed and employable. Active labour market policies help in this respect. Such policies are best designed at the level of the Member State. However, the advantages of policy learning in the European context should not be underestimated. The EU should stimulate the debate and the exchange of information among Member States. EU participation in this field will also generally be less controversial than in the social policy field.

Given the importance of labour market mechanisms as determinants of one's socio-economic position, it would be natural to strive for a better integration of social and employment policy. This is important for the design of European economic and social policy. From the point of view of social exclusion in the EU, framing national action plans for employment and inclusion using two different processes should be reconsidered. Employability, entrepreneurship, adaptability and equal opportunity as EU employment policy objectives also have significance in the social field. The fine-tuning of employment and social inclusion policies could generate returns on both fronts.

Member States, having lost their major instruments for economic stabilisation to the EU, will have to rely more heavily on flexible and dynamic labour markets in order to absorb employment shocks. Flexibilisation is also required to make – and keep – the EU competitive. Flexibilisation, however, requires a well-designed safety net because it will generally have a substantial effect on one's income level. To the extent that flexibilisation drives people out at the lower end of the labour market, increasing their productive capacities – human and social capital – needs policy attention. Flexibilisation also refers to increased dynamics within the labour market. In transitional labour markets, mobility is expected to become more common. Periods of employment might be followed by periods of unemployment. Thus, transitions between employment and caring activities are expected to increase, as are transitions between employment and education, full- and part-time employment, and so on (Schmid, 1998). Adequate safety nets – possibly at a higher than minimum level – might be necessary in order to bridge periods of unemployment, education and care on the transitional labour markets. However, increasing the dynamics in the labour market also necessitates recasting social protection systems to make them more adaptable to new economic situations. The key here is the safeguard of social protection rights when people make transitions in the labour market.

8.5.3   Minimum Income and Investment in Capabilities

Member States seem to recognise the necessity of striking a better balance between economic and social policy. This interplay between economic and social policy will determine the socio-economic outcome. Flanking the economic dimension of the EU with a social dimension is also expected to improve public support for Europe. Harmonisation imposed from the top is not necessary and would encounter a strong protest. In a monetary union, however, something must be developed in order to avoid a downward spiral of social protection and wages. This also holds for the expected effect on the income distribution from EU enlargement (see Chapters 3 and 7). A number of policy tools are required to make our social protection systems 'Euro-proof'. These include agreements in the field of employment policy to operationalise the newly included title on employment in the Treaty of Amsterdam, a federal compensation mechanism to compensate the losers from the integration process and European minimum floors (see also Westerlaken and van Dijk, 1996). Stimulating the Member States to agree upon minimum standards of subsistence is a first step towards meeting this challenge. It could also function as a mechanism to absorb asymmetric shocks. No absolute minima at EU level have to be considered, but Member States should agree on minimum floors that are relative to the economic situations of the individual Member States. These could be linked to the average wage level, for example. Obviously, in order to avoid poverty traps and to circumvent possible disincentive problems, these minimum floors should not be too high.

Nonetheless, there is more to the fight against poverty than the use of minimum income protection schemes. Keeping people employed and employable means that they have to be given adequate marketable skills. The models estimated above do indeed show that human capital has a significant effect on the poverty risk (Chapter 6). A skilled labour force is the key to Europe's economic success, especially in the advent of the knowledge-based economy. This is also endorsed within the framework of the European Employment Strategy. Investing in people's capabilities – that is providing them with the means of action – could be a new road for social policy (Raveaud and Salais, 2001). Improving people's productive capabilities (relating to the economic domain) and social capabilities (relating to the social domain) will serve both economic efficiency and equity. From a long-term perspective, investing in people's capabilities is expected to be fruitful because it makes the labour force more responsive to changing economic conditions. Focusing on the promotion of life chances fits into a preventive approach to social protection. It also corresponds to a role of the State that is in line with positive subsidiarity (see Chapter 2). This preventive approach is believed to be more fruitful than the curative one, based on the reparation of damages caused by the realisation of social and economic risks. Training and activation programmes should be integrated. Shaping the role of the State along the line of positive subsidiarity and the development of capabilities involves more proactive policies focused on developing one's life chances, especially for the long-term excluded. The Commission should encourage developments towards active and human capital-enhancing policies, since that would contribute towards making Europe both social and competitive. The fight against poverty should be accompanied by investments in human capital through education and training programmes.

8.5.4 The Open Method of Co-ordination

In order to progress in the social field in Europe, the decision to co-operate should be left to the Member States. The cultural dependence of such schemes is strong because social protection arrangements have grown historically under the influence of voters and political parties in the Member States of the EU. Social protection schemes reflect the preferences of the population in the various Member States with respect to, among other things, redistribution. In such a context, it follows from the theory of fiscal federalism that a top-down harmonisation is inefficient and also against the principle of subsidiarity. Hence, in the light of the institutional diversity within the EU, harmonisation of social protection schemes does not make much sense. Voluntary co-operation seems the only workable solution, especially in the light of the EU enlargement.[5] It also follows that one must accept a 'multiple-speed' Europe and give room for multilateral agreements. This does not have to be a bad thing, provided that nations can join when they are ready – which is now the case with the EMU construction. This could take the form of open partnerships, where Member States agree on a certain number of policy aims and common strategies without forcing other countries to participate. As long as the agreements do not harm the overall EU objectives, such a solution would be acceptable.

The issue of social exclusion has now been put on the EU agenda. In that respect articles 136 and 137 of the Treaty of Amsterdam are of interest since they make it possible for the Commission to support Member States in various areas. These include the combat against exclusion, the improvement of knowledge, the exchange of information and best practices, the promotion of innovative approaches and the evaluation of experiences. At this time, the EU has no role to play in the delivery of social protection or the combat against exclusion, but it only has a role in facilitating the exchange of information, data, best practices and research. In the wake of the European Employment Strategy, the EU is taking part in the development of the employment policy of the Member States through soft laws, the introduction of national action plans and a peer review monitoring system. The EU does not have any formal competencies in that area, but it plays a stimulating role which it takes seriously. It is also rather effective, since, in that exchange of information no Member State wants to be at the bottom of the class. Madsen et al. (2002) indicate that there is a potential for policy learning and the transfer of policy practice among Member States in the wake of the European Employment Strategy. On the basis of an analysis of the NAPs/employment 1999 and 2000, they note a shift towards more active policies in a number of European countries. Changes in policy practice are associated with positive achievements in terms of employment and social exclusion. Although these changes cannot simply be ascribed to the open method of co-ordination, the authors show that the findings are in line with the hypothesis that policy learning is taking place. Similarly, de la Porte and Pochet (2002) note that the open method of co-ordination in the European Employment Strategy has stimulated the reflection about the existing and projected policies and has stimulated the co-ordination among administrative agencies.

The open method of co-ordination has now been chosen for the setting-up of national action plans in the field of social exclusion, as agreed upon at the

Nice summit. It is expected to increase the policy awareness in this policy field and Member States are now starting to agree upon a number of issues including the setting of poverty targets. This is not to say that the open method of co-ordination is devoid of disadvantages. The method does have a number of drawbacks (Begg and Berghman, 2001). Chassard (2001), for example, points out the deficient democratic legitimacy of the method, as well as the risk that unpopular policy measures might be presented as being imposed from 'Brussels' – potentially casting the Commission in the role of scapegoat. Another issue relates to the sensitivity of such a soft approach of policy convergence to general economic conditions. The underlying risk here is that, following an economic downturn, Member States would diminish their efforts to co-operate. Despite these criticisms, the open method of co-ordination could help to shape co-operation at the EU level. It is possible that the exchange of information through the peer review process induces Member States to copy best practices in such a way that upward convergence can be achieved. Rather than a race to the bottom, this option would strengthen Europe's socio-economic heritage. However, one should not rely solely upon the open method of co-ordination. This process should be accompanied by EU legislation (Vandenbroucke, 2001).

8.6   CONCLUSION

Social integration and economic performance are not contradictory. Social protection is not only a cost factor to the economy. It is also a source of economic welfare. Thus far, the EU has undertaken relatively little in the area of social policy. Although it has some competencies, these are subject to the unanimity rule and the subsidiarity test. Economic subsidiarity entails an efficiency test favouring the most decentralised level of government, unless market failures – such as externalities – and informational problems make higher-tier intervention efficiency-enhancing. There are two types of externalities. First, from a macroeconomic perspective, the consolidation of the EMU limits the possibilities of the Member States to correct for external shocks so that there is a looming risk of fiscal competition. Fiscal competition would lead to a downsizing of the welfare state and a reduction of welfare. Secondly, the EU enlargement is also expected to have effects on the welfare level of the Member States and their ability to conduct their income policy. The EU enlargement is also expected to increase low-skill labour mobility and a possible race to the bottom with respect to wages. This, in turn, could deter investments in human capital.

In order to secure Europe's strong social heritage, co-operation among Member States is necessary. In the short and medium term, imposed co-ordination from the Commission is doomed to fail: it fails to recognise the differences in institutional settings among the various Member States and it is counter to the principle of subsidiarity. Relying on the open method of co-ordination seems to be more fruitful because it leaves the initiative to the Member States. More than a defensive instrument, it is also a constructive instrument on which to base the consolidation of Europe's social model (Vandenbroucke, 2001).

To a large extent, social policy is a domain of experimentation. Learning-by-doing is part of this process. Sharing experience on the effectivity of policy measures is important in this respect. The open method of co-ordination should be the platform for this exchange of information. It seems, for example, that there is something to be learned from the Dutch experience. The country has managed to keep poverty low while, despite its relatively high level of social spending, realising high rates of economic and employment growth in the 1990s. This study has shown that it is crucial to understand the events that trigger poverty entries and exits and persistent poverty. Only then can a policy framework be designed that focuses appropriately on the improvement of people's living conditions. Labour participation and dynamics determine, to a large extent, these living conditions and how they change. Investment in productive and social capabilities – that is the improvement of one's ability to take part in the economic and social process – is crucial for improving one's socio-economic prospects. It also fits within a preventive approach to social policy and is in line with positive subsidiarity. The improvement of social and economic efficiency of social protection systems could be achieved through shifting budgets from passive to active policy and towards human capital formation – especially at the lower end of the labour market – in order to keep people productive. To achieve this, integrating social and employment policy is a necessity. The Dutch and Irish experiences tell us that the involvement of the social partners is required in order to come to a better integration of social and economic policy.[6]

The above elements could be the elements of the European social model. From the point of view of positive subsidiarity, the Community's role in the near future should be to actively stimulate and support the Member States in developing this policy framework. The EU should be supportive of the open method of co-ordination and the platform for the exchange of information of social and employment policy. The EU's role is to encourage learning-by-doing and learning-by-sharing experiences in activation and training programmes for the poor. Merging the EU employment and social inclusion policies would benefit both policy fields since it would increase the credibility of the approach.

NOTES

1. See Jaspers et al. (2002) and Vansteenkiste (1995) for a legal perspective.
2. The open method of co-ordination refers to a process of exchange of information with respect to policy measures and research with the aim to compare and adapt policies in the Member States of the EU.
3. Some signs of autonomous convergence of social protection expenditure, taxation regime and active and passive labour market expenditure (Greve, 1996; Alonso et al., 1998; Broekman et al., 2001).
4. Moral hazard, however, is an informational problem of a different order. Solving it would require careful monitoring of the insuree's behaviour. This could equally well be implemented within a private or public setting.
5. A co-operative solution was shown to be possible within a federal setting (Cremer and Pestieau, 1996).
6. See Muffels and Fouarge (2001), Arents et al. (2001), Hodson (2001).

Appendix 1: A Simple Insurance Model

The aim of social protection is to replace lost income (due to illness, old age, and so on), to supplement income (family benefits) or to prevent income losses (that is by providing information and establishing safety rules). We confine ourselves primarily to the first of these three aims. The following model shows how the private market for social insurance, in the form of minimum protection, is not sustainable. As an illustration, we use the simplified insurance model presented by Atkinson (1989: 112–16). The model considers a worker with the probability p of becoming unemployed and losing his wage income as well as the probability $(1 - p)$ of remaining in work and earning his wage w. In both states, he would get income from capital k. Say δ is the premium paid and b is the social minimum benefit received when unemployed. If employed, the worker would receive an income of $(1 - \delta)w + k$ with a probability $(1 - p)$ and, when unemployed, an income of $b + k$ with a probability of p.

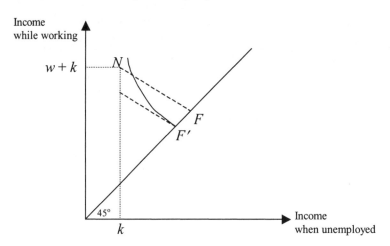

Source: adapted from Atkinson (1989).

Figure A.1.1   Utility and unemployment insurance

In the no-insurance situation, the worker would get $w + k$ if in work and k if unemployed (point N in Figure A.1.1). Supposing there are no administrative costs and that the insurance is actuarially fair (the expectation of net gain is zero), then in the case of full insurance: $(1 - p)\delta w = pb$. The worker is then allowed to move along the line $N–F$, with slope equal to $-p/(1 - p)$, according to his preference.

Assuming the worker is maximising his utility and that utility of income is the same in both situations, then the worker maximises the following function: $(1 - p)$ U$[w(1 - \delta) + k] + p$ U$[b + k]$. In case of risk aversion, the chosen point would be F, the point giving total insurance. Full insurance would be chosen by all risk-averse persons, whatever their degree of risk aversion.

Say the administrative cost per insurance policy equals a, then the amount pa has to be deducted from the benefit paid. This shifts the dashed line in Figure A.1.1 downwards, bringing the full insurance point in F'. Whether or not the point of full insurance is the one that will actually be chosen depends on the degree of risk aversion – that is the curvature of the indifference curve – and the level of the administrative costs relative to the incurred income loss. The person depicted in the figure is better off with full insurance, but if its indifference curves were flatter (if he was less risk-averse) or the administrative costs were higher, he might prefer the no-insurance situation. We see that, in this situation, people take either full insurance or they take no insurance at all.

If administrative costs of State insurance are higher than those of private insurance, as it is sometimes argued, then we can expect more people to choose full insurance. Therefore, the distortion resulting from the administrative costs will be lower in a private minimum protection scheme. However, because of the economies of scale possible with State insurance, this form of insurance might have an advantage over a multiplicity of private insurers. Atkinson also argues that, if compulsory state insurance has lower costs (as they might indeed have, see Gouyette and Pestieau, 1999), it is possible that everybody would be better off and social welfare would therefore rise.

Compulsory state insurance, however, offers less diversity of choice because it does not allow people to opt out. Also, the argument in terms of diversity assumes that perfect competition makes it possible to have a multitude of private insurers from which the customer can choose. What if perfect competition is not sustainable on the insurance market? In order to understand this, consider the situation in which people differ only in their risk of becoming unemployed and that this risk is not readily observable to insurers. One group has a probability p^+ of losing employment while for the other group, this probability equals p^-, with $p^+ > p^-$. Both groups have the same degree of risk aversion. In Figure A.1.2, the indifference curves for both groups are depicted such that in each point the slope of the indifference curve of the high-risk group is higher than the slope of the indifference curve of the low-risk group. The line A–D shows all contracts that would break even if both high and low risks purchase the minimum protection insurance. The slope of this line depends on the probabilities p^+ and p^- and on the proportion of both groups in the population. The line AC^+ is the locus of contracts that would break even if only the high risks purchase insurance and AC^- is the equivalent locus if only the low risks purchase insurance. In such a situation, a problem of adverse selection appears.

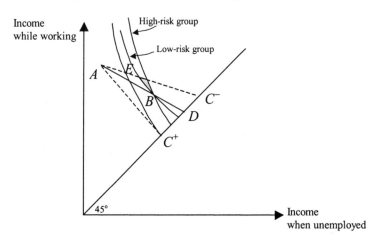

Source: adapted from Atkinson (1989).

Figure A.1.2   Private insurance and sorting equilibrium

Assuming the insurers do not know, ex ante, the risk of their prospective clients, it is impossible to attain a competitive equilibrium, that is a set of insurance contracts such that no other contract exists which, if offered, would make a profit. Supposing an insurer offers a contract as soon as it can make a profit – and that it can do so without influencing the behaviour of other insurers – then a solution could be somewhere on the locus A–D, where both low and high risks purchase the same contract, say B. At that point, however, any contract in the shaded area would attract people from the low-risk group. Insurers then have the possibility to make a profit. This type of pooling equilibrium can, therefore, never be stable.

Alternatively, we can look for a separating equilibrium, with contracts along AC^+ offered to the high-risk group and contracts along AC^- offered to the low-risk group. Here, the constraint is that, for this latter group, the contract lies on the segment A–E, so that the high-risk group will not be attracted. In this case, a contract such as B, would be profitable because it would attract people from the low-risk group.

Appendix 2: Description of the Data

Table A.2.1   Sample size of the three panels

Wave	Netherlands (SEP) Sample size	Valid household income	Germany (GSOEP) Sample size	Valid household income	Great Britain (BHPS) Sample size	Valid household income
1985	11,838	11,696	–	–	–	–
1986	14,042	13,882	13,079	13,076	–	–
1987	13,875	13,844	12,856	12,849	–	–
1988	13,772	13,643	12,212	12,209	–	–
1989	–	–	11,783	11,777	–	–
1990	13,404	13,028	17,304	11,329	–	–
1991	12,278	11,714	16,909	11,512	13,902	11,634
1992	13,426	12,192	16,504	16,497	13,151	11,001
1993	13,083	11,215	16,176	16,171	13,104	10,475
1994	13,029	12,098	16,503	16,490	12,851	10,477
1995	12,791	11,981	16,973	16,960	12,549	10,125
1996	–	–	16,558	16,545	12,720	10,544
1997	–	–	–	–	15,042	10,556

Sources: SEP (1985–95); GSOEP (1986–96); BHPS (1991–7).

Table A.2.2   Sample size for longitudinal analyses

	Netherlands (SEP) Waves[a]	Valid household income	Germany (GSOEP) Waves	Valid household income	Great Britain (BHPS) Waves	Valid household income
Medium-term:						
five years	1985–90	7,470	1986–90	9,486	–	–
	1991–5	6,753	1992–6	12,713	1991–5	7,197
Long term:						
seven years	1988–95	5,722	1990–1996	7,830	1991–7	6,450
ten years	1985–95	3,636	1986–95	7,057	–	–

Note: a) Since 1990 income has been asked retrospectively for the year before interview.

Sources: SEP (1985–95); GSOEP (1986–96); BHPS (1991–7).

Appendix 3: Measuring Inequality

There are a great variety of analytical tools to describe the distribution of income, each of which measures different aspects of inequality. Some measurements are simply common sense, while others rest on complex mathematical constructions. An overview of inequality indices can be found in Coulter (1989) and Cowell (1995). In this study, we use a limited set of inequality indices to measure the degree of inequality of the income distribution in the Netherlands, Germany and Great Britain. The measurements applied are: the percentile ratio, the relative mean deviation, the Gini coefficient, the Theil coefficient and the Atkinson coefficient.

A simple measurement of inequality is the *P75/P25 percentile ratio*. It incorporates information on two particular points in income distribution by relating the income level at the top quarter of income distribution to that at the bottom quarter. Hence, it gives an easily interpretable measurement of the distance between the income of those at the top and those at the bottom of the income distribution.

The *relative mean deviation* (*M*) is the average absolute distance separating one's income from the mean. For a population n with an income distribution vector y ($y_1 \leq y_2 \leq \ldots \leq y_n$) where y_i is the adult equivalent income of the ith recipient ($i = 1, \ldots n$) and μ the average income, M is defined as follows:

$$M(y;n) = \frac{1}{2n\mu} \sum_{i=1}^{n} |y_i - \mu|.$$

Defined as such, the relative mean deviation can be interpreted as the percentage of the income of the rich (income above the mean) that should be redistributed to the poor (income below average) in order to get an equal distribution of income (everyone with an average income). Hence, this measure is also referred to as the *Robin Hood* indicator of inequality.

Another well-known summary index of inequality used in this study is the *Gini coefficient*. The Gini coefficient can be directly derived from the Lorenz curve, which represents the income share enjoyed by the p percentage of the population with the lowest income. Given the same notations as above, the Gini coefficient (*G*) can be computed as follows:

$$G(y;n) = \frac{1}{2n^2\mu} \sum_{i=1}^{n} \sum_{j=1}^{n} |y_i - y_j|.$$

Unlike the relative mean deviation, Gini does not view inequality in terms of deviations from a central measurement of income (such as the mean), but takes the differences between all pairs of income.

Inequality is also computed using the *Theil coefficient*, an index from the generalised entropy family (see Cowell, 1995). Using the notations introduced earlier, the Theil coefficient (*T*) can be computed according to the following formula:

$$T(y;n) = \frac{1}{n} \sum_{i=1}^{n} \frac{y_i}{\mu} \ln \frac{y_i}{\mu}.$$

Generalised entropy indices share a number of interesting properties, one of them being that they are additively decomposable by subgroups. Subgroup decomposability implies that total inequality can be decomposed into 'within-group' and 'between-group' inequality (Shorrocks, 1980):

$$T(y;n) = \sum_{k=1}^{K} \frac{n_k \mu_k}{n\mu} T(y_k;n_k) + \sum_{k=1}^{K} \frac{n_k \mu_k}{n\mu} \ln \frac{\mu_k}{\mu}.$$

The second term measures between-group inequality and $T(y_k;n_k)$ stands for within-group inequality. The first term then represents the weighted sum of within-group inequality with:

$$T(y_k;n_k) = \sum_{i=1}^{n_k} \frac{y_{i,k}}{n_k \mu_k} \ln \frac{y_{i,k}}{\mu_k},$$

where k is the subgroup number ($k = 1, \ldots, K$), n_k the number of individuals in subgroup k, $y_{i,k}$ the equivalent income of the ith person in group k, μ the average income and μ_k the average income in group k.

For all these inequality measurements, it holds that the higher the value, the higher the level of inequality. Although they all have a minimum value of 0, *P75/P25* has no maximum value, $T(y;n)$ has a maximal value of $ln(n)$ and $G(y;n)$ and $M(y;n)$ both a maximal value of 1.

Appendix 4: Model for Poverty Profiles

The model used to estimate the probability of being in one of the poverty profiles is the multinomial logit model. The model estimated distinguishes four poverty states – never poor, transient poor, recurrent poor and persistent poor – where the 'never poor' act as the reference category. The probability of being in either state, as compared to the reference state, is given by the following equation:

$$P(y = j) = \frac{\exp\left(\sum_{k=1}^{K} \beta_{jk} x_k\right)}{1 + \sum_{j=1}^{J-1} \exp\left(\sum_{k=1}^{K} \beta_{jk} x_k\right)},$$

with $J = 4$ (so $j = 0, 1, 2, 3$), $j = 0$ being the reference state and K the number of explanatory variables x. In order to gain a better understanding of the labour market events associated with poverty spells, the analysis was limited to individuals living in a household where both the head and the partner – if any – are of prime working age (aged 25–59). Hence, the results in the remainder of this section are concerned with those who fit the above conditions. As in the previous models, we report the estimated coefficients from the models. Positive (negative) coefficients represent an increased (decreased) risk compared to the reference category. The results are given in Tables A.4.1–A.4.3 for the Netherlands, Germany and Great Britain, respectively.

Some of the variables included in the model indicate the status of the household or household head at one point in time while others indicate changes of that status. Changes in the variables are measured between the beginning and the end of the observation period. In Fouarge and Layte (2003) we improved this procedure by looking at individual, household and labour market characteristics prior to the start of a poverty profile and by assessing the impact of life events occurring in the period just before the beginning to the end of the poverty spell.

Table A.4.1 Parameters for the probability of being in either of the four poverty profiles, the Netherlands, 1990–94

Reference state: Never poor	Transient poor	Recurrent poor	Persistent poor
Personal and household characteristics:			
Age of household head (ref: 45+)			
25–34	0.131	0.524*	−0.435
35–44	−0.363*	−0.337	−0.374
Female head of the household (ref: male)	0.871**	0.378	0.778
Number of adults (ref: two adults)			
One adult	0.255	0.003	−0.850
Three adults or more	1.067**	1.515**	0.766*
Number of children (ref: no child)			
One child	0.684**	0.653*	1.528**
Two children	1.247**	0.943**	1.855**
Three children	1.701**	1.679**	2.991**
Marital status of the household head (ref: married)			
Separated head	0.035	0.127	−0.626
Unmarried head	−0.010	0.441*	0.189
Single parent (ref: not single parent)	−0.261	−1.000*	−1.238
Socio-economic characteristics:			
Educational level of household head (ref: average educational level)			
Low educated head	0.674**	0.326	0.699*
High educated head	0.046	0.017	−0.157
Total hours worked by the household	−0.044**	−0.064**	−0.083**
Number of employed persons in the household			
	0.095	−0.606*	−0.037
Household head is out of employment (ref: employed head)			
	0.322	0.275	1.420**
Household formation events:			
Separation (ref: no change marital status)	2.242**	1.983**	1.912**
Labour market events:			
Change in number of hours worked by the household			
Fewer hours worked	1.162**	0.820*	1.728**
More hours worked	0.491*	0.150	−0.427
Change in number of employed persons in the household (ref: no change)			
Fewer employed in the household	0.770**	1.304**	0.482
More employed in household	−0.623**	−0.010	−0.866
Constant	−3.359**	−2.814**	−5.169**

Note: * significant at 5%; ** significant at 1%.

Source: SEP.

Table A.4.2   Parameters for the probability of being in either of the four poverty profiles, Germany, 1991–5

Reference state: Never poor	Transient poor	Recurrent poor	Persistent poor
Personal and household characteristics:			
Age of household head (ref: 45+)			
25–34	0.044	0.015	0.234
35–44	0.179	−0.177	−0.044
Female head of the household (ref: male)	−0.236*	0.216	0.766**
Number of adults (ref: two adults)			
One adult	0.097	0.644**	0.133
Three adults or more	0.360	1.399**	0.798**
Number of children (ref: no child)			
One child	−0.108	0.420**	0.056
Two children	0.460**	0.273	0.378
Three children	0.340*	1.036**	0.307
Marital status of the household head (ref: married)			
Separated head	0.775**	−0.248	−0.347
Unmarried head	0.864**	1.081**	0.492*
Single parent (ref: not single parent)	1.102**	2.063**	1.287**
Socio-economic characteristics:			
Educational level of household head (ref: average educational level)			
Low educated head	−0.185	0.161	−0.258
High educated head	−0.947**	−0.458**	−1.515**
Total hours worked by the household	−0.016**	−0.029**	−0.022**
Number of employed persons in the household			
	−0.250*	−0.894**	−2.062**
Household head is out of employment (ref: employed head)			
	0.634**	0.400*	0.271
Household formation events:			
Separation (ref: no change marital status)	1.299**	1.408**	1.273**
Labour market events:			
Change in number of hours worked by the household			
Fewer hours worked	0.031	0.136	0.932**
More hours worked	0.264	−0.521**	0.235
Change in number of employed persons in the household (ref: no change)			
Fewer employed in the household	1.445**	1.507**	1.869**
More employed in household	−0.387**	−0.490*	−1.152**
Constant	−2.001**	−2.106**	−2.324**

Note: * significant at 5%; ** significant at 1%.

Source: GSOEP.

Table A.4.3   Parameters for the probability of being in either of the four poverty profiles, Great Britain, 1991–5

Reference state: Never poor	Transient poor	Recurrent poor	Persistent poor
Personal and household characteristics:			
Age of household head (ref: 45+)			
25–34	0.243	0.520**	0.818**
35–44	0.115	0.147	0.423
Female head of the household (ref: male)	−0.274	−0.213	0.170
Number of adults (ref: two adults)			
One adult	−0.161	0.016	−0.489
Three adults or more	1.003**	1.294**	2.253**
Number of children (ref: no child)			
One child	0.692**	1.167**	−0.349
Two children	0.867**	1.667**	1.220**
Three children	1.321**	2.211**	2.327**
Marital status of the household head (ref: married)			
Separated head	1.078**	0.865**	1.259**
Unmarried head	0.612**	0.703**	0.791**
Single parent (ref: not single parent)	0.198	0.384	0.829*
Socio-economic characteristics:			
Educational level of household head (ref: average educational level)			
Low educated head	0.475**	0.550**	1.301**
High educated head	−0.497*	−0.064	0.168
Total hours worked by the household	−0.013**	−0.003	−0.011
Number of employed persons in the household			
	−0.686**	−1.891**	−2.192**
Household head is out of employment (ref: employed head)			
	0.352*	0.571**	0.098
Household formation events:			
Separation (ref: no change marital status)	1.071**	1.001**	0.836**
Labour market events:			
Change in number of hours worked by the household			
Fewer hours worked	0.547*	0.897**	0.658*
More hours worked	0.488*	0.930**	−0.069
Change in number of employed persons in the household (ref: no change)			
Fewer employed in the household	1.395**	2.094**	2.149**
More employed in household	−0.010	−0.747**	−0.358
Constant	−2.436**	−2.914**	−3.781**

Note: * significant at 5%; ** significant at 1%.

Source: BHPS.

References

Abramovici, G. (2003), 'The social protection in Europe', *Statistics in Focus: Population and Social Condition*, 2003-3.

Acemoglu, D. and J.-S. Pischke (1998), Beyond Becker: training in imperfect labor markets, Cambridge: NBER Working Paper No. 6740.

Adema, W. (2001), Net social expenditure, 2nd edition, Paris: OECD Labour Market and Social Policy Occasional Paper No. 52.

Alonso, J., M.-A. Galindo and S. Sosvilla-Rivero (1998), 'Convergence of social protection benefits across EU countries', *Applied Economic Letters*, 5, 153–5.

Altonji, J. (1986), 'Intertemporal substitution in labor supply: evidence from micro data', *Journal of Political Economy*, 94 (2), S176–S215.

Andersen, T. (2002), 'International integration, risk and the welfare state', *Scandinavian Journal of Economics*, 104 (2), 343–64.

Andersen, T. (2003), 'European integration and the welfare state', *Journal of Population Economics*, 16, 1–19.

Aoki, M. (1990), 'Towards an economic model of the Japanese firm', *Journal of Economic Literature*, 28 (1), 1–27.

Arents, M., M. Cluitmans and M. Pepping (2001), Marktwerking en vernieuwing in het activeringsbeleid: Buitenlandse lessen voor Nederland, Den-Haag: Servicecentrum Uitgevers, OSA-publicatie A180.

Arjona, R., M. Ladaique and M. Pearson (2001), Growth, inequality and social protection, Paris: OECD Labour Market and Social Policy Occasional Paper No. 51.

Arrow, K. (1972), 'Gifts and exchanges', *Philosophy and Public Affairs*, 1, 343–62.

Arts, W. and J. Gelissen (2001), 'Welfare states, solidarity and justice principles: does the type really matter?', *Acta Sociologica*, 44 (4), 283–300.

Atkinson, A. (1989), *Poverty and Social Security*, London: Harvester Wheatsheaf.

Atkinson, A. (1995), *Incomes and the Welfare State*, Cambridge: Cambridge University Press.

Atkinson, A. (1996), 'Growth and the welfare state', *New Economy*, 3 (3), 182–6.

Atkinson, A. (1999), *The Economic Consequences of Rolling Back the Welfare State*, Cambridge: The MIT Press.

Atkinson, A. and G. Mogensen (1993), *Welfare and Work Incentives: A North European Perspective*, Oxford: Oxford University Press.

Atkinson, A. and J. Stiglitz (1980), *Lectures on Public Economics*, London: McGraw-Hill.

Atkinson, A., F. Bourguignon and C. Morrisson (1992), *Empirical Studies of Earnings Mobility*, London: Harwood.

Atkinson, A., L. Rainwater and T. Smeeding (1995), Income distribution in advanced economies: the evidence from the Luxembourg Income Study (LIS), Luxembourg: LIS Working Paper Series, Working Paper No. 120.

Atkinson A., B. Cantillon, E. Marlier and B. Nolan (2002), *Indicators for Social Inclusion in the European Union*, Oxford: Oxford University Press.

Atkinson A., E. Marlier and B. Nolan (2003), Indicators and targets for social inclusion in the European Union, Dublin: ESRI Working Paper No. 151.

Autor, D., L. Katz and A. Krueger (1998), 'Computing inequality: have computers changed the labour market?', *The Quarterly Journal of Economics*, **113** (4), 1169–213.

Bane, M. and D. Ellwood (1986), 'Slipping into and out of poverty: the dynamics of spells', *Journal of Human Resources*, **21** (1), 1–23.

Bardasi, E., S. Jenkins and J. Rigg (1999), Derived current and annual net household income variables, BHPS waves 1–7, University of Essex: Institute for Social Economic Research.

Barr, N. (1987), *The Economics of the Welfare State*, London: Weidenfeld & Nicolson.

Barr, N. (1989), 'Social insurance as an efficiency device', *Journal of Public Policy*, **9** (1), 59–82.

Barr, N. (1992), 'Economic theory and the welfare state: a survey and interpretation', *Journal of Economic Literature*, **30** (2), 741–803.

Barro, R. and X. Sala-i-Martin (1995), *Economic Growth*, New York: Mc Graw-Hill.

Bayoumi, T. and P. Masson (1995), 'Fiscal flows in the United States and Canada: lessons for monetary union in Europe', *European Economic Review*, **39** (2), 253–74.

Becker, G. (1981), 'Altruism, egoism, and genetic fitness: economics and sociobiology', *Journal of Economic Literature*, **14** (3), 817–26.

Beckerman, W. (1979), 'The impact of income maintenance payments on poverty in Britain, 1975', *The Economic Journal*, **89**, 261–79.

Beer, P. de (2001), *Over Werken in de Postindustriële Samenleving*, Den Haag: Sociaal en Cultureel Planbureau.

Begg, I. and J. Berghman (2001), 'The future role of the EU in dealing with social exclusion: policy perspectives', in D. Mayes, J. Berghman and R.

Salais (eds), *Social Exclusion and European Policy*, Cheltenham, UK and Northampton, MA, USA: Edward Elgar, pp. 306–26.

Begg, I. and F. Nectoux (1995), 'Social protection and economic union', *Journal of European Social Policy*, 5 (4), 285–302.

Bekkers, V., H. van den Hurk and G. Leenknegt (1995), *Subsidiariteit en Europese Integratie*, Zwolle: Tjeenk Willink.

Berghman, J. (1995). 'Social exclusion in Europe: policy context and analytical framework', in G. Room (ed.), *Beyond the Threshold: The Measurement and Analysis of Social Exclusion*, Bristol: The Policy Press, pp. 19–28.

Beugelsdijk, S. and A. van Schaik (2001), Social capital and regional economic growth, Tilburg University: CentER Discussion Paper No. 2001-102.

Beugelsdijk, S., H. de Groot and A. van Schaik (2002), Trust and economic growth, Rotterdam University: Tinbergen Institute Discussion Paper No. TI2002-049/3.

Bird, E. (2001), 'Does the welfare state induce risk-taking?', *Journal of Public Economics*, 80 (3), 357–83.

Blank, R. (1994), *Social Protection Versus Economic Flexibility*, Chicago: University of Chicago Press.

Blundel, R. and A. Lewbel (1991), 'The information content of equivalence scales', *Journal of Econometrics*, 50 (1–2), 49–68.

Boadway, R. and D. Wildasin (1984), *Public Sector Economics*, Boston: Little, Brown & Company.

Böheim, R. and M. Taylor (2000), The search for success: do the unemployed find stable employment?, University of Essex: ISER Working Paper No. 2000-5.

Bonoli, G. (1997), 'Classifying welfare states: a two dimension approach', *Journal of Social Policy*, 26 (3), 351–72.

Borjas, G. (1998), Immigration and welfare magnets, Cambridge: NBER Working Paper No. 6813.

Bouget, D. (1998), 'The Juppé Plan and the future of the French social welfare system', *Journal of European Social Policy*, 8 (2), 155–72.

Bradbury, B., S. Jenkins and J. Micklewright (2001), *The Dynamics of Child Poverty in Industrialised Countries*, Cambridge: Cambridge University Press.

Broekman, P., W. van Vliet, R. de Mooij and H. Vollebergh (2001), 'Evaluatie venootschapsbelasting', *Economisch Statistisch Berichten*, 4294, 130–32.

Brown, C. and W. Oates (1987), 'Assistance to the poor in a federal system', *Journal of Public Economics*, 32 (3), 307–30.

Buchanan, J. (1950), 'Federalism and fiscal equity', *American Economic*

Review, **40** (4), 583–99.

Buhmann, B., L. Rainwater, G. Schmaus and T. Smeeding (1988), 'Equivalence scales, well-being, inequality, and poverty: sensitivity estimates across ten countries using the Luxembourg Income Study (LIS) database', *Review of Income and Wealth* **34**, 115–42.

Burkhauser, R., B. Butrica and M. Daly (1999), 'The PSID–GSOEP equivalent file: a product of cross-national research', in W. Voges (ed.), *Dynamic Approaches to Comparative Social Research: Recent Developments and Applications*, Aldershot: Ashgate, pp. 53–66.

Callan, T., B. Nolan, C. Whelan and J. Williams (1996), *Poverty in the 1990s: Evidence from the 1994 Living in Ireland Survey*, Dublin: Oak Tree Press.

Cantillon, B., I. Marx and K. Van den Bosch (1996), Armoede, arbeidsmarkt en sociale zekerheid in de landen van de OESO, Antwerp: Centre for Social Policy.

Cantillon, B., I. Marx and K. Van den Bosch (2002), The puzzle of egalitarianism: about the relationships between employment, wage inequality, social expenditures and poverty, Antwerp: Centre for Social Policy.

Cappellari, L. and S. Jenkins (2002), 'Who stays poor? Who becomes poor? Evidence from the British Household Panel Survey', *The Economic Journal*, **112**, c60–c67.

Card, D. and A. Krueger (1995), *Myth and Measurement: The New Economics of the Minimum Wage*, Princeton: Princeton University Press.

CBS (1991), *Sociaal-economisch panelonderzoek: inhoud, opzet en organisatie*, Voorburg/Heerlen: Centraal Bureau voor de Statistiek.

Chassard, Y. (2001), 'European integration and social protection: from the Spaak report to the open method of co-ordination', in D. Mayes, J. Berghman and R. Salais (eds), *Social Exclusion and European Policy*, Cheltenham, UK and Northampton, MA, USA: Edward Elgar, pp. 277–305.

Chassard, Y. and O. Quintin (1993), 'Towards a convergence of policies', in J. Berghman and B. Cantillon (eds), *The European Face of Social Security*, Aldershot: Avebury, pp. 337–55.

Chiu, W. (1998), 'Income inequality, human capital accumulation and economic performance', *The Economic Journal*, **108**, 44–59.

Coleman, J. (1986), *Individual Interests and Collective Action*, Cambridge: Cambridge University Press.

Coote, N. (1989), 'Catholic social teaching', *Social Policy and Administration*, **23** (2), 150–60.

Cornelisse, P. and K. Goudswaard (2001), On the convergence of social protection systems in the European Union, Leiden University: Department of Economic Research Memorandum 2001.02.

Coulter, P. (1989), *Measuring Inequality: A Methodological Handbook*,

Boulder: Westview Press.

Coulter, F., F. Cowell and S. Jenkins (1992), 'Equivalence scale relativities and the extent of inequality and poverty', *The Economic Journal*, **102**, 1067–82.

Cowell F. (1995), *Measuring Inequality*, London: Harvester Wheatsheaf.

Creedy, J. (1996), *Fiscal Policy and Social Welfare: An Analysis of Alternative Tax and Transfer Systems*, Cheltenham, UK and Brookfield, USA: Edward Elgar.

Cremer, H. and P. Pestieau (1996), 'Distributive implications of European integration', *European Economic Review*, **40**, 747–57.

Cremer, H., V. Fourgeaud, M. Leite Monteiro, M. Marchand and P. Pestieau (1995), Mobility and redistribution: a survey, Université Catholique de Louvain: CORE Discussion Paper No. 9566.

Deleeck, H., K. Van den Bosch and L. De Lathouwer (1992), *Poverty and the Adequacy of Social Security in the EC*, Aldershot: Avebury.

Desai, M. (1990), *Poverty and Capability: Towards an Empirically Implementable Measure*, London School of Economics: Development Economics Programme.

Dirven, H.-J. and J. Berghman (1991), Poverty, insecurity of subsistence and relative deprivation in the Netherlands: report 1991, Tilburg University: Department of Social Security Studies, Report No. 16.

Dirven, H.-J. and D. Fouarge (1996), Income mobility and deprivation dynamics among the elderly in Belgium and the Netherlands, Tilburg University: WORC Paper No. 96.05.005/2.

Dirven, H.-J. and D. Fouarge (1998), 'Impoverishment and social exclusion: a dynamic perspective on income and relative deprivation in Belgium and the Netherlands', in H.-J. Andress (ed.), *Empirical Poverty Research in a Comparative Perspective*, Aldershot: Ashgate, pp. 257–81.

Dirven, H.-J., D. Fouarge and R. Muffels (1998), 'Poverty in the Netherlands', in J. Dixon and D. Macarov (eds), *Poverty: A Persistent Global Reality*, London: Routledge, pp. 136–70.

Dowrick, S. and J. Quinggin (1994), 'International comparisons of living standards and tastes: a revealed-preference analysis', *The American Economic Review*, **84** (1), 332–41.

Duncan, G. and M. Hill (1985), 'Conceptions of longitudinal households: fertile or futile?', *Journal of Economic and Social Measurement*, **13**, 361–75.

Duncan, G. and W. Rodgers (1991), 'Has children's poverty become more persistent?', *American Sociological Review*, **56**, 538–50.

Duncan, G., B. Gustafsson, R. Hauser, G. Schmauss, H. Messinger, R. Muffels, B. Nolan and J.-C. Ray (1993), 'Poverty dynamics in eight countries', *Journal of Population Economics*, **6** (3), 215–34.

Eijsbouts, W. (1991), 'Soevereiniteit en subsidiariteit', *Theoretische Geschiedenis*, **18** (4), 479–91.

Esping-Andersen, G. (1990), *The Three Worlds of Welfare Capitalism*, Cambridge: Polity Press.

Esping-Andersen, G. (1996), *Welfare States in Transition: National Adaptations in Global Economies*, London: Sage.

Esping-Andersen, G. (1999), *Social Foundations of Post-industrial Economics*, Oxford: Oxford University Press.

European Commission (1997), Modernising and improving social protection in the European Union, COM(97) 102, Brussels: European Commission.

European Commission (1998), On the implementation of the Recommendation 92/441/EEC of 24 June 1992 on common criteria concerning sufficient resources and social assistance in social protection schemes, COM(98) 774 final, Brussels: European Commission.

European Commission (1999), A concerted strategy for modernising social protection, COM(99) 347 final, Brussels: European Commission.

European Commission (2000a), Social policy agenda, COM(2000) 379 final, Brussels: European Commission.

European Commission (2000b), Building an inclusive Europe, COM(2000) 79, Brussels: European Commission.

European Commission (2000c), Structural indicators, COM(2000) 594 final, Brussels: European Commission.

European Commission (2000d), *The Budget of the European Union: How is your Money Spent?*, Luxembourg: Office for Official Publications of the European Communities.

European Commission (2002a), *Joint Report on Social Inclusion*, Luxembourg: Office for Official Publications of the European Communities.

European Commission (2002b), *Industrial Relations in Europe 2002*, Luxembourg: Office for Official Publications of the European Communities.

European Commission (2003), Mid-term review of the social policy agenda, COM(2003) 312 final, Brussels: European Commission.

European Council (2000a), Presidency conclusions, Lisbon European Council, 23–24 March 2000.

European Council (2000b), Presidency conclusions, Santa Maria da Feira European Council, 19–20 June 2000.

European Council (2000c), Presidency conclusions, Nice European Council, 7–9 December 2000.

Eurostat (1996), *European Community Houshold Panel (ECHP): Methods*, vol. I, Luxembourg: Office for Official Publications of the European Communities.

Eurostat (1997), 'Income distribution and poverty in EU12-1993', *Statistics in Focus: Population and Social Condition*, 1997-6.

Eurostat (1998), 'Analysis of income distribution in 13 EU Member States', *Statistics in Focus. Population and Social Condition*, 1998-11.

Eurostat (2000a), *The Social Situation of the European Union 2000*, Luxembourg: Office for Official Publications of the European Communities.

Eurostat (2000b), *European Social Statistics: Income, Poverty and Social Exclusion*, Luxembourg: Office for Official Publications of the European Communities.

Eurostat (2000c), *Eurostat 2000 Yearbook: A Statistical Eye on Europe*, Luxembourg: Office for Official Publications of the European Communities.

Eurostat (2001), *The Social Situation of the European Union 2001*, Luxembourg: Office for Official Publications of the European Communities.

Ferrera, M. (1996), 'The "southern model" of welfare in social Europe', *Journal of European Social Policy*, **6** (1), 17–37.

Ferrera, M., A. Hemerijck and M. Rhodes (2000), The future of social Europe: Recasting work and welfare in the new economy, report for the Portugese presidency of the European Union, Lisbon.

Filer, R., D. Hamermesh and A. Rees (1996), *The Economics of Work and Pay*, New York: HarperCollins College Publishers.

Føllesdal, A. (1998), 'Survey article: subsidiarity', *Journal of Political Philosophy*, **6** (2), 190–218.

Foster, J., J. Greer and E. Thorbecke (1984), 'A class of decomposable poverty measures', *Econometrica*, **52** (3), 761–66.

Fouarge, D. (2002), *Minimum Protection and Poverty in Europe: An Economic Analysis of the Subsidiarity Principle within EU Social Policy*, Amsterdam: Thela Thesis.

Fouarge, D. (2003), Costs of non-social policy: towards an economic framework of quality social policies – and the costs of not having them, report for the Employment and Social Affairs DG.

Fouarge, D. and H.-J. Dirven (1995), 'Income dynamics among the elderly: results of an international comparative study', in *Actes des quinzièmes Journées de l'Association d'Economie Sociale*, vol. I, Nancy: Berger-Levrault GTI, pp. 409–29.

Fouarge, D. and M. Kerkhofs (2000), 'Krappe markt remt flexibilisering', *Economisch Statistische Berichten*, **4240**, 80–82.

Fouarge, D. and R. Layte (2003), Duration of poverty spells in Europe, University of Essex: EPAG-Working Paper No. 2003-47.

Fouarge, D. and R. Muffels (2000), Persistent poverty in the Netherlands,

Germany and the UK: a model-based approach using panel data for the 1990s, University of Essex: EPAG Working Paper No. 2000-15.

Frank, R. (1987), 'If *Homo Economicus* could choose his own utility function, would he want one with a conscience?', *American Economic Review*, **77** (4), 593–604.

Fuente, A. de la and A. Ciccone (2002), Human capital in a global and knowledge-based economy, report at the demand of the Employment and Social Affairs DG.

Gabszewicz, J. and T. van Ypersele (1996), 'Social protection and political competition', *Journal of Public Economics*, **61**, 193–208.

Geelhoed, L. (1991), 'Het subsidiariteitsbeginsel: een communautair principe?', *Sociaal-Economische Wetgeving*, **7/8**, 422–35.

Gelauff, G. and J. Graafland (1994), *Modelling Welfare State Reform*, Amsterdam: North-Holland.

Gelissen, J. (2002), *Worlds of Welfare, Worlds of Consent? Public Opinion on the Welfare State*, Leiden: Brill Academic Publisher.

Gerven, W. van (1992), 'De beginselen subsidiariteit, evenredigheid en samenwerking in het europese gemeenschapsrecht', *Rechtskundig Weekblad* **36**, 1241–6.

Giscard d'Estaing, V. (1990), Report of the committee of institutional affairs on the principle of subsidiarity, A3-0267/90.

Goedhart, T., V. Halberstadt, A. Kapteyn and B. Van Praag (1977), 'The poverty line: concept and measurement', *The Journal of Human Resources*, **12** (4), 503–20.

Goodin, R.E., B. Headey, R. Muffels and H.-J. Dirven (1999), *The Real Worlds of Welfare Capitalism*, Cambridge: Cambridge University Press.

Gottschalk, P. and T. Smeeding (1997), 'Cross-national comparisons of earnings and income inequality', *Journal of Economic Literature*, **35**, 633–87.

Gourinchas, P. (1997), 'Federal transfers, decentralization and the labor market', *Annales d'Economie et de Statistique*, **45**, 251–74.

Gouyette, C. and P. Pestieau (1999), 'Efficiency of the welfare state', *Kyklos*, **52** (4), 537–53.

Greve, B. (1996), 'Indications of social policy convergence in Europe', *Social Policy and Administration*, **30** (4), 348–67.

Gustafsson, B. and M. Lindblom (1993), 'Poverty lines and poverty in seven European countries, Australia, Canada and the USA', *Journal of European Social Policy*, **3** (1), 21–42.

Hagenaars, A., K. de Vos and M. Zaidi (1994), *Poverty Statistics in the Late 1980s: Research Based on Micro-data*, Luxembourg: Office for Official Publications of the European Communities.

Halleröd, B. (1998), 'Poor Swedes, poor Britons: a comparative analysis of relative deprivation', in H.-J. Andress (ed.), *Empirical Poverty Research in a Comparative Perspective*, Aldershot: Ashgate, pp. 283–311.

Headey, B., R. Goodin, R. Muffels and H.-J. Dirven (1997), 'Welfare over time: three worlds of welfare capitalism in panel perspective', *Journal of Public Policy*, **17**, 329–59.

Headey, B., R. Muffels, R. Goodin and H.-J. Dirven (2000), 'Is there a trade-off between economic efficiency and a generous welfare state? A comparison of best cases of "the three worlds of welfare capitalism"', *Journal of Social Indicators Research*, **50** (2), 115–57.

Hirsch Ballin, E. and R. Steenvoorde (2000), Catholic social thought on citizenship: no place for exclusion, paper presented at the 12th Annual Meeting on Socio-economics, LSE, 1–10 July 2000, London.

Hochman, H. and J. Rodgers (1969), 'Pareto optimal redistribution', *The American Economic Review*, **59** (4), 542–57.

Hodson, D. (2001), 'Social inclusion through social partnerships: the case of Ireland', in D. Mayes, J. Berghman and R. Salais (eds), *Social Exclusion and European Policy*, Cheltenham, UK and Northampton, MA, USA: Edward Elgar, pp. 170–87.

Hoffman, M. (1981), 'Is altruism part of human nature', *Journal of Personality and Social Psychology*, **40** (1), 121–37.

Immervoll, H., C. O'Donoghue and H. Sutherland (1999), An introduction to EUROMOD, University of Cambridge: EUROMOD Working Paper No. EM0/99.

Jäntti, M. and S. Danzinger (2000), 'Income poverty in advanced countries', in A. Atkinson and F. Bourguignon (eds), *Handbook of Income Distribution*, vol. I, Amsterdam: Elsevier, pp. 309–78.

Jaspers, T., D. Siegers and S. Vansteenkiste (2002), Subsidiariteit en Minimumbescherming, Universiteit Utrecht: AWSB Onderzoeksrapport.

Jehoel-Gijsbers, G., H. Scholten and A. Vissers (1995), Sociale zekerheid en arbeidsparticipatie: inventarisatie en evaluatie van Nederlands empirish onderzoek, OSA-werkdocument W126, Den-Haag: Sdu DOP.

Jenkins, S. (2000), 'Modelling household income dynamics', *Journal of Population Economics*, **13** (4), 529–67.

Jordan, B. (1996), *A Theory of Poverty and Social Exclusion*, Cambridge: Polity Press.

Kakwani, N. (1986), *Analysing Redistribution Policies*, Cambridge: Cambridge University Press.

Kapteyn, A. and B. Van Praag (1976), 'A new approach to the construction of family equivalence scales', *European Economic Review*, **7**, 313–35.

Kapteyn, A., P. Kooreman and R. Willemse (1985), 'Some methodological issues in the implementation of subjective poverty definitions', *The Journal of Human Resources*, **23** (2), 222–42.

Kennedy, B., I. Kawachi, D. Prothrow-Stith, K. Lochner and V. Gupta (1998), 'Social capital, income inequality, and firearm violent crime', *Social Science and Medecine*, **47**, 7–17.

Kersbergen, K. van (1995), *Social Capitalism: A Study of Christian Democracy and the Welfare State*, London: Routledge.

Kleinman, M. and D. Piachaud (1993), 'European social policy: conceptions and choices', *Journal of European Social Policy*, **3** (1), 1–19.

Knack, S. and P. Keefer (1997), 'Does social capital have an economic payoff? A cross-country investigation', *The Quarterly Journal of Economics*, **112** (4), 1251–88.

Krueger, A. (2000), 'From Bismark to Maastricht: the march to European Union and the labour compact', *Labour Economics*, **7** (2), 117–34.

Kuyper, A. (1880), Souvereiniteit in eigen kring, Rede ter inwijding van de Vrije Universiteit. Amsterdam: Kruyt.

Layte, R. and T. Callan (2001), 'Unemployment, welfare benefits and the financial incentive to work', *The Economic and Social Review*, **32** (2), 103–29.

Layte, R., C. Whelan, B. Maître and B. Nolan (2001), 'Explaining levels of deprivation in the European Union', *Acta Sociologica*, **44** (2), 105–22.

Lee, K. (1998), 'Uncertain income and redistribution in a federal system', *Journal of Public Economics*, **69** (3), 413–33.

Le Grand, J. (1990), 'Equity versus efficiency: the elusive trade-off', *Ethics*, **100** (3), 554–68.

Leibfried, S. (1992), 'Towards a European welfare state? On integrating poverty regimes into the European Community', in Z. Ferge and J. Kolberg (eds), *Social Policy in a Changing Europe*, Frankfurt am Main: Campus Verlag, pp. 245–79.

Lejour, A. (1995), Integrating and desintegrating welfare states? A qualitative study to the consequences of economic integration on social insurance, Tilburg University: Centre for Economic Research, Dissertation Series.

Lejour, A., R. de Moij and R. Nahuis (2001), EU enlargement: economic implications for countries and industries, Den Haag: CPB Document No. 011.

Lemmens, R. (1992), The socio-economic panel survey: content, design and organisation, Eurostat seminar 'Training of European Statisticians', 9–19 June 1992, Berlin.

Lenaerts, K. and P. van Ypersele (1994), 'Le principe de subsidiarité et son contexte: étude de l'article 3b du traité CE', *Cahiers de Droit Européen*, **1–2**, 3–85.

Leo XIII (1891), *Rerum Novarum*, Internet source: http://www.vatican.va /holy_father/leo_xiii/encyclicals/documents/hf_lxiii_enc_15051891_rerum -novarum_en.html

Lillard, L. and R. Willis (1978), 'Dynamic aspects of earnings mobility', *Econometrica*, **46** (5), 985–1012.

MacGillivray, A., S. Lingayah and S. Zadek (1996), Social protection as a productive factor: exploiting new accounting frameworks and new techniques of measurement, New Economics Foundation.

MaCurdy, T. (1981), 'An empirical model of labor supply in a life-cycle setting', *Journal of Political Economy*, **89** (6), 1059–85.

Madsen, P., P. Munch-Madsen and K. Langhoff-Roos (2002), 'Employment policies and social exclusion: an analysis of the performance of European employment regimes', in R. Muffels, P. Tsakloglou and D. Mayes (eds), *Social Exclusion in European Welfare States*, Cheltenham, UK and Northampton, MA, USA: Edward Elgar, pp. 235–63.

Maître, B. and B. Nolan (1999), Income mobility in the European Community Household Paney Survey, University of Essex: EPAG Working Paper No. 4.

Matsaganis, M. and P. Tsakloglou (2001), 'Social exclusion and social policy in Greece', in D. Mayes, J. Berghman and R. Salais (eds), *Social Exclusion and European Policy*, Cheltenham: Edward Elgar, pp. 188–203.

Mayes, D. and M. Virén (2002), 'Macro-economic factors and policies and the development of social exclusion', in R. Muffels, P. Tsakloglou and D. Mayes (eds), *Social Exclusion in European Welfare States*, Cheltenham, UK and Northampton, MA, USA: Edward Elgar, pp. 21–50.

Mejer, L. and G. Linden (2000), 'Persistent income poverty and social exclusion in the European Union', *Statistics in Focus: Population and Living Conditions*, 2000-13.

Millon-Delsol, C. (1990), 'Le principe de subsidiarité: origines et fondements', *Cahiers de l'Institut la Boétie*, **4**, 4–11.

Millon-Delsol, C. (1992), *L'État Subsidiaire. Ingérence et Non Ingérence de l'État: Le Principe de Subsidiarité aux Fondements de l'Histoire Européenne*, Paris: Presses Universitaires de France.

Ministry of Social Affairs (1996), De Nederlandse verzorgingsstaat in internationaal en economisch perspectief, The Hague: Sdu Uitgevers.

Mitchell, D. (1991), *Income Transfers in Ten Welfare States*, Aldershot: Avebury.

Mitchell, O. (1998), 'Administrative costs in public and private retirement systems', in M. Feldstein (ed.), *Privatizing Social Security*, Chicago: University of Chicago Press, pp. 403–56.

Moffit, R. (1992), 'Incentive effects of the U.S. welfare system: a review', *Journal of Economic Literature*, **30**, 1–61.

Mooij, R. de (2000), 'Internationalisering en Europese integratie', in CPB/SCP, Trends, dilemma's en beleid: essays over ontwikkeling op langere termijn, Den Haag: Centraal Planbureau.

Poverty and Subsidiarity in Europe

238   *Poverty and Subsidiarity in Europe*

238

Poverty and Subsidiarity in Europe

238 Poverty and Subsidiarity in Europe

238 Poverty and Subsidiarity in Europe

238   Poverty and Subsidiarity in Europe

Muffels, R. (1993), Welfare economic effects of social security. Essays on poverty, social security and labor markets: evidence from panel data, Tilburg University: Series on Social Security Studies, Report No. 21.

Muffels, R. and D. Fouarge (2001), 'Social exclusion and poverty: definition, public debate and empirical evidence in the Netherlands', in D. Mayes, J. Berghman and R. Salais (eds), *Social Exclusion and European Policy*, Cheltenham, UK and Northampton, MA, USA: Edward Elgar, pp. 93–123.

Muffels, R. and D. Fouarge (2002a), 'Do European welfare regimes matter in explaining social exclusion?', in R. Muffels, P. Tsakloglou and D. Mayes (eds), *Social Exclusion in European Welfare States*, Cheltenham, UK and Northampton, MA, USA: Edward Elgar, pp. 202–32.

Muffels, R. and D. Fouarge (2002b), 'Employment regimes and labour market attachment: evidence from the ECHP', in R. Muffels, P. Tsakloglou and D. Mayes (eds), *Social Exclusion in European Welfare States*, Cheltenham, UK and Northampton, MA, USA: Edward Elgar, pp. 51–77.

Muffels, R. and D. Fouarge (2002c), 'Woking profiles and employment regimes in Europe', *Journal of Applied Social Science Studies*, **122** (1), 85–110.

Muffels, R. and D. Fouarge (2004), 'The role of European welfare states in explaining resources deprivation', *Social Indicators Research*, **68** (3), 299–330.

Muffels, R., D. Fouarge and E. Snel (1999), 'Langdurige, hardnekkige armoede', *Economische Statistische Berichten*, **4199**, 296–8.

Muffels, R., E. Snel, D. Fouarge and S. Kariotys (1998), 'Armoedecarrières: dynamiek en determinanten van armoede', in G. Engbersen, J. Vrooman and E. Snel (eds), *Effecten van Armoede: Derde Jaarrapport Armoede en Sociale Uitsluiting*, Amsterdam: Amsterdam University Press, pp. 45–65.

Musgrave, R. (1959), *The Theory of Public Finance: A Study in Public Economy*, New York: McGraw-Hill.

Nord, M. (1998), 'Poor people on the move: county-to-county migration and the spatial concentration of poverty', *Journal of Regional Science*, **38** (2), 329–51.

Nozick, R. (1974), *Anarchy, State and Utopia*, Oxford: Blackwell.

Oates, W. (1972), *Fiscal Federalism*, New York: Harcourt Brace Jovanovich, Inc.

Oates, W. (2001), 'Fiscal competition and European Union: contrasting perspectives', *Regional Science and Urban Economics*, **31**, 133–45.

OECD (1994), *The tax/benefit position of production workers: Annual report 1990–1993*, Paris: Organisation for Economic Co-operation and Development.

OECD (1998), *Benefits systems and work incentives*, Paris: Organisation for

Economic Co-operation and Development.

OECD (1999), *Employment Outlook*, Paris: Organisation for Economic Co-operation and Development.

OECD (2000), *Employment Outlook*, Paris: Organisation for Economic Co-operation and Development.

OECD (2001), *Employment Outlook*, Paris: Organisation for Economic Co-operation and Development.

Okun, A. (1975), *Equality and Efficiency: the Big Trade-off*, Washington, DC: The Brookings Institution.

Oorschot, W. van and E. Smolenaars (1993), Local income assistance policies: the Dutch case and a European impression, Tilburg University: WORC Paper No. 93.07.011/2B.

O'Shea, E. (1996), 'The European principle of subsidiarity and Christian social doctrine', in J. Pacolet (ed.), *Social Protection and the European Economic and Monetary Union*, Aldershot: Avebury.

Pauly, M. (1973), 'Income redistribution as a local public good', *Journal of Public Economics*, **2**, 35–58.

Pedroso, P. (1997), 'Achieving integration of all within society', Bulletin Luxembourgeois des Questions Sociales. Report of the conference on Modernising and Improving Social Protection in Europe, pp. 59–61.

Pierson, C. (1998), *Beyond the Welfare State? The New Political Economy of Welfare*, Cambridge: Polity Press.

Pius XI (1931), *Quadragesimo Anno*, Internet source: http://www.vatican.-va/holy_father/pius_xi/encyclicals/documents/hf_pxi_enc_19310515_qua dragesimo-anno_en.html

Pollak, R. and T. Wales (1979), 'Welfare comparisons and equivalence scales', *American Economic Review*, **69**, 216–21.

Porte, C. de la and P. Pochet (2002), *Building Social Europe through the Open Method of Co-ordination*, Brussels: PIE Peter Lang.

Portes, A. (1998), 'Social capital: its origins and applications in modern sociology', *Annual Review of Sociology*, **24**, 1–24.

Putnam, R. (1993), *Making Democracy Work: Civic Tradition in Modern Italy*, Princeton, NJ: Princeton University Press.

Ranjault, P. (1992), 'On the principle of subsidiarity', *Journal of European Social Policy*, **1**, 49–52.

Ravallion, M. (2001), 'On assessing the efficiency of the welfare state: a comment', *Kyklos*, **54** (1), 115–24.

Raveaud, G. and R. Salais (2001), 'Fighting against social exclusion in a European knowledge-based society: what principles of action?', in D. Mayes, J. Berghman and R. Salais (eds), *Social Exclusion and European Policy*, Cheltenham, UK and Northampton, MA, USA: Edward Elgar, pp. 47–71.

Rawls, J. (1971), *A Theory of Justice*, Cambridge, MA: Belknap Press.

Recommandation du Conseil 92/441/CEE. Recommandation portant sur les critères communs relatifs à des ressources et prestations suffisantes dans les systémes de protection sociale. *Journal Officiel des Communautés Européennes*.

Recommandation du Conseil 92/442/CEE. Recommandation relative à la convergence des objectifs et politiques de protection sociale. *Journal Officiel des Communautés Européennes*.

Rendall, M. and A. Speare (1993), 'Comparing economic well-being among elderly Americans', *Review of Income and Wealth*, **39** (1), 1–21.

Riel, B. van (2001), 'Arbeidsmobiliteit in de EU, nu en straks', *Economisch Statistische Berichten*, **4301**, 276–8.

Ringen, S. (1988), 'Direct and indirect measures of poverty', *Journal of Social Policy*, **17** (3), 351–65.

Rodgers, J. and J. Rodgers (1993), 'Chronic poverty in the United States', *The Journal of Human Resources*, **28** (1), 25–54.

Rodrik, D. (1998), 'Why do more open economies have bigger governments?', *Journal of Political Economy*, **106** (5), 997–1032.

Rodrik, D. (1999), 'Where did all the growth go? External shocks, social conflict, and growth collapse', *Journal of Economic Growth*, **4** (4), 385–412.

Roebroek, J. (1993), The imprisoned state: the paradoxical relationship between state and society, Tilburg University: Department of Social Security Studies, Report No. 20.

Rubery, J., J. Humphries, C. Fagan, D. Grimshaw and M. Smith (1998), Equal opportunities as a productive factor, Report for Policy and Perspective group of DGV, European Commission.

Sala-i-Martin, X. and J. Sachs (1991), Fiscal federalism and optimum currency areas: evidence for Europe from the United States, Cambridge: NBER Working Paper No. 3855.

Schmid, G. (1998), Transitional labour markets: a new European employment strategy, Berlin: WZB Discussion Paper FS I 98-206.

Schokkaert, E. and Van Ootegem (1990), Sen's concept of the living standard applied to the Belgian unemployed, Louvain: CES, Recherches Economiques de Louvain.

Schwarze, J. (1996), 'How income inequality changed in Germany following reunification: an empirical analysis using decomposable inequality measures', *Review of Income and Wealth*, **42** (1), 1–11.

SCP (1996), *Sociaal en cultureel rapport 1996*, Rijswijk: Sociaal en Cultureel Planbureau.

SCP (1998), *Sociale en culturele verkenningen 1998*, Rijswijk: Sociaal en Cultureel Planbureau.

Sen, A. (1976), 'Poverty: an ordinal approach to measurement', *Econometrica*, **44** (2), 219–31.

Sen, A. (1979), 'Issues in the measurement of poverty', *Scandinavian Journal of Economics*, **81**, 285–307.

Sen, A. (1983), 'Poor relatively speaking', *Oxford Economic Papers*, **35**, 153–69.

Sen, A. (1985), *Commodities and Capabilities*, Amsterdam: North-Holland.

Sen, A. (1992), *Inequality Reexamined*, Oxford: Clarendon Press.

SER (2001), Arbeidsmobiliteit in de EU, Advies 01/04, Den Haag: Sociaal Economische Raad.

Shorrocks, A. (1980), 'The class of additively decomposable inequality measures', *Econometrica*, **48** (3), 613–25.

Sinn, H.-W. (1993), How much Europe? Subsidiarity, centralization and fiscal competition, London: Centre for Economic Policy Research, Discussion Paper Series No. 834.

Sinn, H.-W. (1995), 'A theory of the welfare state', *Scandinavian Journal of Economics*, **97** (4), 495–526.

Sinn, H.-W. (1996), 'Social insurance, incentives and risk taking', *International Tax and Public Finance*, **3**, 259–80.

Sinn, H.-W. (1997), 'The selection principle and market failure in systems competition', *Journal of Public Economics*, **66**, 247–74.

Smeeding, T., P. Saunders, J. Coder, S. Jenkins, J. Fritzell, A. Hagenaars and M. Wolfson (1993), 'Poverty, inequality and family living standards across seven nations: the effect of non-cash subsidies for health, education and housing', *Review of Income and Wealth*, **39**, 229–56.

Smeeding, T., M. O'Higgins and L. Rainwater (1990), *Poverty, Inequality and Income Distribution in Comparative Perspective*, London: Harvester Wheatsheaf.

Smit, L. (2001), 'Migratie is schijnantwoord', *Economisch Statistische Berichten*, **4300**, 256–8.

Smith, A. (1974), *The Theory of Moral Sentiments*, Oxford: Clarendon Press.

Smith, A. (1976), *An Inquiry into the Nature and Causes of the Wealth of Nations*, Oxford: Clarendon Press.

Snower, D. (1996), 'The low-skill, bad-job trap', in A. Booth and D. Snower (eds), *Acquiring Skills: Market Failures, their Symptoms and Policy Responses*, Cambridge: Cambridge University Press, pp. 109-24.

Spicker, P. (1991), 'The principle of subsidiarity and the social policy of the European Community', *Journal of European Social Policy*, **1** (1), 3–14.

Stevens, A. (1994), 'The dynamics of poverty spells: updating Bane and Ellwood', *American Economic Review*, **84** (2), 34–7.

Stevens, A. (1999), 'Climbing out of poverty, falling back in: measuring the persistence of poverty over multiple spells', *Journal of Human Resources*,

34 (3), 557–88.

Stevens, M. (1996), 'Transferable training and poaching externalities', in A. Booth and D. Snower (eds), *Acquiring Skills: Market Failures, their Symptoms and Policy Responses*, Cambridge: Cambridge University Press, pp. 19–40.

Stiglitz, J. (1988), *Economics of the Public Sector*, New York: W. W. Norton & Company.

Svallfors, S. (1997), 'Worlds of welfare and attitudes to the redistribution: a comparison of eight western nations', *European Sociological Review*, **13** (3), 283–304.

Tanzi, V. and L. Schuknecht (1997), 'Reconsidering the fiscal role of government: the international perspective', *American Economic Review*, **87** (2), 164–8.

Taylor, M. (ed.) with J. Brice, N. Buck and E. Prentice-Lane (1999), British Household Panel Survey user manual volume A: introduction, technical report and appendices, Colchester: University of Essex.

Taylor-Gooby, P. (2002), 'Open markets and welfare values: welfare values, inequality and social change in the silver age of the welfare state', Social Values, Social Policies: Annual Conference of the European Social Policy Research Network, Tilburg University, 29–31 August 2002.

Temple, J. (2000), Growth effects of education and social capital in the OECD countries, Paris: OECD, Economics Department Working Papers No. 263.

Temple, J. and P. Johnson (1998), 'Social capability and economic growth', *The Quarterly Journal of Economics*, **113**, 965–90.

Theeuwes, J. and I. Woittiez (1992), Advising the minister on the elasticity of labour supply, Leiden University: Research Memorandum No. 92.06.

Thurow, L. (1971), 'The income distribution as a pure public good', *Quarterly Journal of Economics*, **85**, 327–36.

Tiebout, C. (1956), 'A pure theory of local expenditures', *Journal of Political Economy*, **64**, 416–24.

Titmuss, R. (1971), *The Gift Relationship*, London: Allen & Unwin.

Titmuss, R. (1974), *Social Policy: An Introduction*, London: Allen & Unwin.

Townsend, P. (1979), *Poverty in the United Kingdom*, London: Penguin Books.

Tsakloglou, P. and F. Papadopoulos (2002), 'Identifying population groups at high risk of social exclusion: evidence from the ECHP', in R. Muffels, P. Tsakloglou and D. Mayes (eds), *Social Exclusion in European Welfare States*, Cheltenham, UK and Northampton, MA, USA: Edward Elgar, pp. 135–69.

Van den Bergh, R. (1994), *Subsidiariteit Rechtseconomisch Bekeken: Adieu Bruxelles?*, Arnhem: Gouda Quint.

Van den Bosch, K. (2001), *Identifying the Poor Using Subjective and Consensual Measures*, Aldershot: Ashgate.

Van den Bosch, K., T. Callan, J. Estivill, P. Hausman, B. Jeandidier, R. Muffels and J. Yfantopoulos (1993), 'A comparison of poverty in seven European countries and regions using subjective and relative measures', *Journal of Population Economics*, **6** (3), 235–59.

Vandenbroucke, F. (2001), 'Samen werken aan duurzame rechtvaardigheid', *Economisch Statistische Berichten*, **4329**, 776–8.

Van Hoorebeeck, B., R. Van Dam and K. Van den Bosch (2000), Bevindingen van een exploratieve studie naar de verschillen tussen de ECHP-dataset van Eurostat en de originele Belgische PSBH-data, Antwerpen: Centrum voor Sociaal Beleid Berichten.

Van Praag, B., A. Hagenaars and H. van Weeren (1982), 'Poverty in Europe', *Review of Income and Wealth*, **28**, 345–59.

Vansteenkiste, S. (1995), *Sociale Zekerheid, Federalisme en de Europese Gemeenschap*, Leuven: Acco.

Vleminckx, K. and J. Berghman (2001), 'Social exclusion and the welfare state: an overview of conceptual issues and policy implications', in D. Mayes, J. Berghman and R. Salais (eds), *Social Exclusion and European Policy*, Cheltenham, UK and Northampton, MA, USA: Edward Elgar, pp. 27–46.

Wagner, G., R. Burkhauser and F. Behringer (1993), 'The English language public use file of the German Socio-Economic Panel', *The Journal of Human Resources*, **28**, 429–33.

Walker, R. (1994), *Poverty Dynamics: Issues and Examples*, Aldershot: Avebury.

Wellisch, D. and D. Wildasin (1996), 'Decentralised income redistribution and immigration', *European Economic Review*, **40**, 187–217.

Westerlaken, A. and J. van Dijk (1996), 'Sociaal beleid voor Europa', *Economisch Statistische Berichten*, **4086**, 1032–5.

Whelan, C., R. Layte and B. Maître (2001a), Persistent deprivation in the European Union, University of Essex: EPAG Working Paper No. 23.

Whelan, C., R. Layte and B. Maître (2001b), What is the scale of multiple deprivation in the European Union?, University of Essex: EPAG Working Paper No. 19.

Whelan, C., R. Layte, B. Maître and B. Nolan (2001c), Persistent income poverty and deprivation in the European Union: an analysis of the first three waves of the European Community Household Panel, University of Essex: EPAG Working Paper No. 17.

Wildasin, D. (1989), 'Interjurisdictional capital mobility: fiscal externality and a corrective subsidy', *Journal of Urban Economics*, **25**, 193–212.

Wildasin, D. (1997), 'Income distribution and redistribution within federations', *Annales d'Economie et de Statistique*, **45**, 291–313.

Wildeboer Schut, J., J. Vrooman and P. de Beer (2000), *De Maat van de Verzorgingstaat*, Den Haag: Sociaal en Cultureel Planbureau.

Wolff, E. (1990), 'Wealth holdings and poverty status in the U.S.', *Review of Income and Wealth*, **36** (2), 143–65.

Woolcock, M. (2001), 'The place of social capital in understanding social and economic outcomes', *Canadian Journal of Policy Research*, **2**, 11–17.

Index